POSTCARD HISTORY SERIES

Elyria

IN VINTAGE POSTCARDS

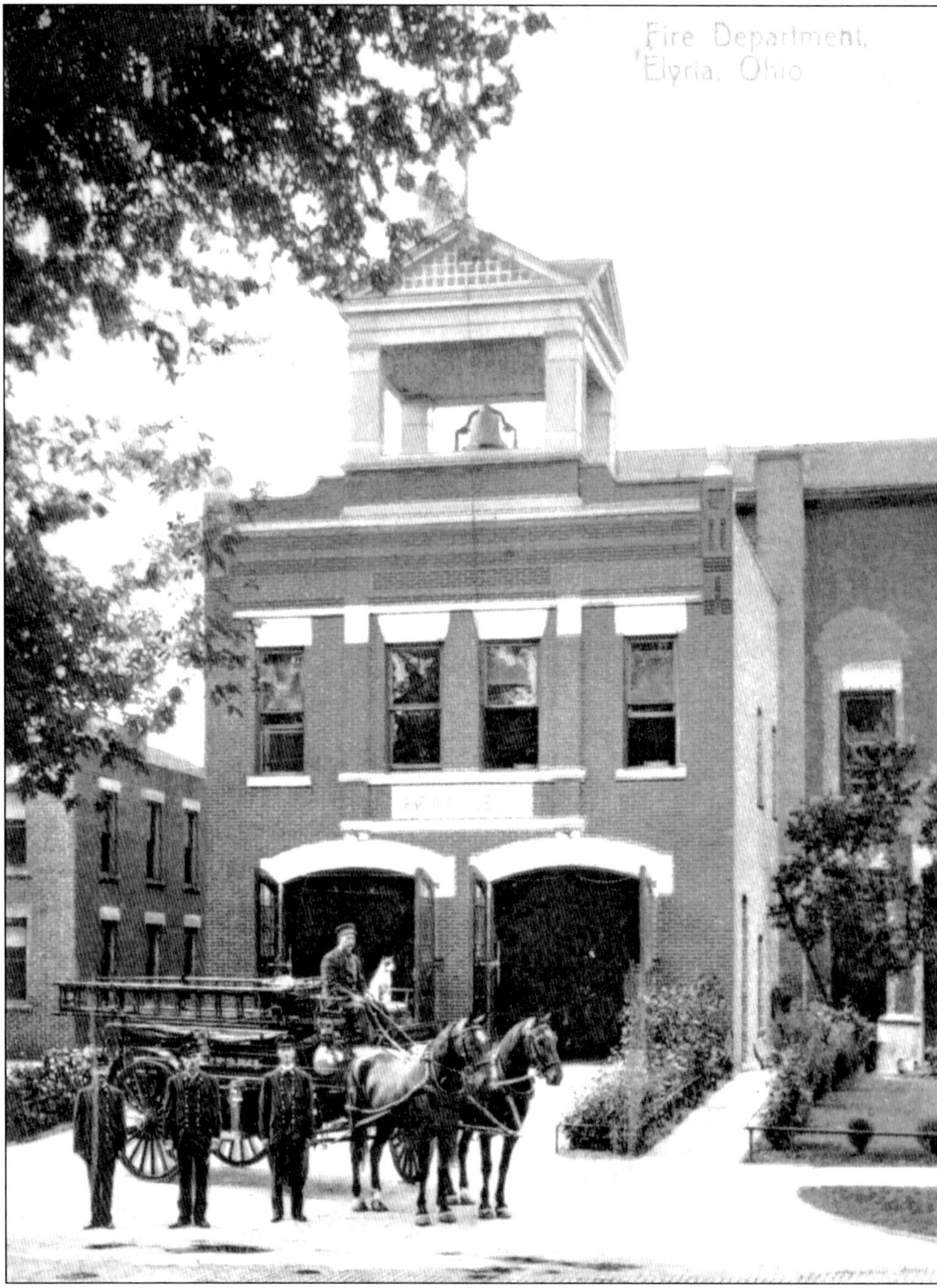

ELYRIA FIRE DEPARTMENT. Elyria's first fire station was built behind the city hall facing Second Street as part of major renovations to the city hall in 1904. When the new fire station was completed, the horses and firefighting equipment were housed on the ground floor, while the men lived upstairs. Until 1906, Elyria's firefighters were volunteers. The city used horse-drawn wagons until 1920. The building remained here for almost a hundred years, but was torn down to make way for a new city hall.

POSTCARD HISTORY SERIES

Elyria
IN VINTAGE POSTCARDS

Benjamin J. and Anne Fischer Mancine

ARCADIA
PUBLISHING

ISBN 978-0-7385-3270-7

Published by Arcadia Publishing
Charleston, South Carolina

Printed in the United States of America

Library of Congress Catalog Card Number: 2004105011

For all general information contact Arcadia Publishing at:
Telephone 843-853-2070
Fax 843-853-0044
E-mail sales@arcadiapublishing.com
For customer service and orders:
Toll-Free 1-888-313-2665

Visit us on the Internet at www.arcadiapublishing.com

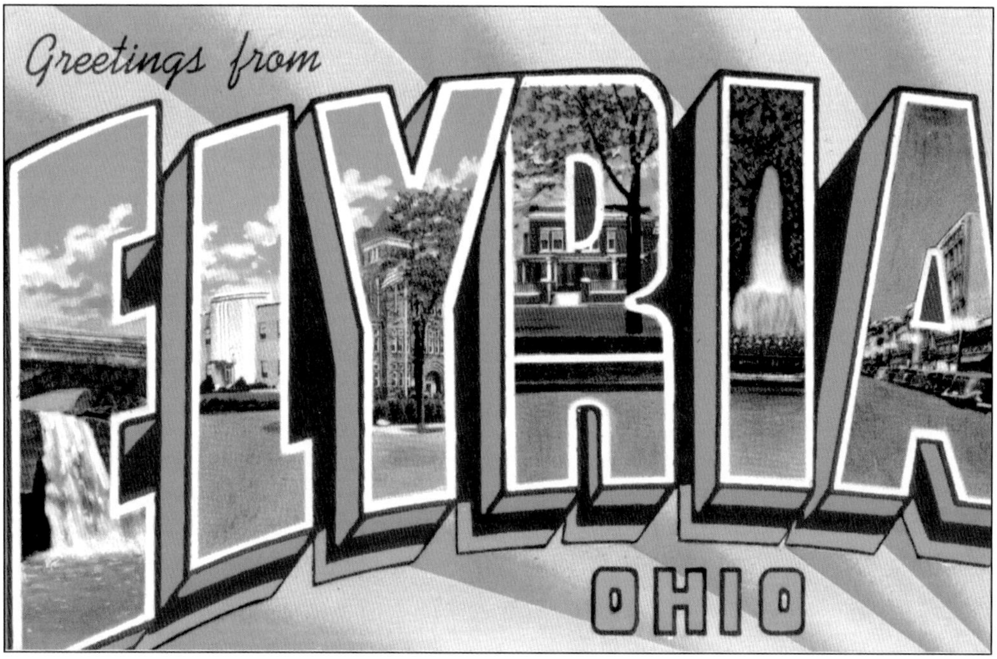

"**Greetings From Elyria Ohio.**" This classic block-letter postcard *circa* 1955 shows six well-known Elyria scenes: West Falls, Bendix-Westinghouse, Elyria High School, Elyria Memorial Hospital, Ely Park Fountain, and Broad Street at night. This popular postcard was reprinted in several formats over the years.

Contents

ACKNOWLEDGMENTS

The authors would like to acknowledge the excellent reference materials available to us in the Ohio Room of the Main Library of the Elyria Public Library system. We always learn something new there. We also want to acknowledge our former neighbor and *Chronicle-Telegram* columnist for many years, Connie Davis. She has been an inspiration to us throughout the writing of this book, and we turned to her columns many times for interesting, factual information.

A part of the proceeds from the sale of this book will be donated to the Lorain County Historical Society, under the directorship of our friend, Bill Bird.

This book is for Tom and Julie, still our best collaborations.

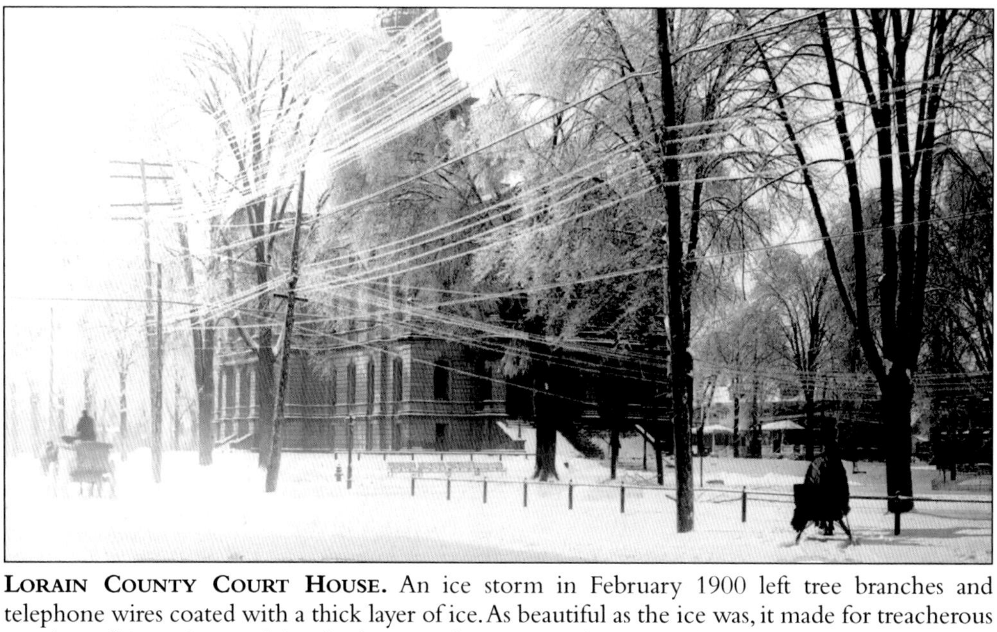

LORAIN COUNTY COURT HOUSE. An ice storm in February 1900 left tree branches and telephone wires coated with a thick layer of ice. As beautiful as the ice was, it made for treacherous travel conditions. A man drives his horse and wagon south on Middle Avenue to the left, while a horse-drawn sleigh waits by the park.

Introduction

Like many of Ohio's earliest towns, Elyria is located on a river that encouraged industry and helped the city grow. In addition, the city's two 40-foot waterfalls aided milling operations, and its proximity to Lake Erie further promoted travel and trade. Elyria grew quickly, and the postcards in this volume pick up her story about 90 years after her founding in 1817. As the seat of Lorain County government, Elyria was already home to nearly 9,000 people by 1900. As Elyria continued to grow in the early years of the 20th century, photographers were there to record her progress, and many of their best photographs were made into postcards.

It was at about this time that a "postcard craze" began sweeping the country. People across the nation enthusiastically traded cards with family and friends, even with total strangers, to add to their collections. In addition, in those days of twice-a-day mail delivery, postcards were often used to convey everyday messages, much the way the telephone and email are used today. The postcards with views of the hospital in particular, contain poignant messages concerning a loved one's illness or the joyous news of a new baby. The end result of this volume of mail was the preservation of images of buildings and landmarks of the day. These postcards offer us a glimpse of long-vanished buildings and places, but at the same time, familiar buildings of today are also represented. The county court house, for example, is easily recognizable, but sports an impressive cupola in the earliest cards.

The earliest postcards were actual photographs with the word "Postcard" stamped on the back. Color postcards were soon introduced, at first printed in Germany, then after the start of World War One, here in the States. By the late 1940s, the postcard craze had largely ended. By the late 1950s, the "photo-chrome" card was developed and is still in use today, although largely restricted to the tourist industry. Examples of each of these types of cards are included in this book. There are no postcards of Elyria currently in print, and even the brightly colored chrome cards of the 1960s can only be found at local flea markets or postcard shows.

It may come as a surprise that we have found more than 600 unique postcard views of this single city. It has certainly been a surprise to us. The occasional unfamiliar postcard we come across is a source of great interest to us. This book represents the very best of our collection. We've included views of Elyria's now-defunct movie theaters and hotels as they looked in their prime. You will see pedestrian bridges across the Black River, old mills, and even an early hydroelectric plant. You may find the school you attended or the church where you worshiped. There are buildings destroyed by fire, bridges destroyed by flood, train wrecks, and snowstorms. We even include rare images taken *inside* Elyria's early businesses, schools, and churches.

So join us now as we explore Elyria in the early to mid-20th century—a world where trolleys still run on the site of today's four-lane highways, and early cars share dirt streets with horse-drawn wagons. See the succession of fountains that have graced the town square. See how little the city's two waterfalls and beautiful Cascade Park has changed in 100 years, or how much has changed on Broad Street. We know you'll find it a fascinating journey!

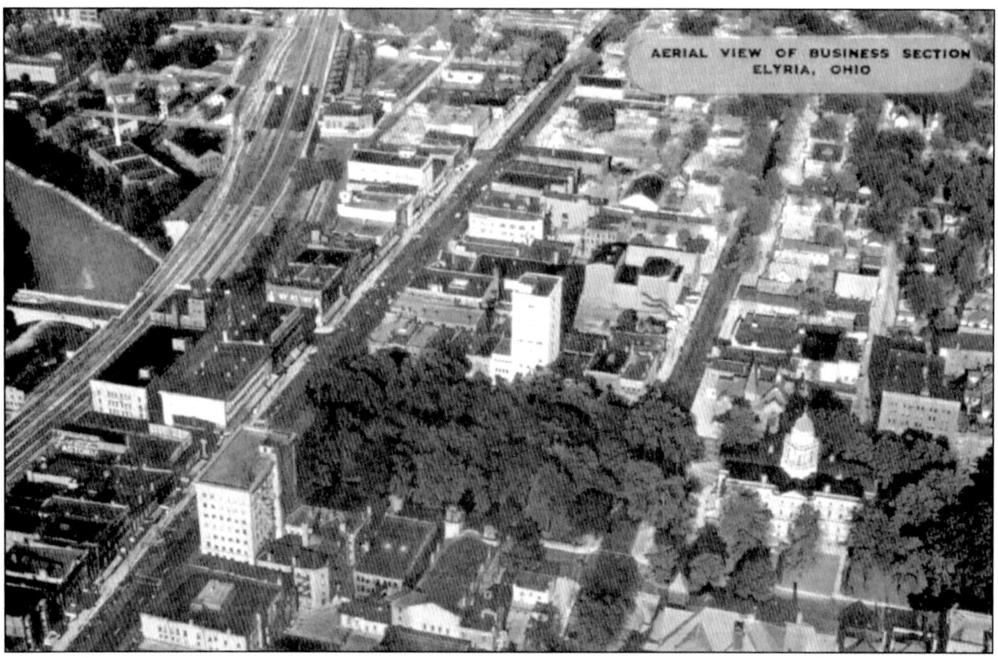

AERIAL VIEW OF DOWNTOWN ELYRIA. Broad Street heads east from the lower left-hand corner of this postcard. Landmark buildings surrounding the trees of Ely Square include EST Bank, Lorain County Savings and Trust, and the county court house before the cupola was removed. The east branch of the Black River at left abuts the New York Central railroad tracks, then flows under the Washington Avenue Bridge.

One

UP AND DOWN BROAD STREET

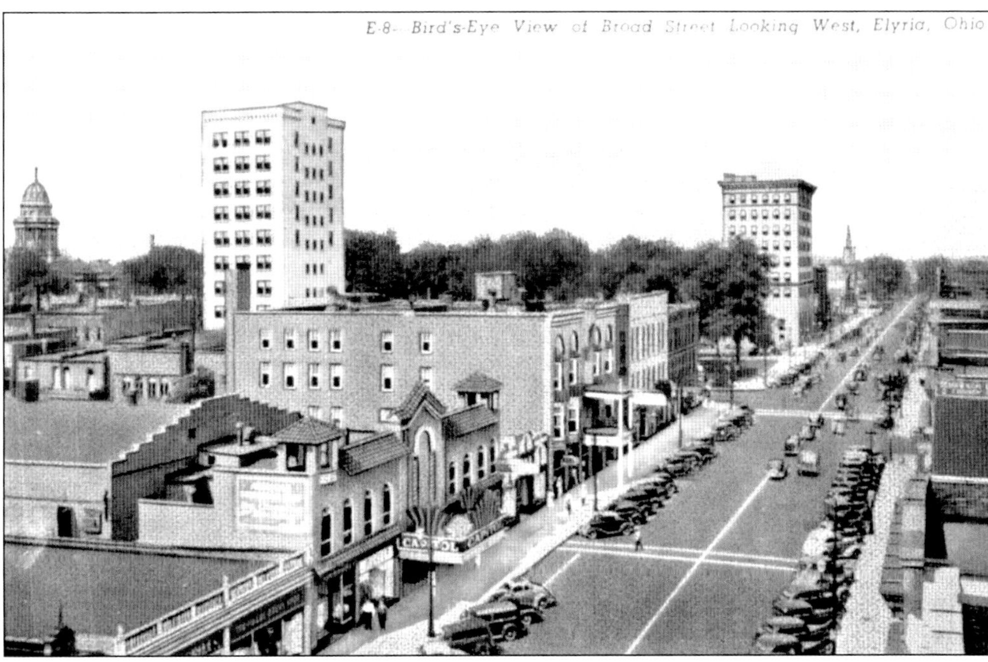

BROAD STREET LOOKING WEST. Probably taken from the top of the J.C. Penney building in the early 1940s, this view captures much of the heart of Elyria: the Lorain County Court house, both bank towers, the Style Center, Capitol Theater, the Graystone Hotel, Ely Square, and Saint John's Lutheran Church in the distance.

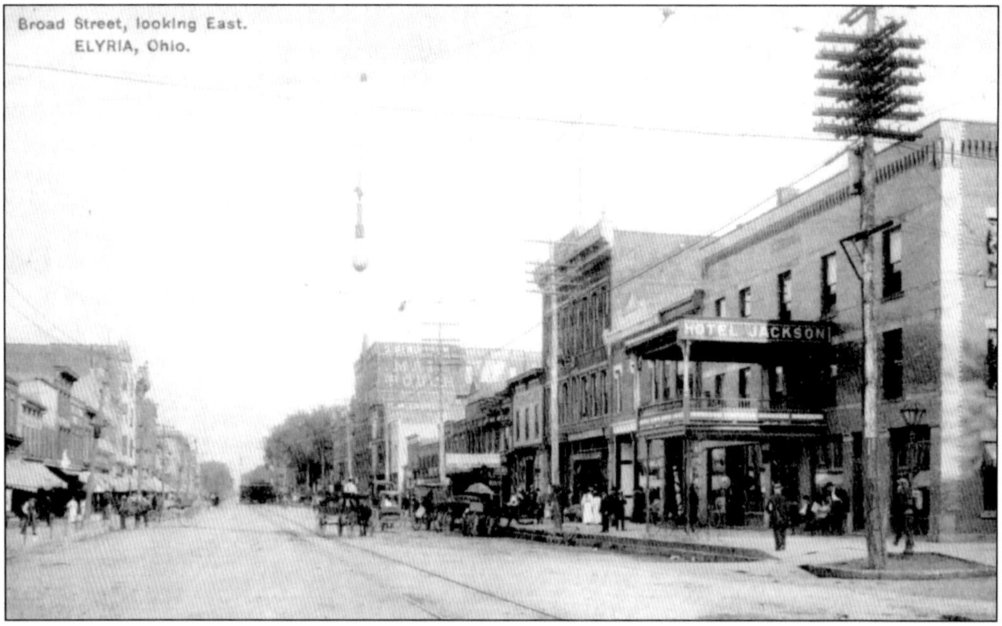

West Broad Street, from West Avenue. We begin our postcard tour of Broad Street at West Avenue in the first decade of the 20th century. Hotel Jackson, at right, survived on this corner until the 1970s. Today, all the buildings on the right (south) side of West Broad Street down to the large building in the distance are gone; the area serves as a bank parking lot.

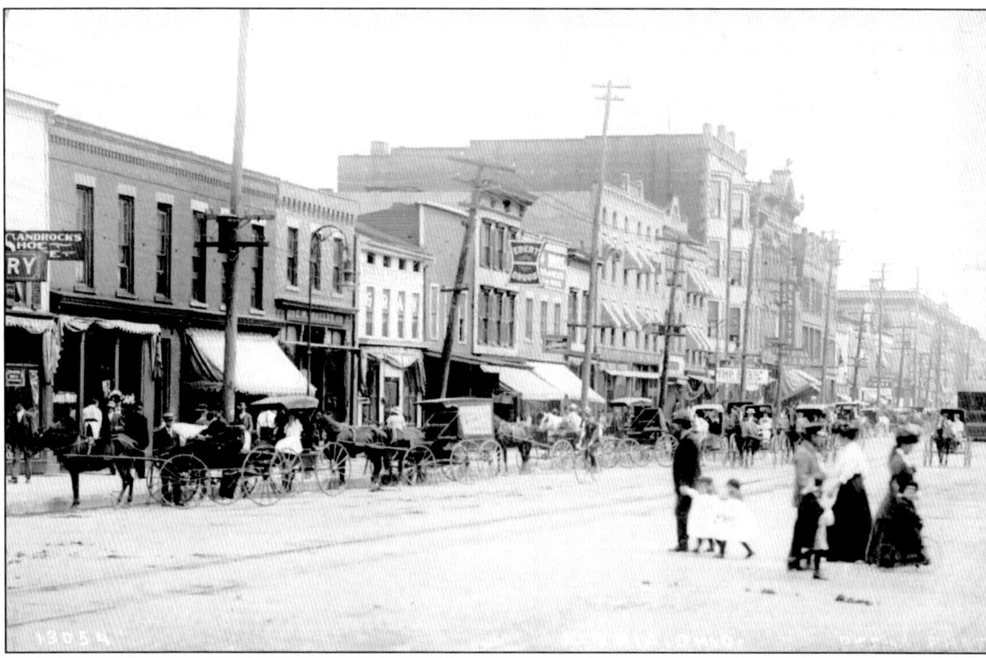

West Broad Street, North Side. This interesting view of the north side of West Broad Street was captured about 100 years ago. Horse-drawn carts and carriages lined the streets where cars park today, and the city's interurban train ran down the center of the street. Broad Street was then known as Main Street.

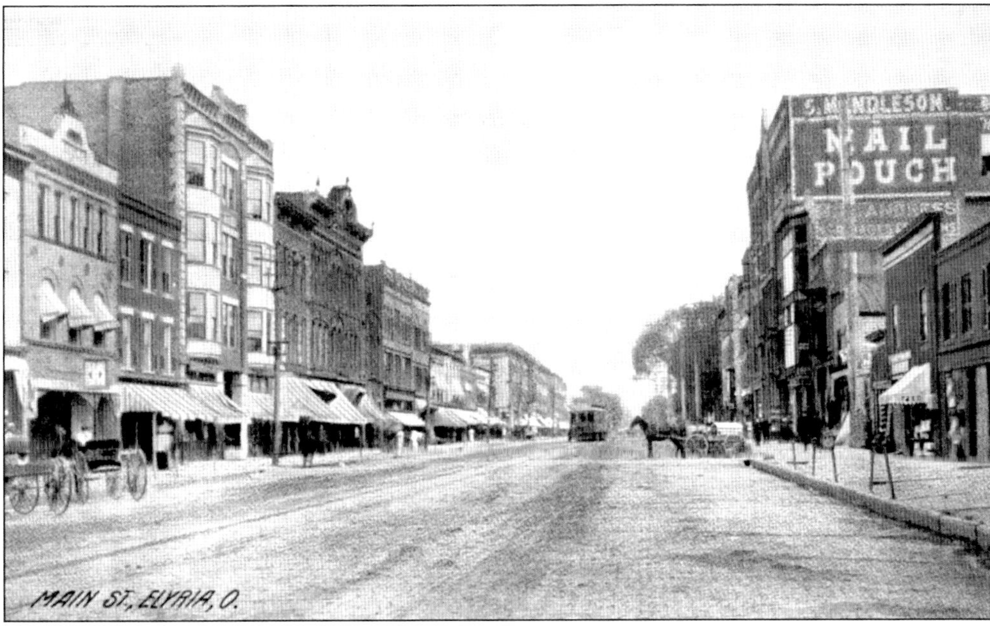

WEST BROAD STREET, LOOKING EAST. The large building at right, sporting the Mail Pouch sign, is the (original) Elyria Block, home of the Elyria Business College. Across the street, the building with the ornate roof line would later house the Dreamland Theater and Thom McAnn shoe store and is today the site of a McDonalds restaurant. The building with the three-story bay windows is the Nichols Block.

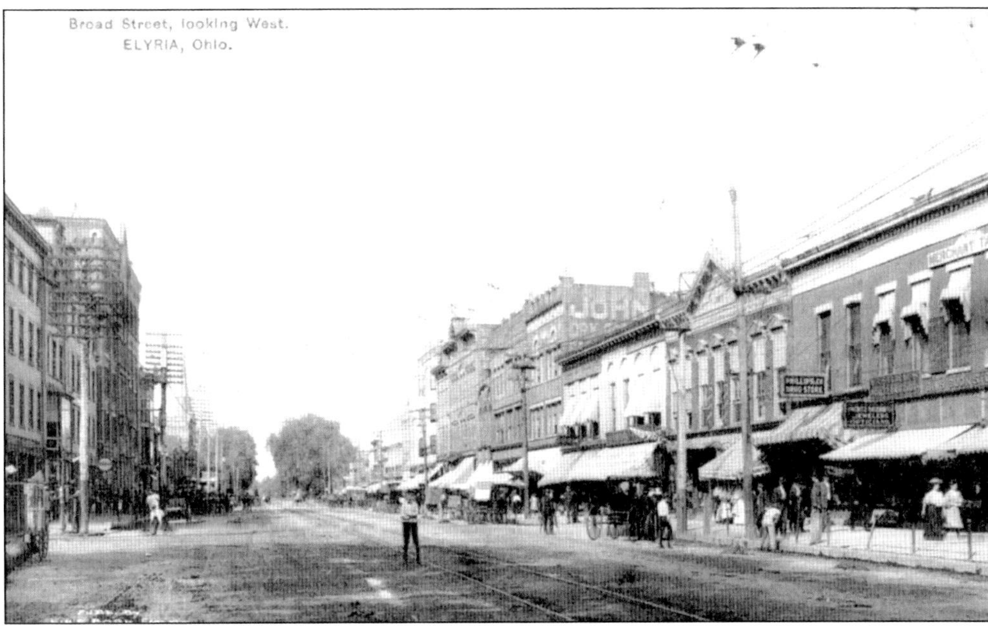

BROAD STREET, LOOKING WEST. The building with the sign on its side is the Fortress Block, built about 1834, and was home to John Lersch Dry Goods for many years. In the 1950s and 1960s, it housed Bear's Furniture. The Phillips Drugs Store and Robinson-Hancock stores are at right.

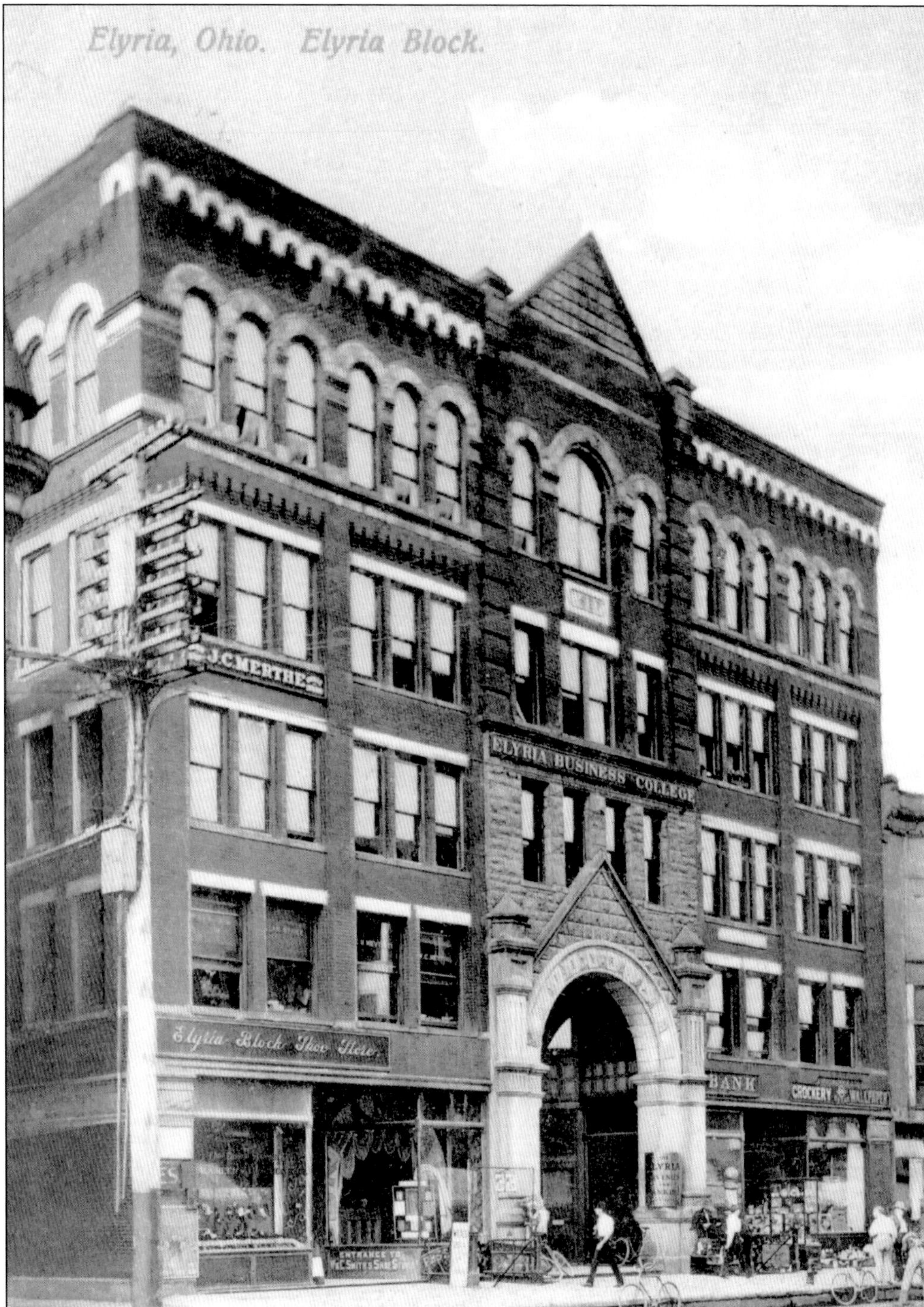

Elyria Block, Original Building. Located on the south side of West Broad Street behind the Hotel Andwur, the Elyria Block was home to the Elyria Business College, an early secretarial training school. The building also housed the J.C. Merthe clothing store, and Elyria Savings and Banking (later Elyria Savings and Trust)

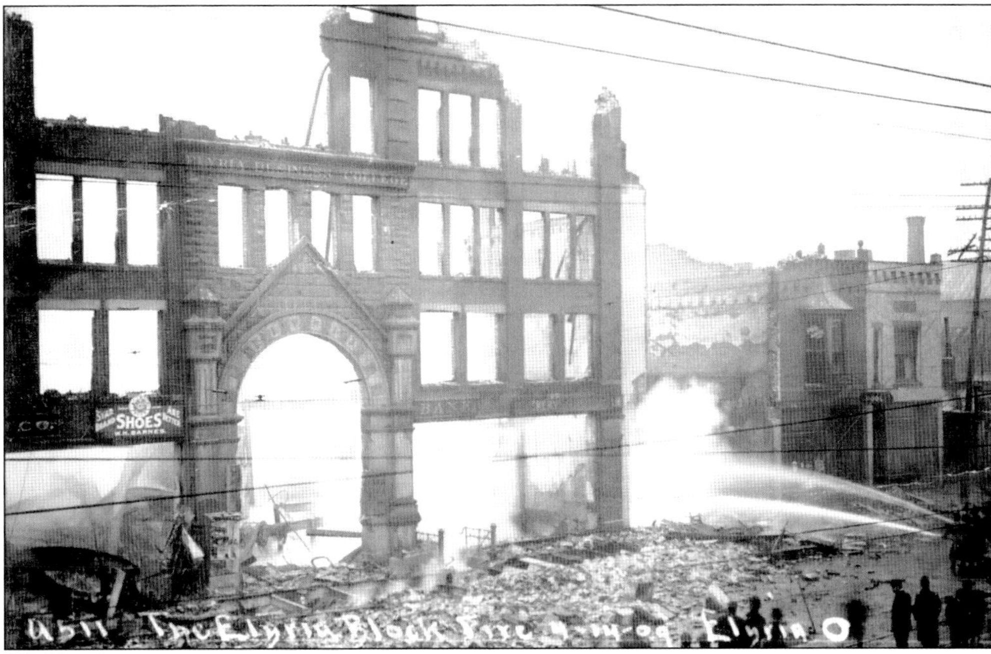

ELYRIA BLOCK FIRE. On April 14, 1909, the Elyria Block burned to the ground. Here, fire fighters aim their hoses at the remains of a horse livery next door. A ladder truck was wrecked during the fire, presumably hampering fire-fighting efforts.

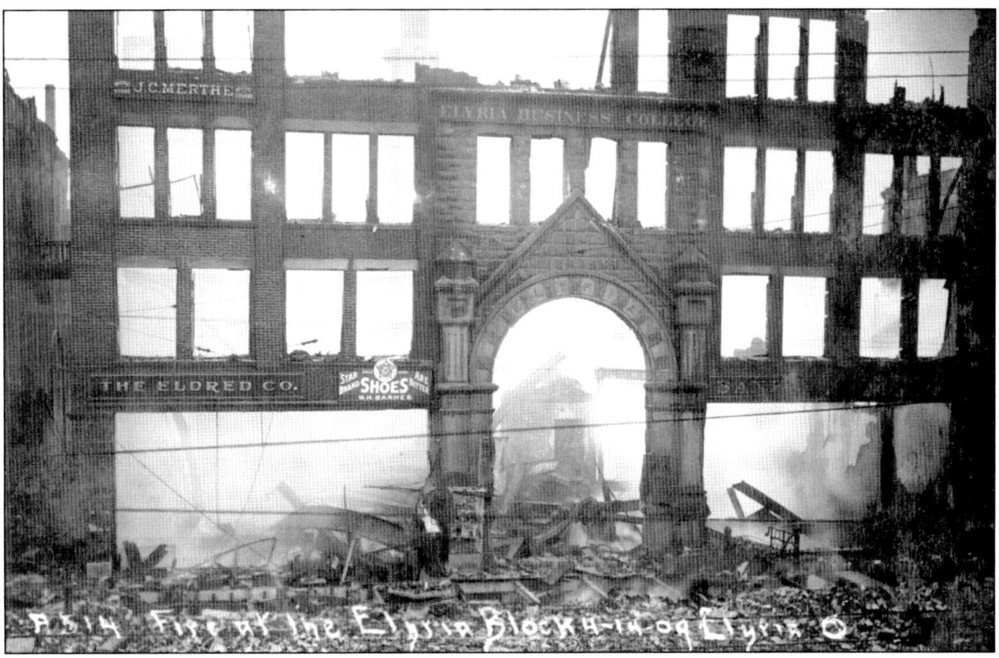

ELYRIA BLOCK FIRE, CLOSE-UP. Other than the building's façade, the only structure to survive the fire was the vault of the Elyria Savings and Banking Company. It was later used by the bank to advertise security for depositors. The Elyria Business College moved to Second Street, and after several more moves, it finally closed its doors in 1962.

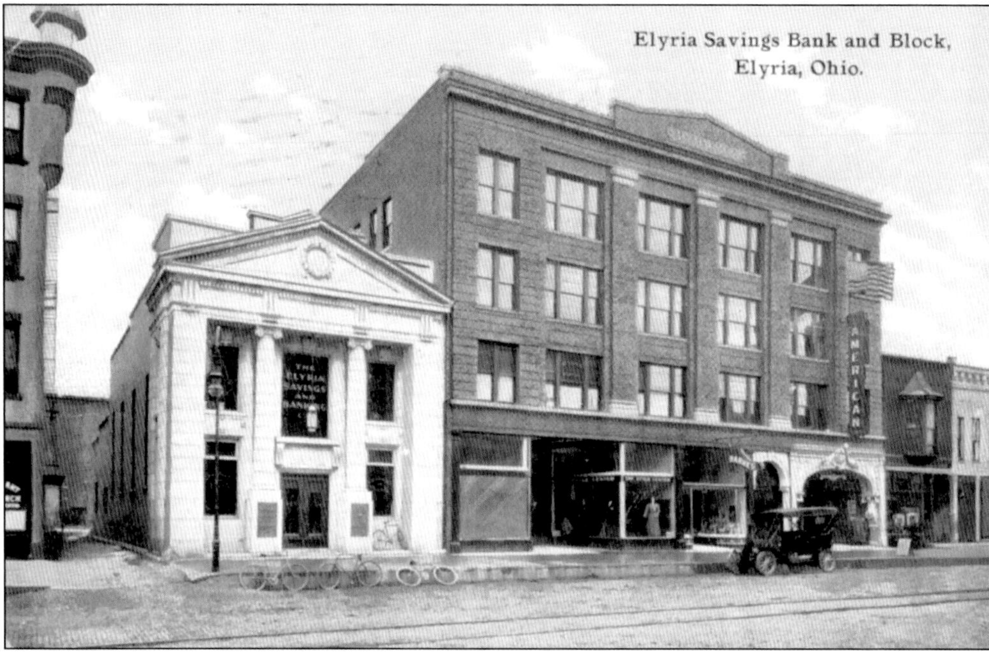

New Elyria Block. The Elyria Block was quickly rebuilt after the fire. It housed the Elyria Style Center (original location) and the American movie theater. The Elyria Savings and Banking Company built a new bank between the Elyria Block and the Andwur Hotel.

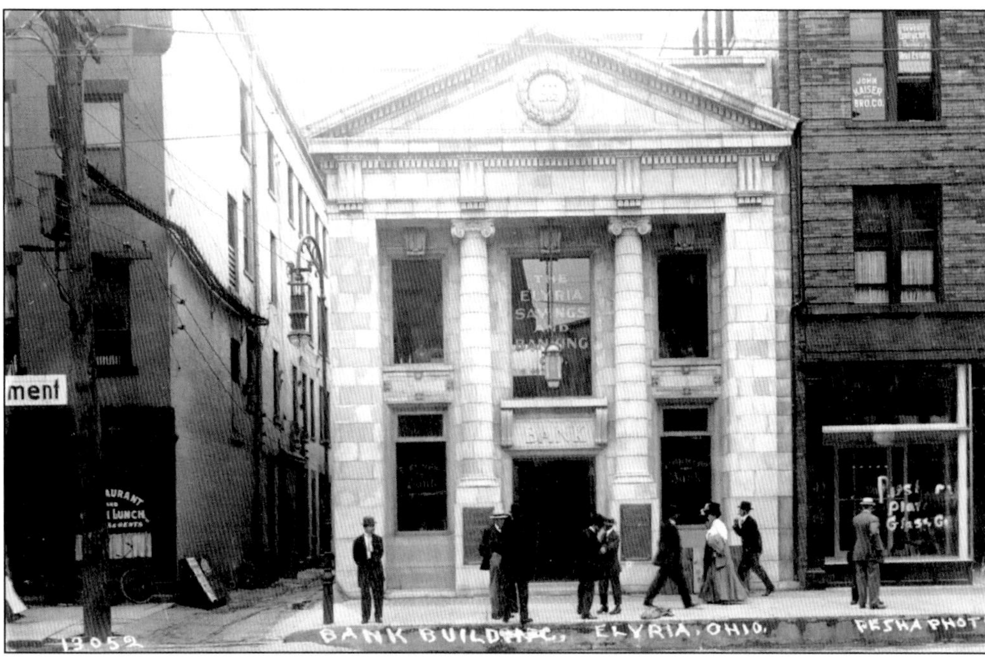

Elyria Savings and Banking Company. After being burned out of the Elyria Block, the bank that would eventually become Elyria Savings and Trust moved to a temporary location. It moved once more before this building was ready at 508 West Broad. In 1923, the EST Bank tower was built on the site of Hotel Andwur, seen here at left.

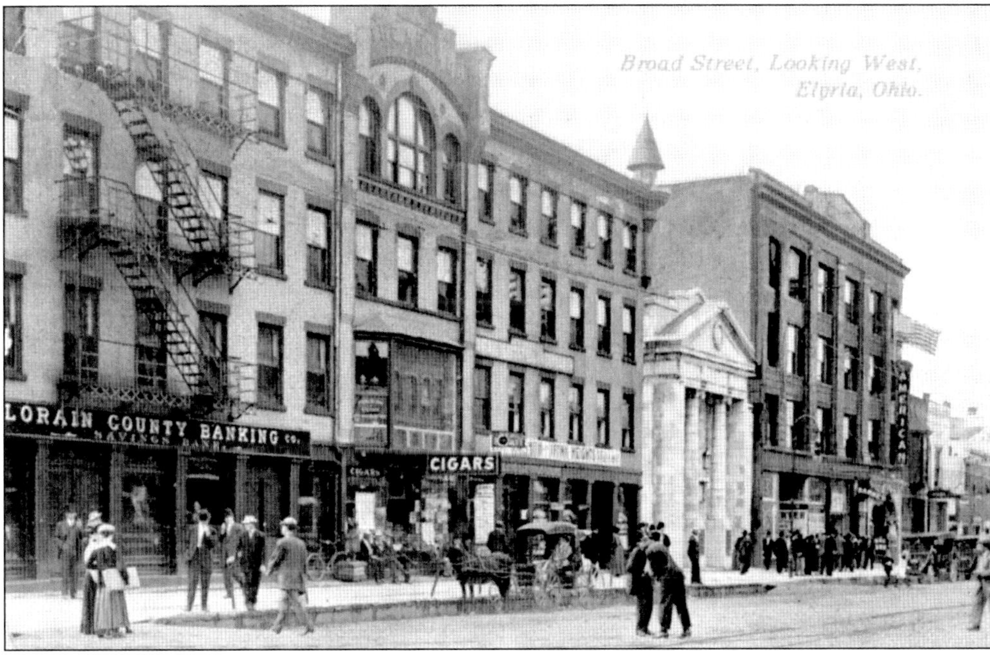

WEST BROAD STREET, SOUTH SIDE. This area, from Hotel Andwur at left to the American Movie Theater in the Elyria Block at right, was a hub of commerce in the 1910s. The Lorain County Bank, which would later build one of two bank towers in Elyria, was at this time located on the ground floor of Hotel Andwur.

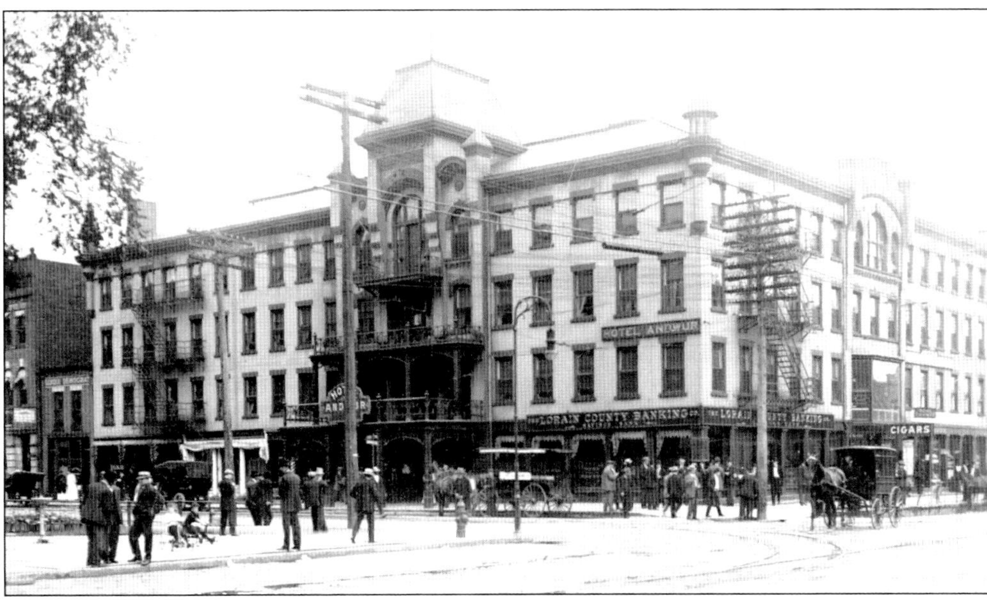

HOTEL ANDWUR. Fire destroyed the Beebe House hotel on this site in 1892. With its strategic location on the corner of Broad and Court Streets, next door to Elyria's main interurban stop, Hotel Andwur thrived for many years. In 1923, the Elyria Savings and Trust bank built an office tower on this corner, but the left-most portion of the hotel remained as Hotel Sederis. The Sederis was torn down in 1973.

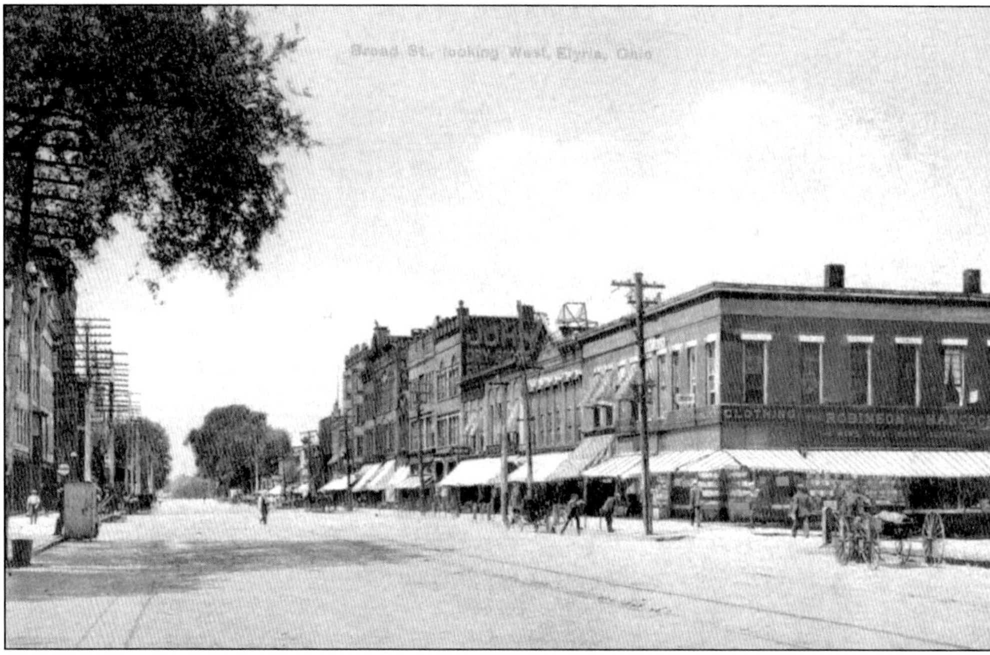

Intersection of Broad and Mill Streets. This corner was home to the Robinson and Hancock men's and boy's clothing store for many years. More recently, the Bell Company, a fine men's clothier, was located here. Mill Street later became Lodi Street, then Lake Avenue.

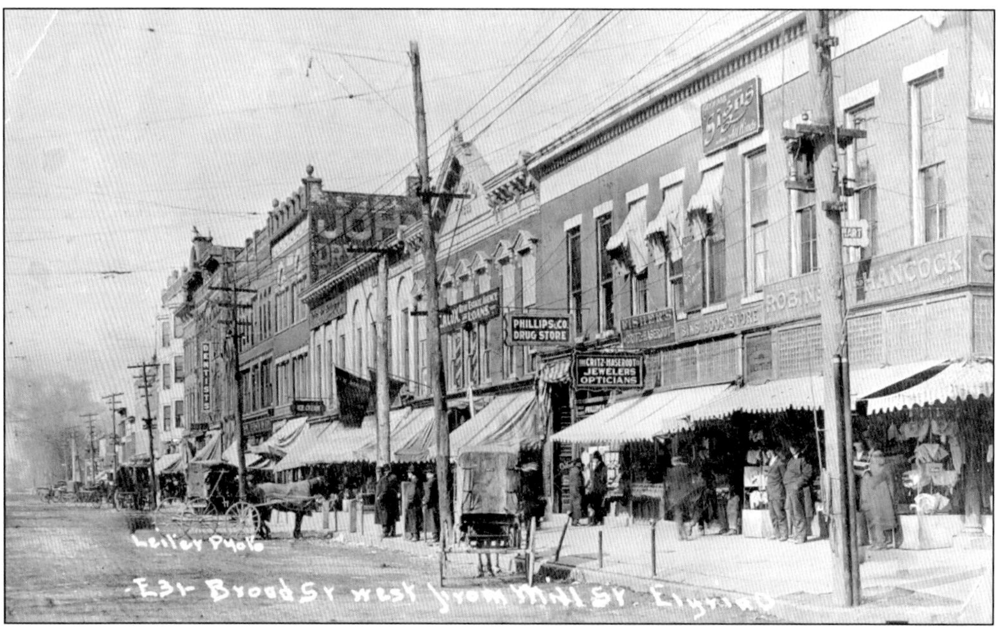

Robinson-Hancock and Bin's Bookstore. Charles Hancock and Theodore Robinson opened their Elyria store in 1903. Next door, J.C. Bin's Book Store sold books, magazines, newspapers, stationery, and picture frames and published many of the postcards included in this book. Down the block from Bin's was Phillip's Drug Store, which operated from this site into the early 1960s.

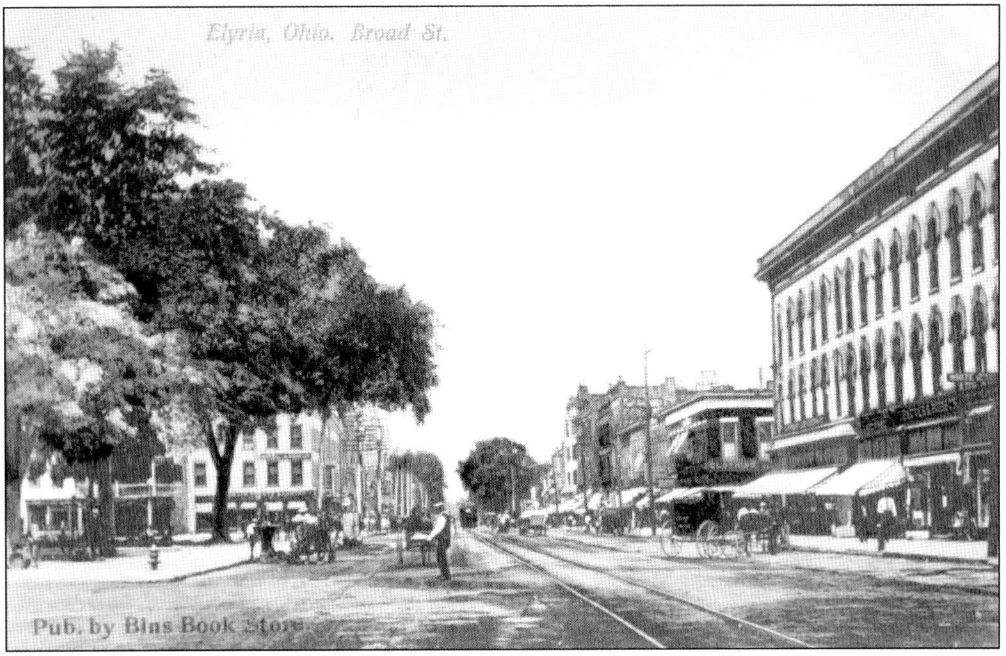

BROAD STREET AT ELY SQUARE. This card provides a view looking west down Broad Street from the center of town around 1910. Elyria's town square is at left, with the Commercial Block at right. Hotel Andwur is barely visible behind the trees.

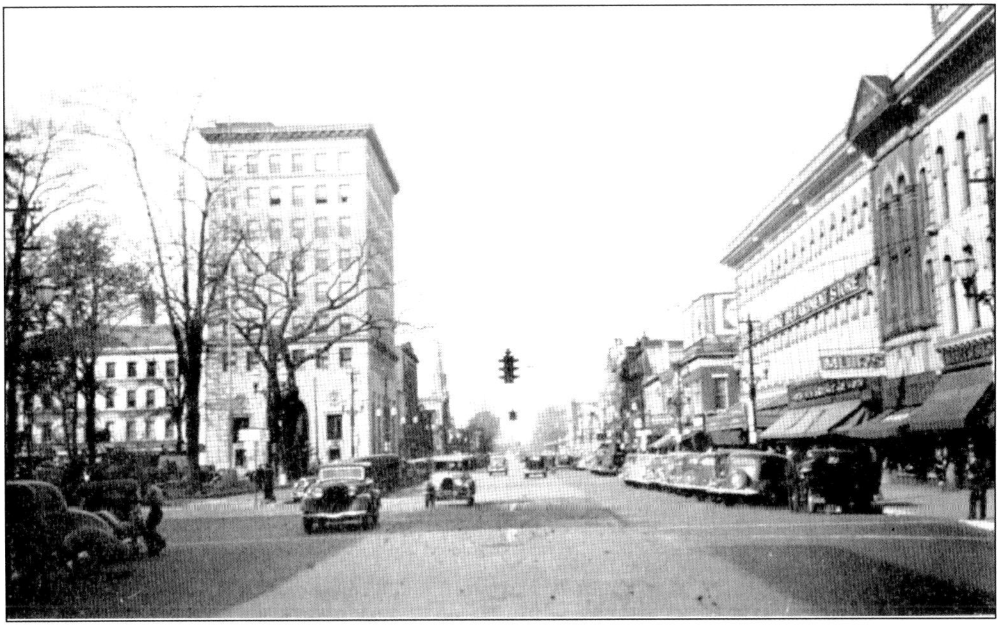

BROAD STREET AT ELY SQUARE. By the late 1930s, this similar view down Broad Street shows the Elyria Savings and Trust (EST) bank building where the Andwur Hotel once stood. Half of the old hotel remained in business as the Hotel Sederis, seen here at left.

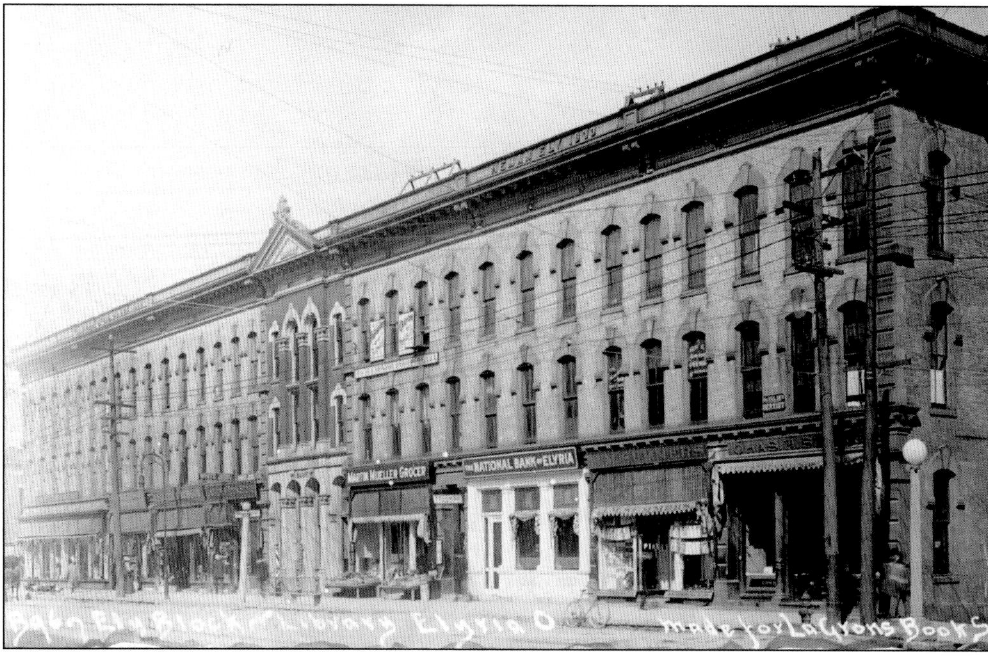

COMMERCIAL AND ELY BLOCKS, 1910S. In 1873, this stretch of Broad Street between Lodi Street and Washington Avenue was the site of the worst fire in Elyria's history. The site was quickly rebuilt in 1874, with the Commercial Block at left, the Center Block housing the Elyria Library, and the Ely Block at right.

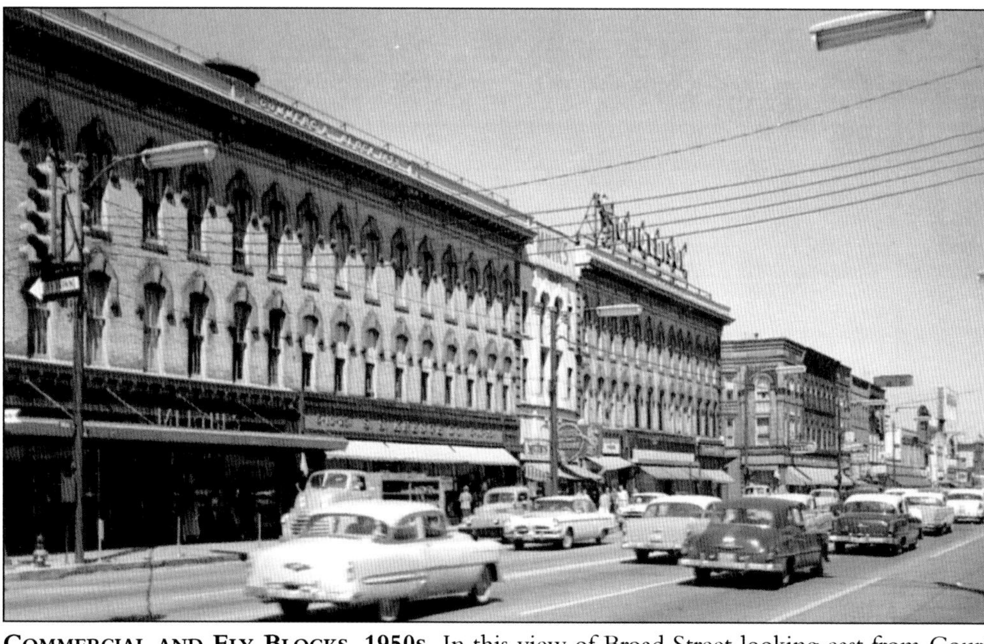

COMMERCIAL AND ELY BLOCKS, 1950S. In this view of Broad Street looking east from Court Street, the Commercial Block is home to Merthe's and Kresge's. The library in the center building has been replaced by Muir's, and the Ely Block at the intersection of Washington Avenue houses Ohio Edison and Standard Drug, among other businesses.

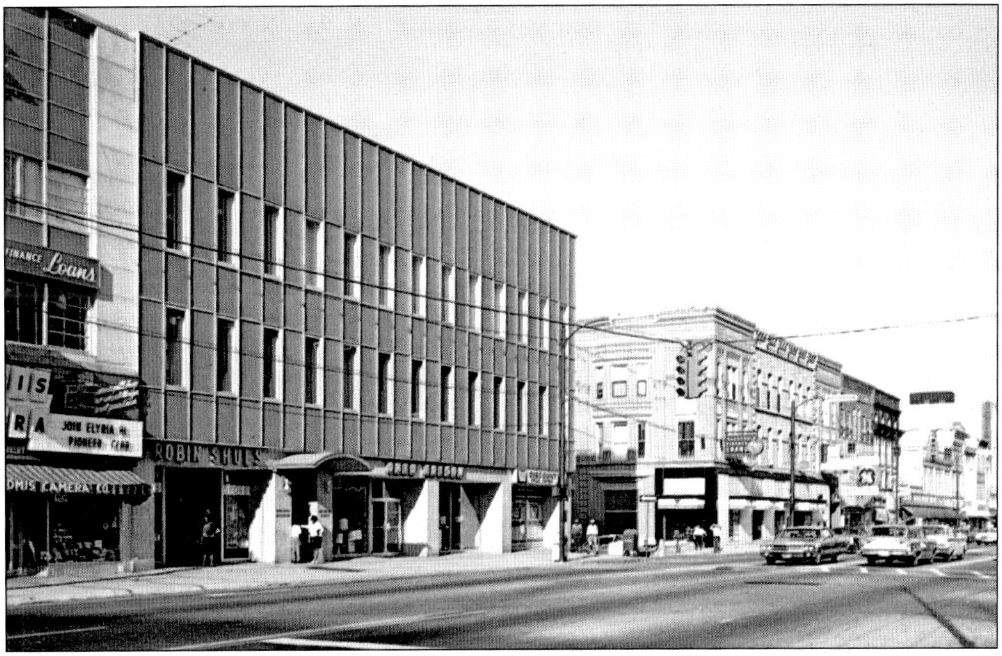

COMMERCIAL AND ELY BLOCKS, 1960S. Around 1960, the Ely Block got a new blue façade and was renamed the Robinson Building. At this time, Loomis Camera occupied the center block, and Revco was on the west side of the Washington Avenue intersection. The Century Block is just right of center in this view.

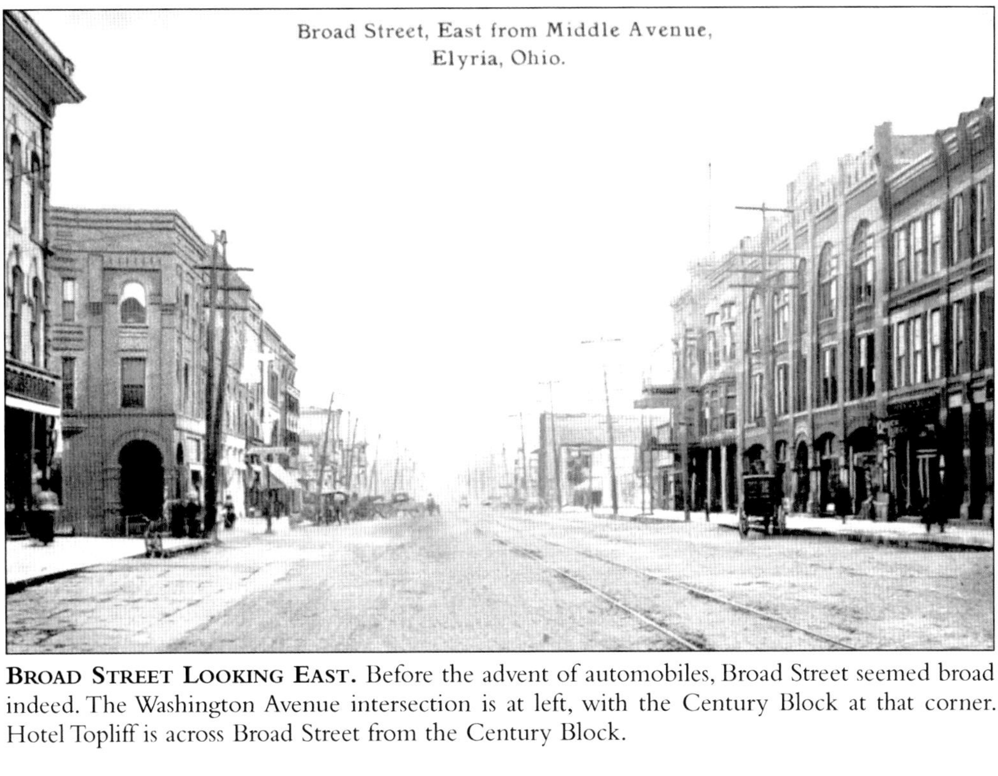

BROAD STREET LOOKING EAST. Before the advent of automobiles, Broad Street seemed broad indeed. The Washington Avenue intersection is at left, with the Century Block at that corner. Hotel Topliff is across Broad Street from the Century Block.

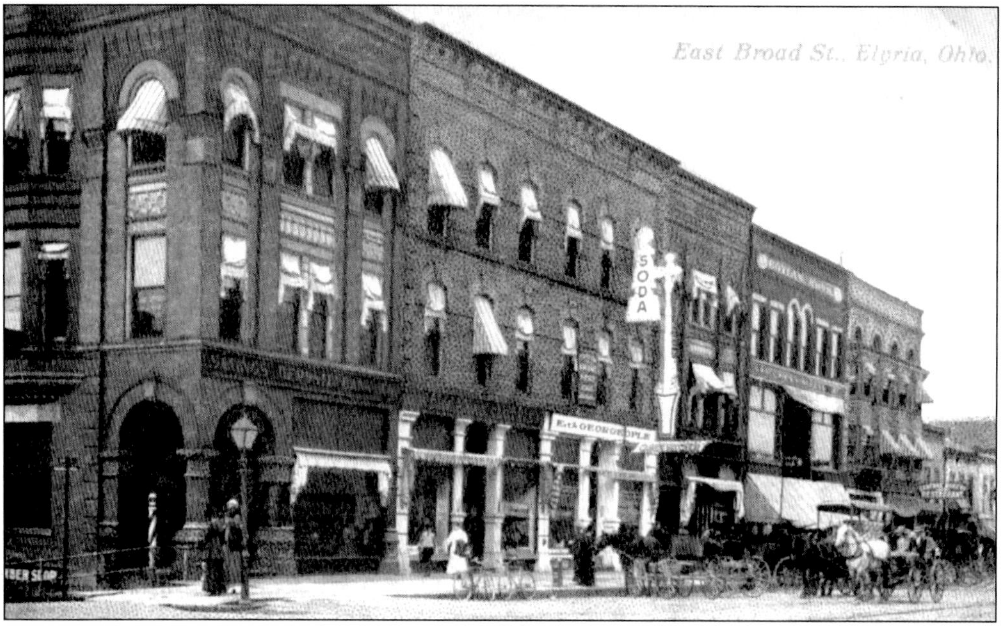

MUSSEY AND CENTURY BLOCKS. On the northeast corner of Broad Street and Washington Avenue, the two-part Century Block sandwiched the Mussey Block like bookends. The Mussey Block was built in 1873. These blocks primarily housed barbers, doctors, lawyers, insurance companies, and other professional offices. A soda shop sign can be seen in this view from the 1910s. Woolworth's and then the Fay Company later located here.

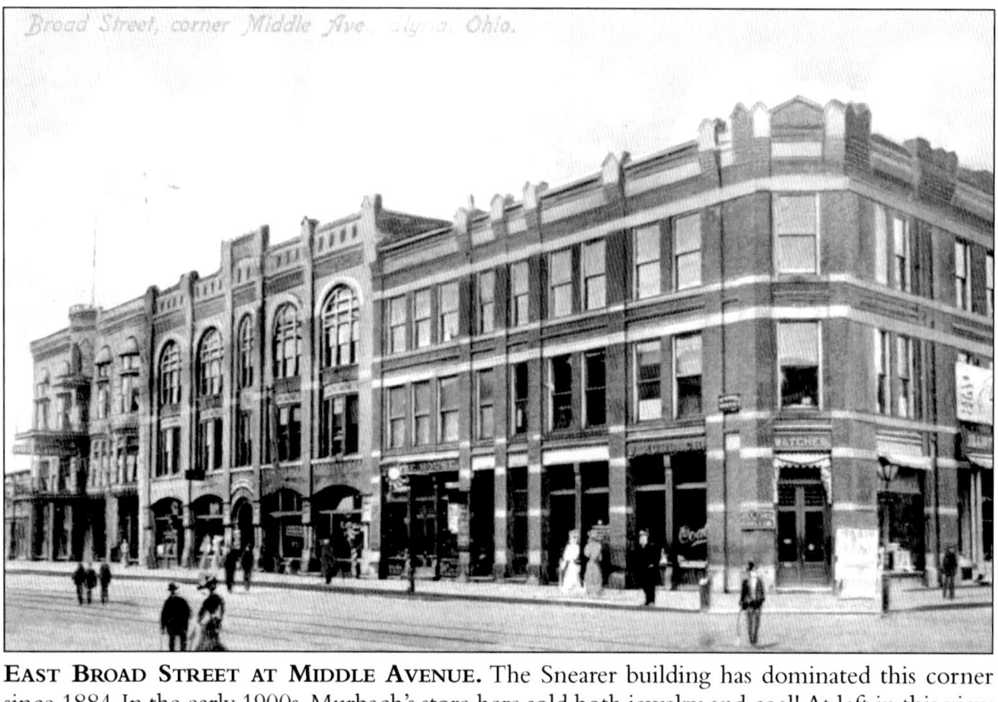

EAST BROAD STREET AT MIDDLE AVENUE. The Snearer building has dominated this corner since 1884. In the early 1900s, Murbach's store here sold both jewelry and coal! At left in this view is Hotel Topliff. The building between the hotel and Snearer block was replaced in 1935.

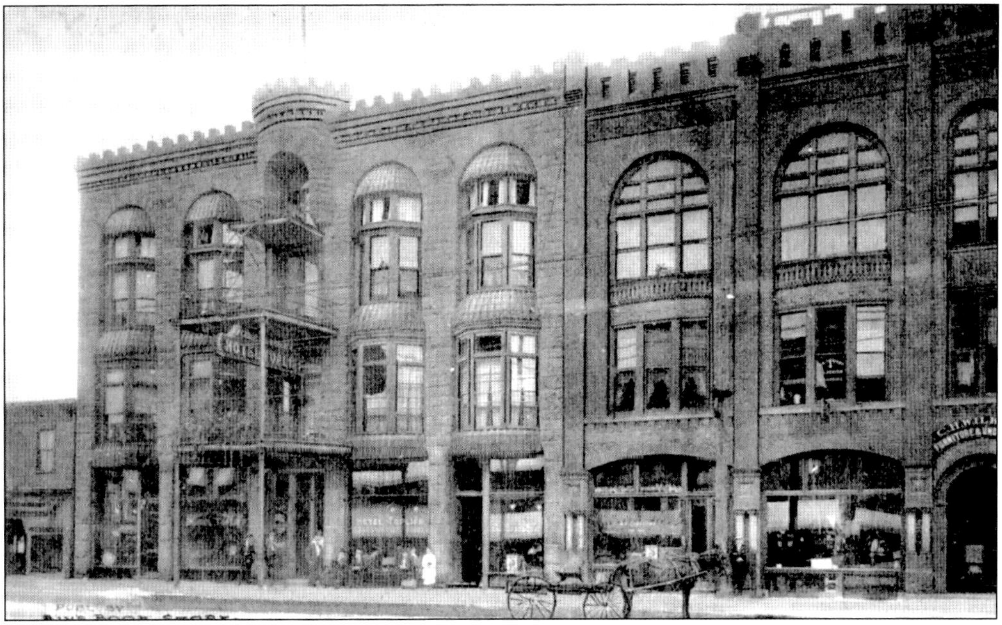

HOTEL TOPLIFF. The elegant Hotel Topliff on the south side of Broad Street was founded by John A. Topliff, Elyria maker of buggies and wagons. A barbershop and restaurant occupied the ground floor. The hotel was subsequently run as Hotel Newell and later the Graystone Hotel, until being demolished for retail space in the 1970s.

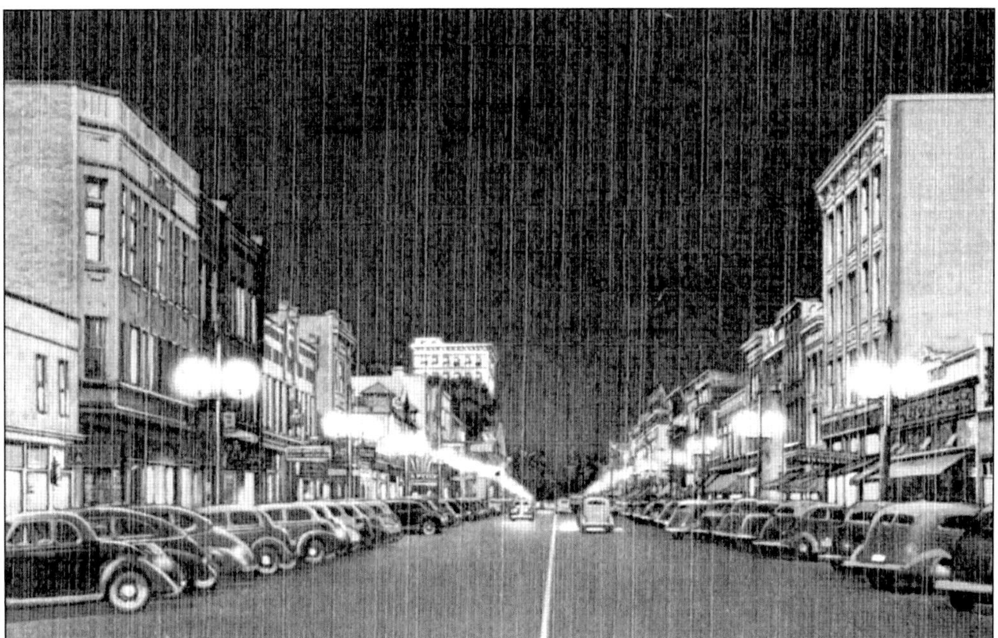

BROAD STREET LOOKING WEST. In this early 1940s view, the Elyria Savings and Trust bank building can be seen in the distance. Sears is the tall building at left, and J.C. Penney's is at right. By this time, parallel parking, with four lanes of traffic, had been replaced by diagonal parking with two lanes of traffic. Broad Street was Ohio Route 20 through Elyria.

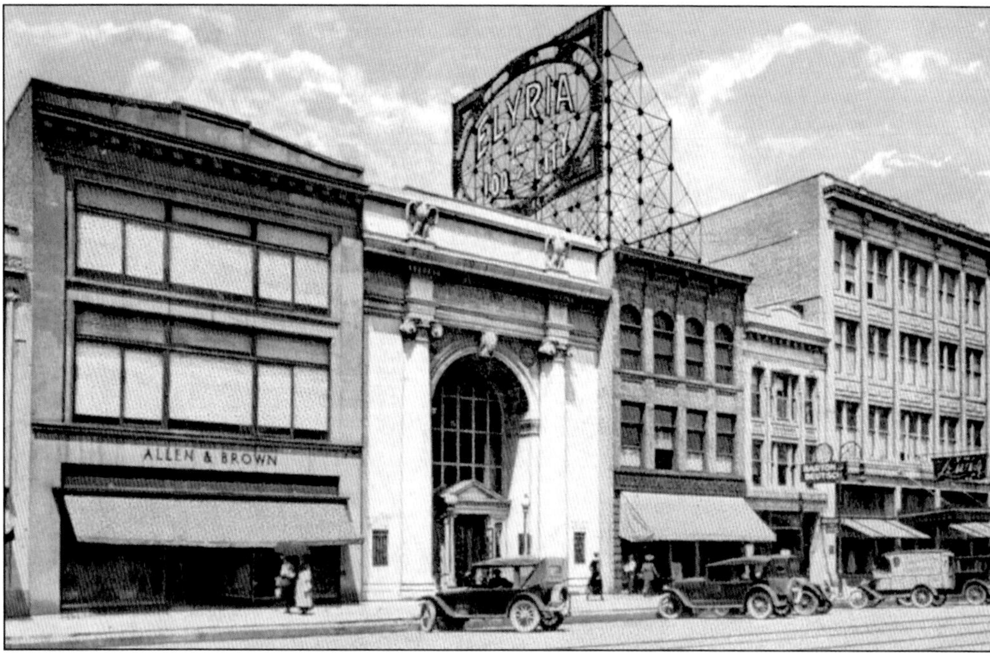

Broad Street, North Side. The white, neo-classic bank building was built in 1917 by the Savings Deposit Bank and Trust Company. It became the First National Bank Of Elyria in 1963 and closed around 2000. The large electric sign bears the city's one-time slogan, "Elyria, The 100% City." The sign was later changed to advertise Elyria Dry Goods Company.

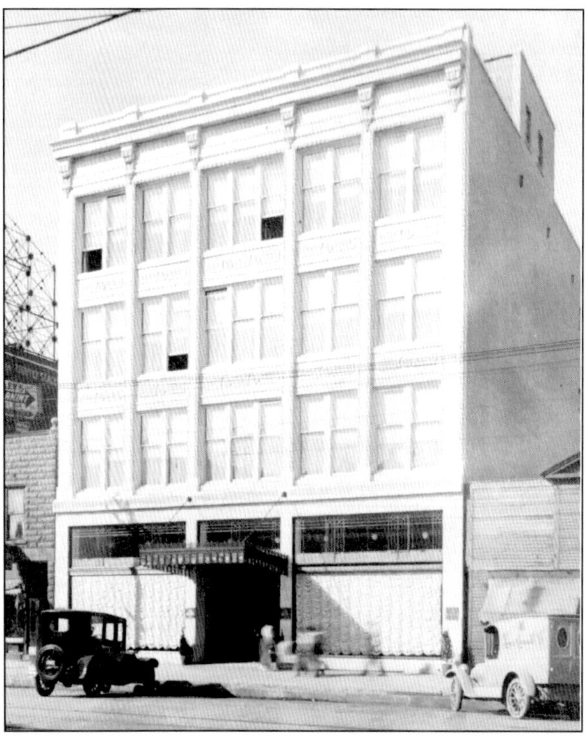

Lewis Mercantile Building. Located on the north side of Broad Street, the Lewis Mercantile store is more familiar to Elyrians as the J.C. Penney building. It was across the street from the Sears building. This building now houses Shane Furniture.

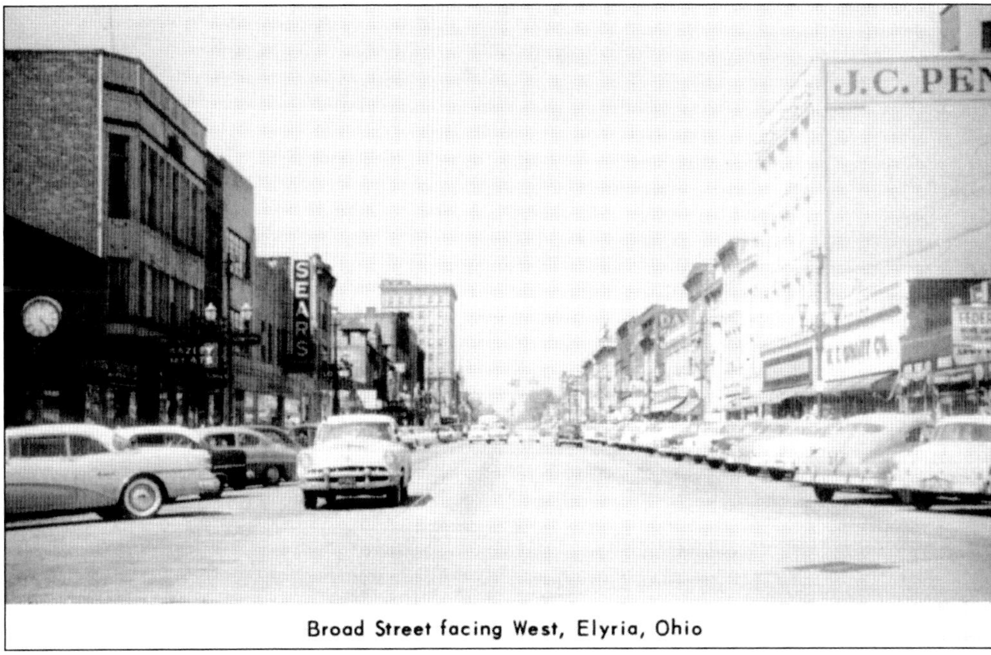

BROAD STREET, 1940S. With Sears on the south side and Penney's and Grants on the north side, this section of Broad Street was the heart of Elyria's shopping district for many years. Parking was at a premium on a sunny afternoon.

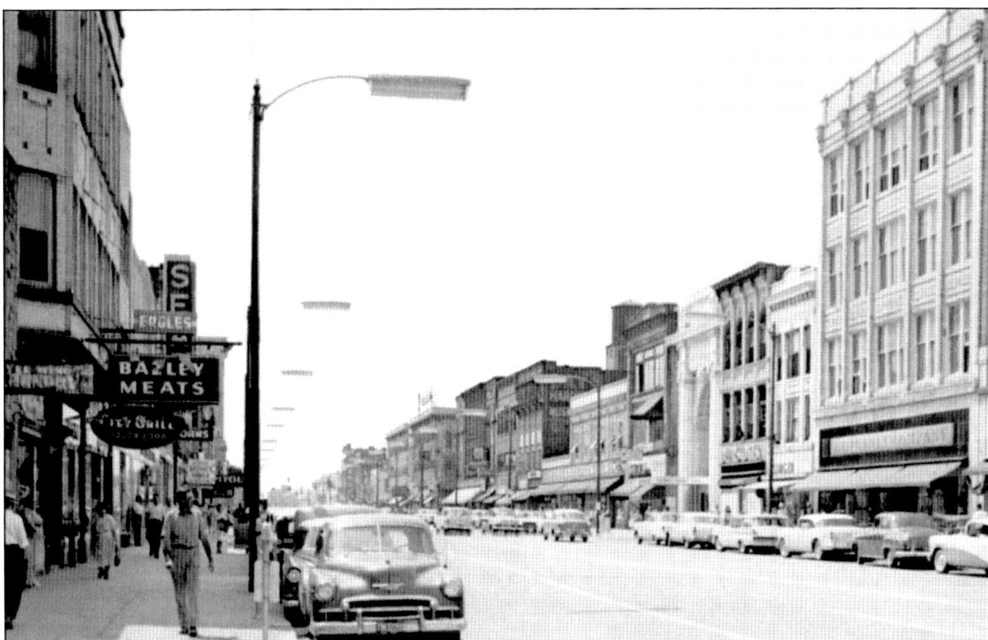

BROAD STREET, 1950S. J.C. Penney's is on the right, as it looked prior to receiving a new façade. Neisner's Five and Dime is near the center of this postcard. After the Midway Mall opened in the mid-1960s, Sears, Penney's, Grant's, and many other merchants closed their downtown stores.

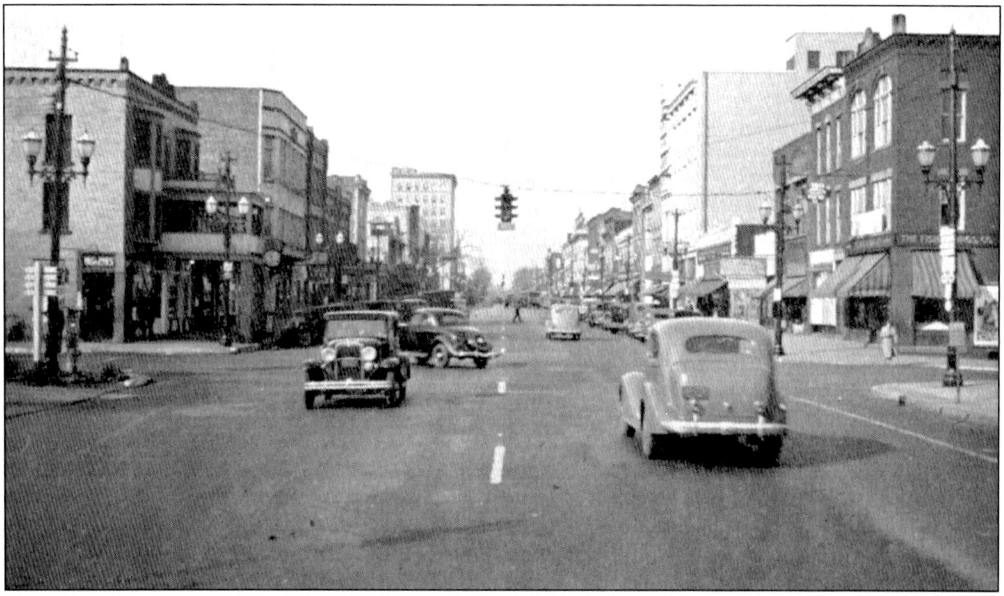

Intersection, Broad Street and East Avenue. This 1930s view shows the Weddell House hotel on the southwest corner with Eddie's Cigar Store on the ground floor. The building on the northwest corner housed Weiss Shoe Store for many years. The Post Office would be just off to the right in this view, on the northeast corner of Broad Street and East Avenue.

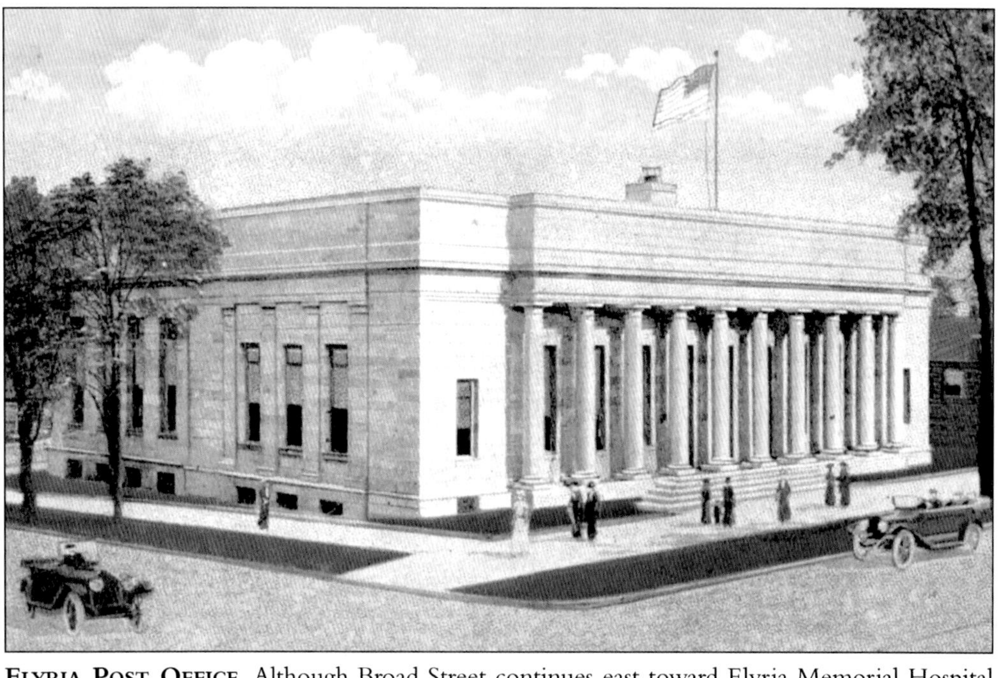

Elyria Post Office. Although Broad Street continues east toward Elyria Memorial Hospital and the Eastern Heights residential neighborhood, the old post office is the last of the grand public downtown buildings. Built in 1918 on the corner of Broad Street and East Avenue, it stood vacant from 1981 until 2001, when it was beautifully restored and renovated by Fifth Third Bank.

Two

Hospital and Eldercare

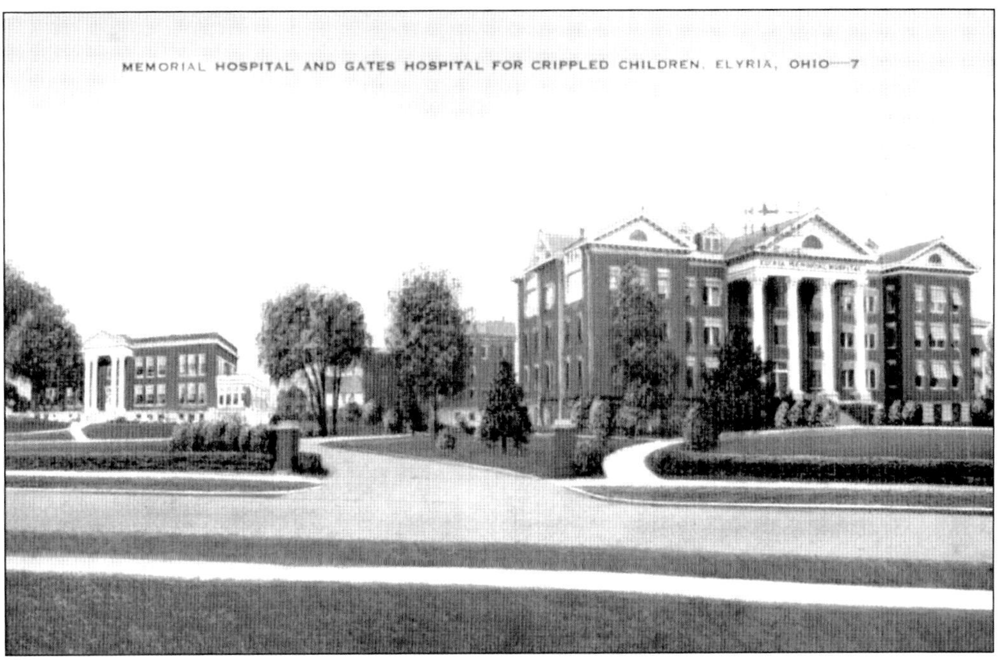

Elyria Memorial Hospital Complex. From across East River Street, we see three of the four buildings that were a part of the hospital complex by the 1920s. Gates Hospital for Crippled Children is to the left rear, with M.B. Johnson School of Nursing in the center, and the main hospital building in front.

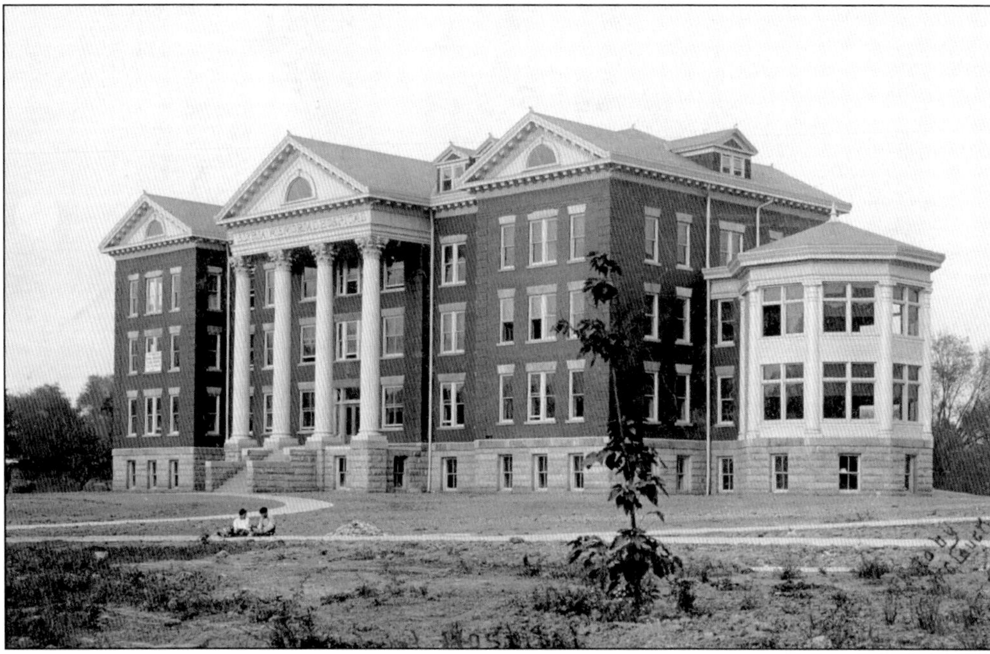

ELYRIA MEMORIAL HOSPITAL. The newly completed hospital, not yet landscaped, stands alone in this early postcard. It opened in October 1908 in memory of the nine people killed in a Memorial Day streetcar accident the previous year.

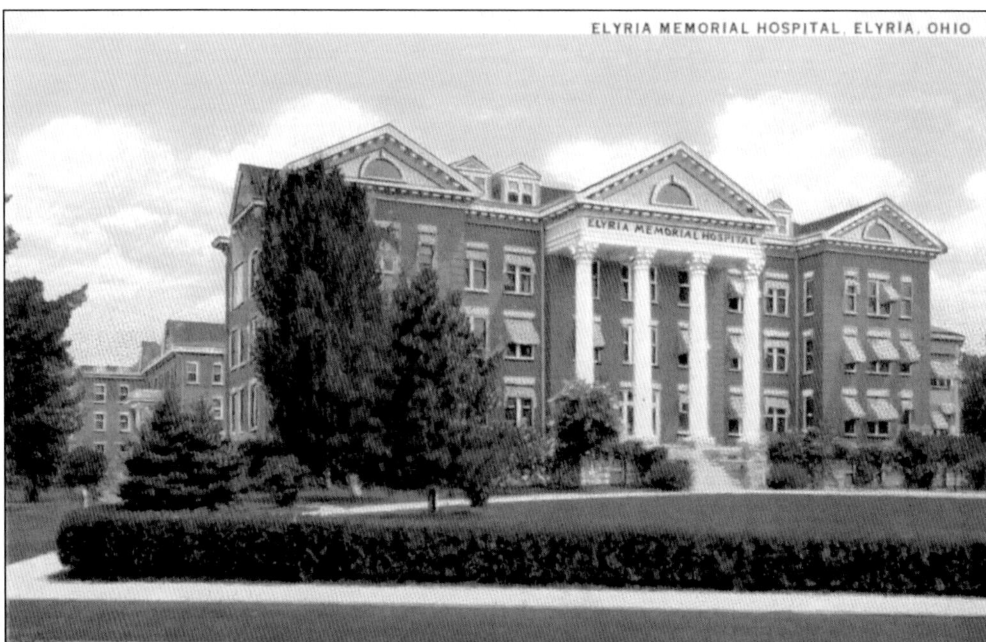

ELYRIA MEMORIAL HOSPITAL. This handsome brick building was erected on the site of an old brickyard on East River Street. If one looks closely at the hospital today, it is possible to discern the shape of this old building among the many additions.

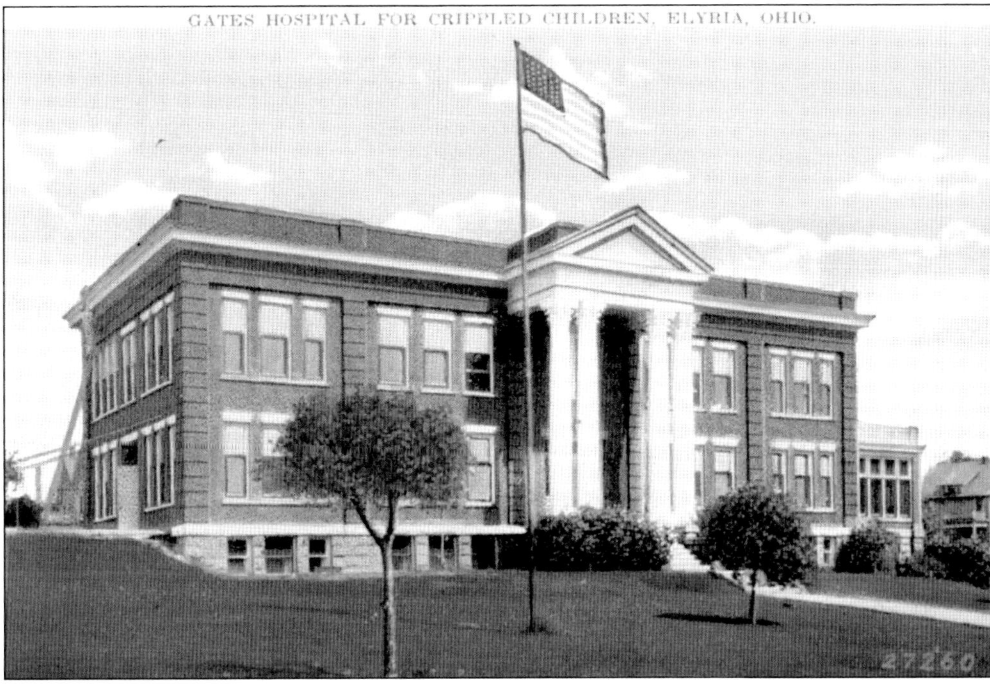

GATES HOSPITAL FOR CRIPPLED CHILDREN. The first of its kind in the nation, the Gates Hospital for Crippled Children opened its doors in 1915. Edgar F. Allen, a local businessman, spearheaded fundraising efforts for the project after a survey revealed large numbers of crippled children under the age of 13. Allen's work led to the founding of the Easter Seals Society.

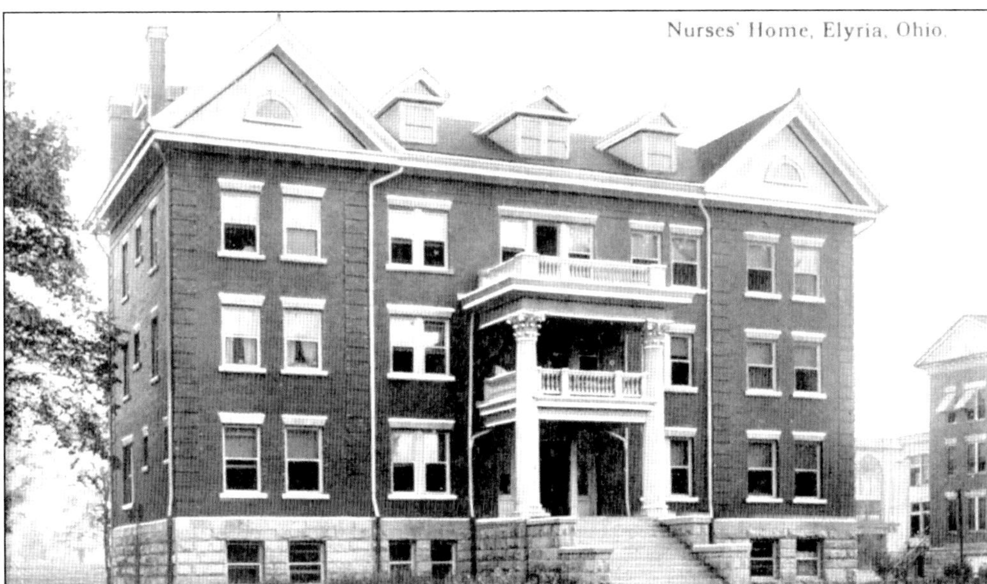

M.B. JOHNSON SCHOOL OF NURSING RESIDENCE HALL. The M.B. Johnson School of Nursing opened in 1908. It was one of a handful of programs in the U.S. to offer a three-year course in nursing. This residence hall was built for the student nurses in 1909. The nursing school and dormitory were later razed to make way for the Gates Medical Center building.

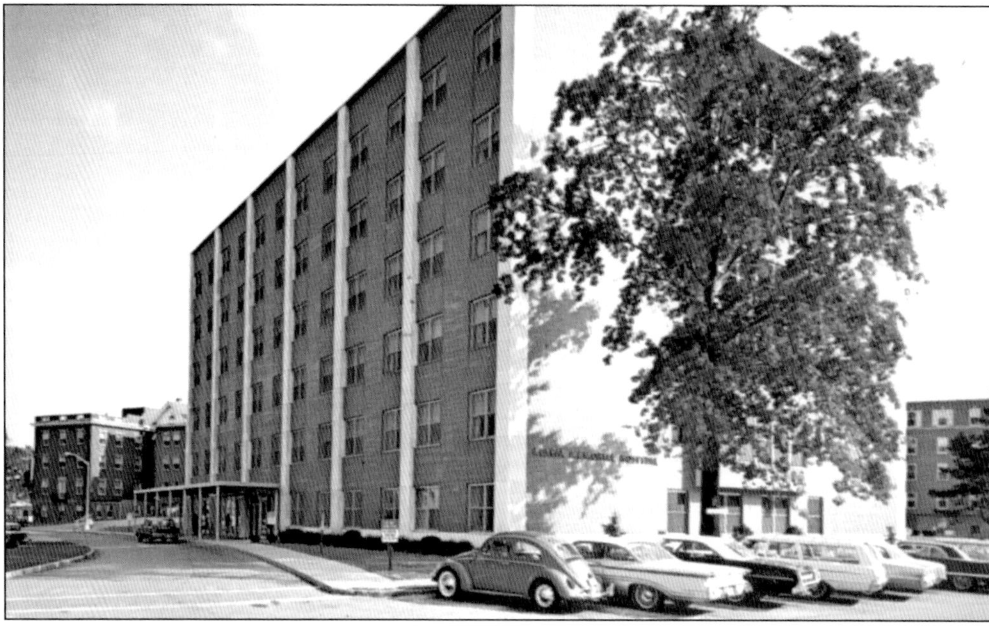

West Building of EMH. This view of the hospital is familiar to many Elyrians. After this addition in 1964, the hospital remained unchanged until four floors were added in 1978. Here, the original hospital buildings can be seen in the background at either side.

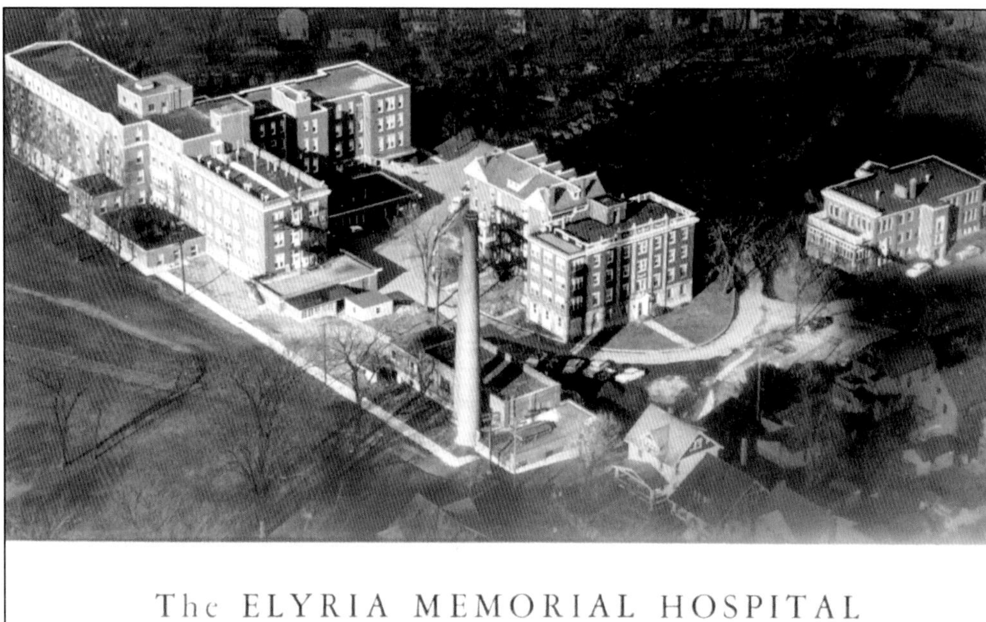

Elyria Memorial Hospital, Aerial View. The original buildings of the hospital can all be seen in this aerial shot. To the far right is Gates Hospital for Crippled Children. The M.B. Johnson School of Nursing is next to Gates with the nurses' residence hall behind and perpendicular to it. The original hospital building, with its 1953 addition, is at top left. Part of the field adjoining McKinley School can be seen at lower left.

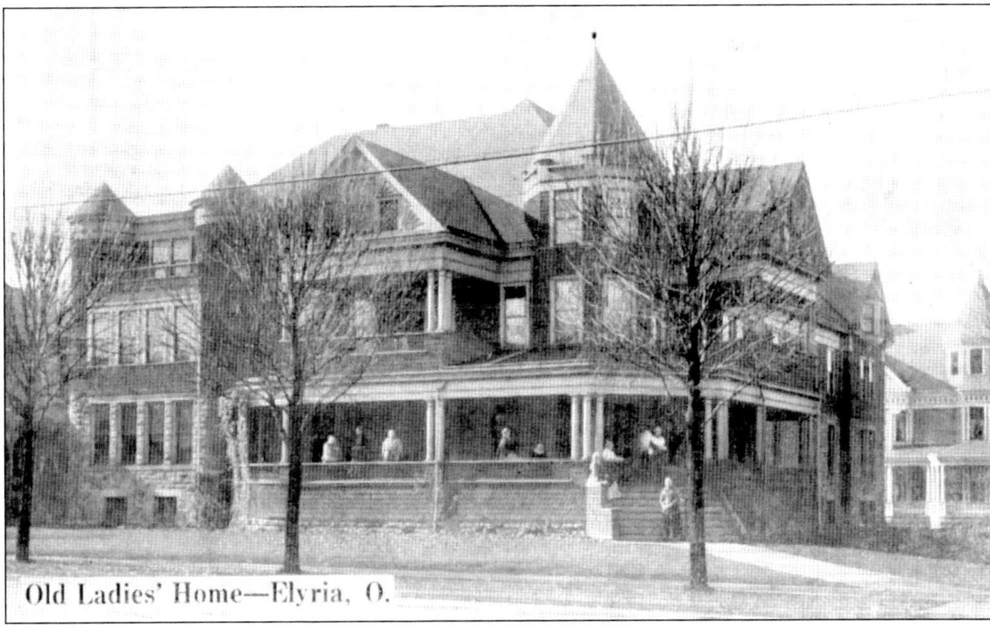

OLD LADIES' HOME. The Old Ladies' Home Association was established in 1901. The association purchased land and built this home on the corner of Second Street and West Avenue (where Ed Thome's Sohio station later stood). In 1907, the Northern Ohio Conference of Methodist Churches took over operations.

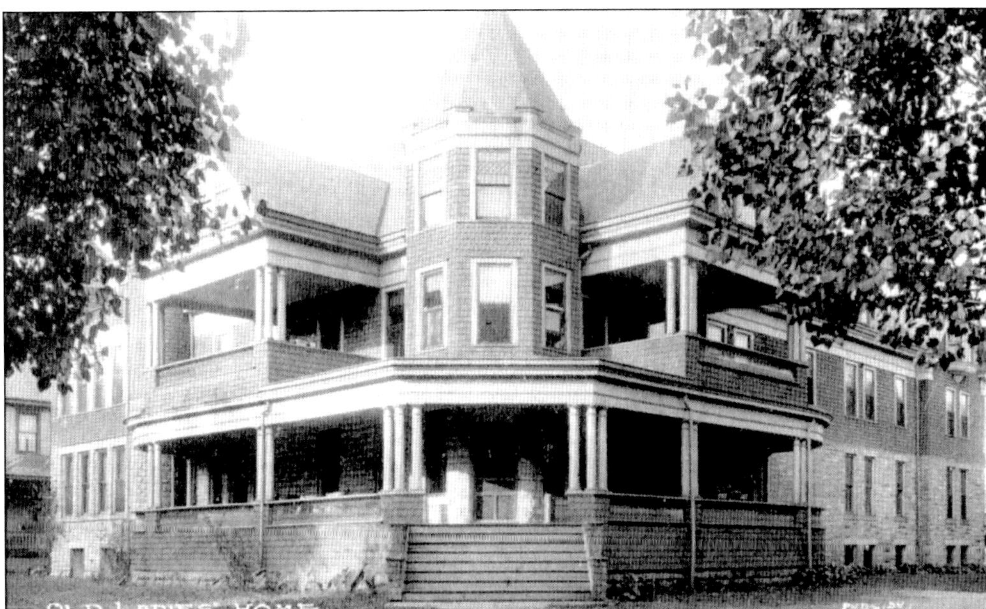

OLD LADIES' HOME. The large stone and frame house had "room for 21 old ladies," as one old postcard reads, and served as the Old Ladies' Home until 1923. At that time, the Conference purchased the Boyd and Wick homes on West Avenue, and the facility became known as The Elyria Home of the Aged, later the Elyria Methodist Home.

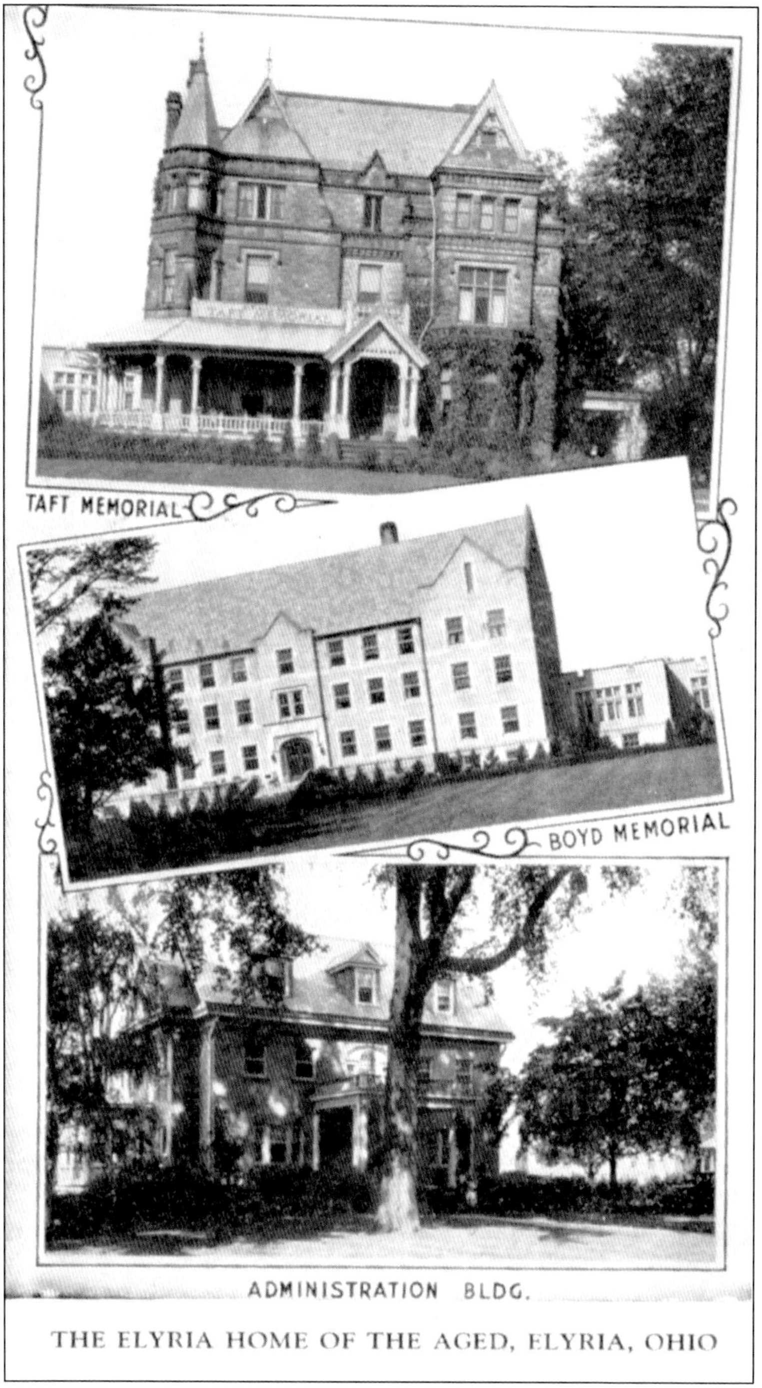

ELYRIA HOME OF THE AGED. This postcard shows the three original buildings of the Methodist Home. At top is the old George Ely mansion, renamed Taft Memorial in honor of Charles Taft, a benefactor. A new structure, Boyd Memorial was named for Mr. and Mrs. D.C. Boyd, two other contributors. The Administration Building, in the bottom view, was the former Henry Wick homestead at the corner of West Avenue and 8th Street.

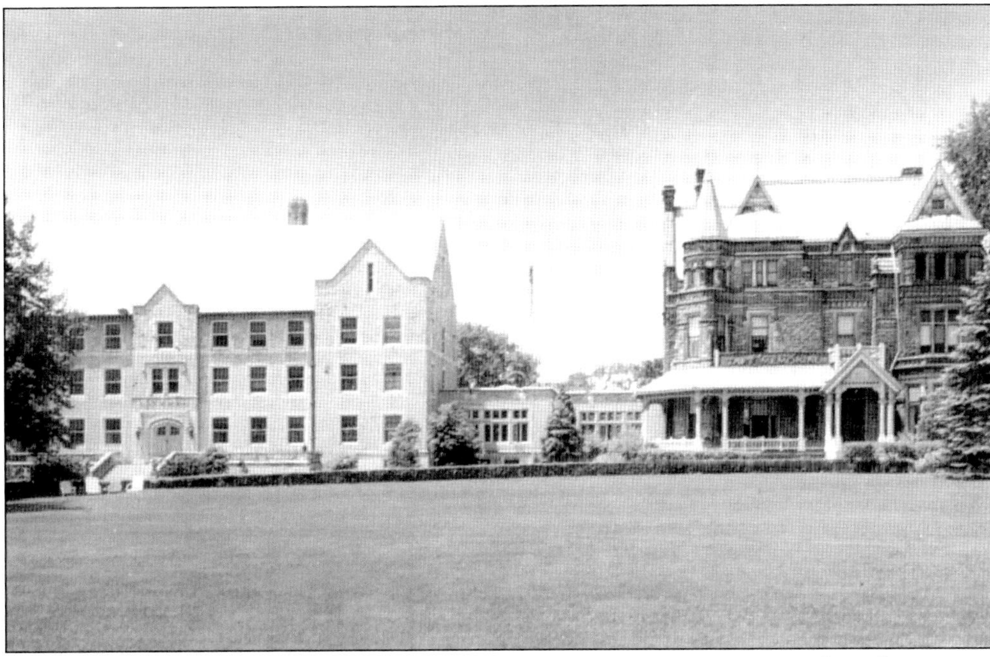

BOYD AND TAFT HALLS. Boyd Hall, at left, was the first building constructed on the new site in 1927. The main dining room was in Boyd Hall until 1967 when it moved to Memorial Hall, which was built where Taft Hall stands in this postcard. Memorial Hall has since been replaced as well.

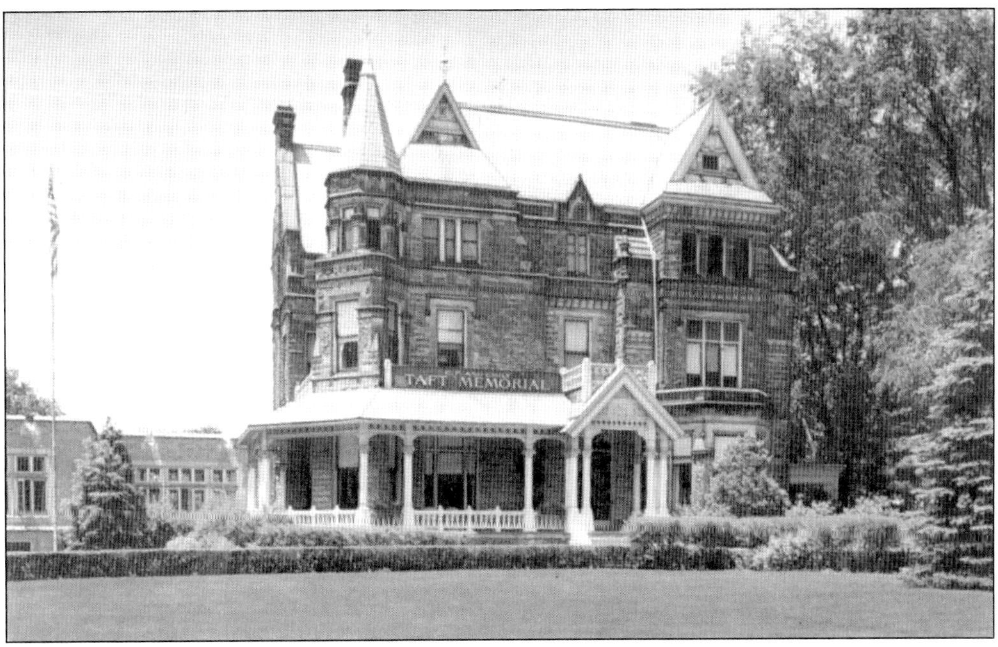

TAFT HALL. This lovely old stone mansion was originally built in 1894 by George Ely, a grandson of Heman Ely, the founder of Elyria. It served as an integral part of the Methodist Home until the mid-1960s when it was demolished to make way for Memorial Hall.

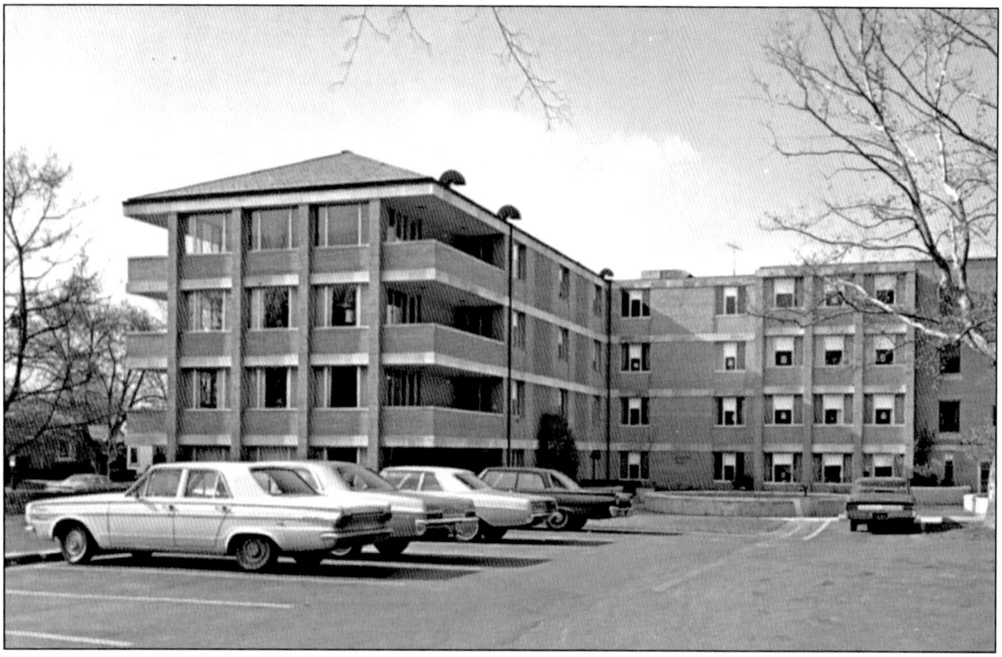

REEDER HALL. Reeder Hall, constructed in 1962, was named after one of the first superintendents of the home, Dr. Glezen A. Reeder. It was built where the Henry Wick homestead building once stood and provided housing for some 40 additional residents.

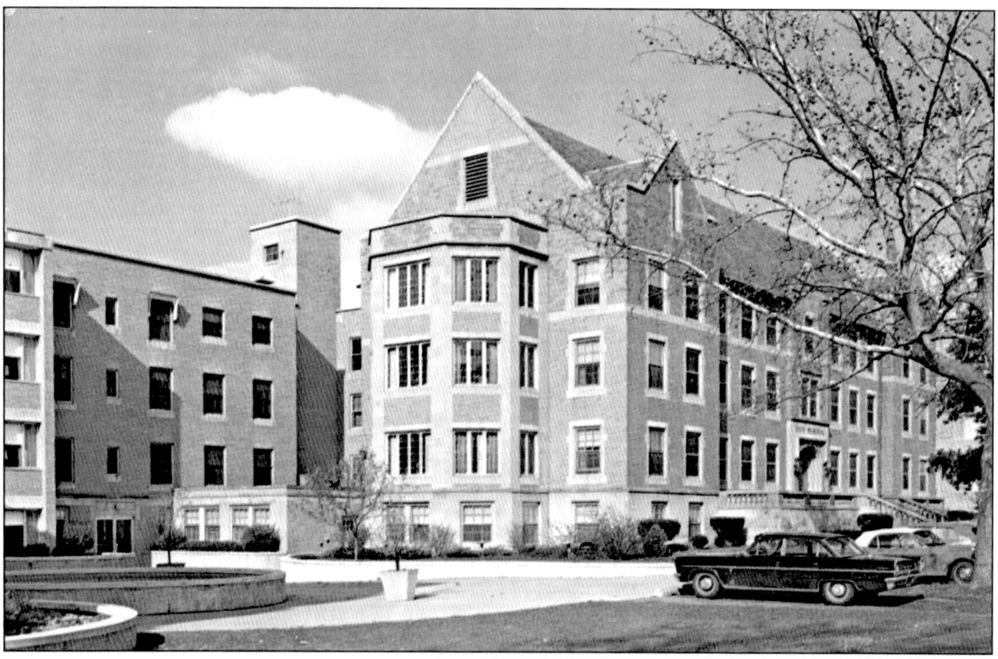

WESLEY AND BOYD HALLS. Looking from a different angle, we can see Wesley Hall to the left behind Boyd Hall. Wesley Hall was built in 1952, at the same time that the Chapel was constructed. An adjoining courtyard included the simple fountain at left.

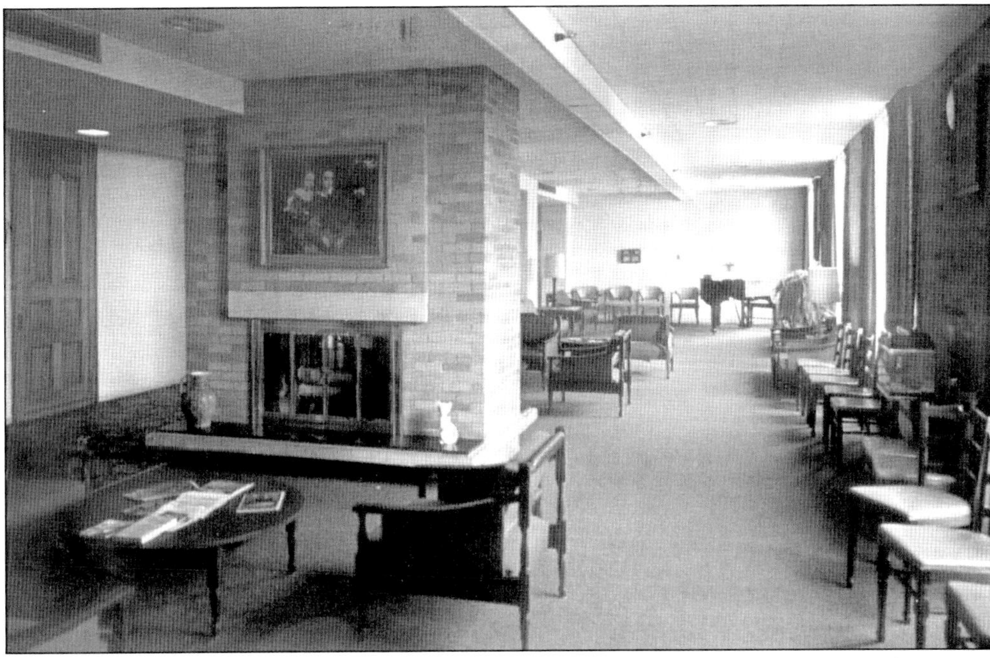

MEMORIAL HALL, TAFT LOUNGE. When Memorial Hall was built in 1967, some elements of Taft Hall, which formerly stood on the site, were included in the new construction as a way of preserving its memory. The Taft Lounge, adjoining the main dining room, was a popular gathering place for residents.

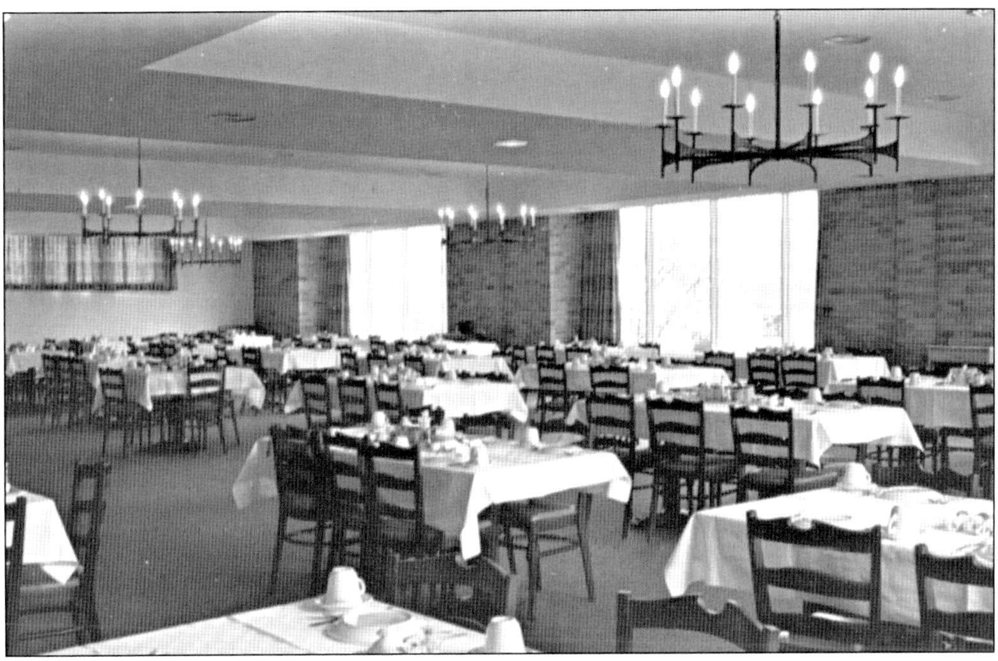

MEMORIAL HALL, MAIN DINING ROOM. The large plate-glass windows of the main dining room overlooked the scenic cottage area behind the main buildings. About 200 residents could dine in comfort in this attractive room.

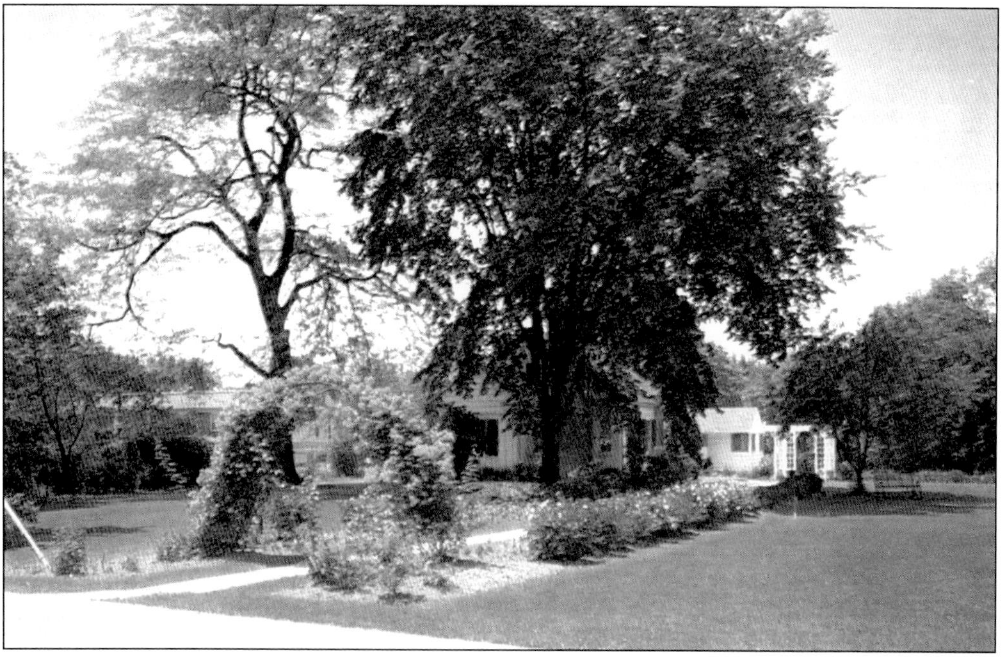

ENTRANCE TO "THE COTTAGES." Many Elyrians will remember passing under this flowering arbor entrance to the Cottages at the Methodist Home. The 10 attractively maintained cottages were on a horseshoe-shaped path with the woods and river behind.

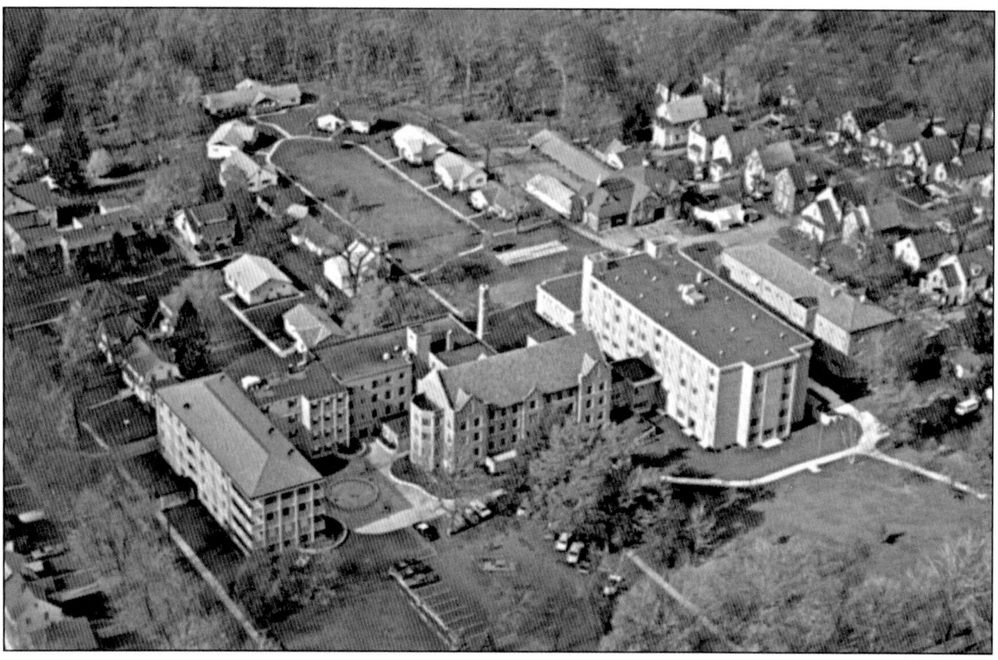

METHODIST HOME, AERIAL VIEW. This postcard provides a clear overview of the Methodist Home and grounds **circa** 1970. The grounds comprised about 11 acres, including the woods behind the cottages. Reeder Hall, Wesley Hall, and Boyd Hall to the left are still in use today. Memorial Hall and the building to its right have since been replaced.

Three

Around the Square

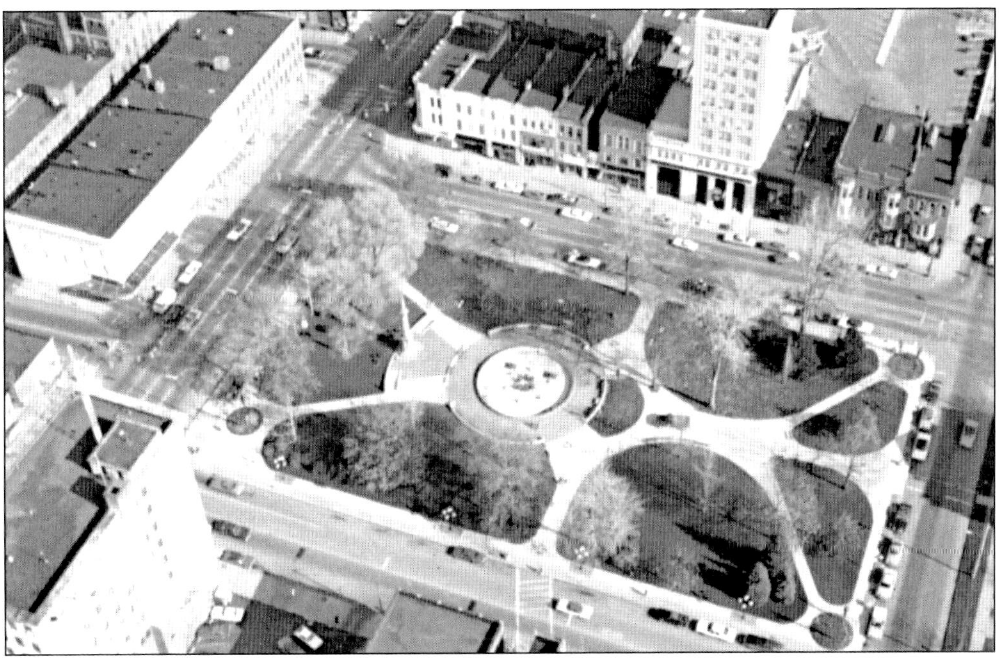

Ely Square, Aerial View. This aerial view of the park in spring offers an opportunity to see the entire park before the trees have leafed out. When this shot was taken some time in the mid-1970s, the fountain had recently been remodeled, but the gazebo had not yet been built.

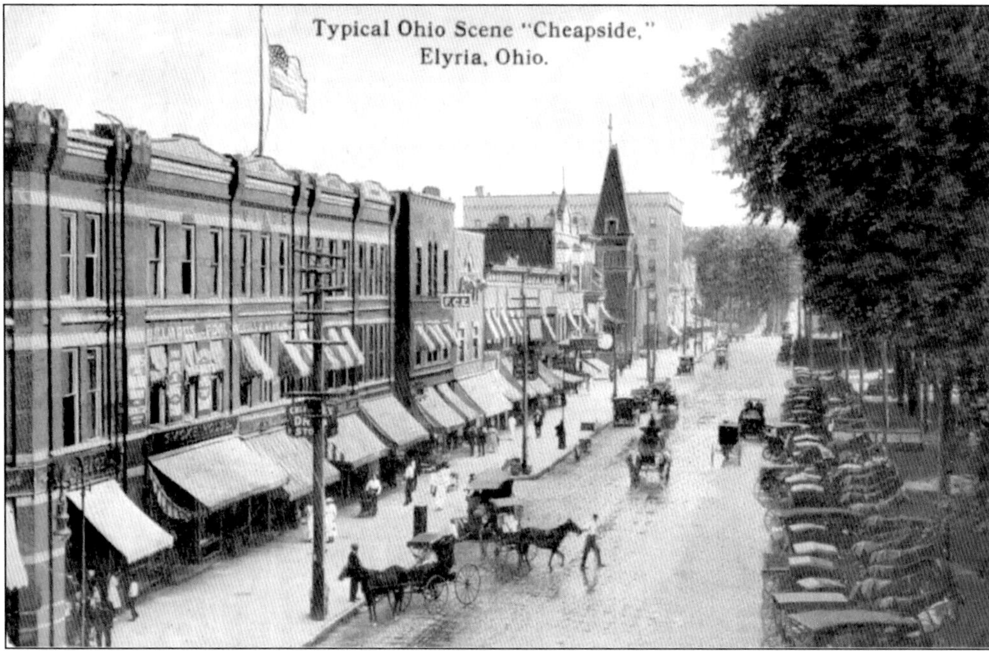

CHEAPSIDE LOOKING SOUTH. This must have been what Cheapside (currently Middle Avenue) looked like on a typical business day in the 1910s. A few automobiles are mixed in with the buggies parked in the shade of the trees in the square. The steeple of the First Baptist Church can be seen in the distance.

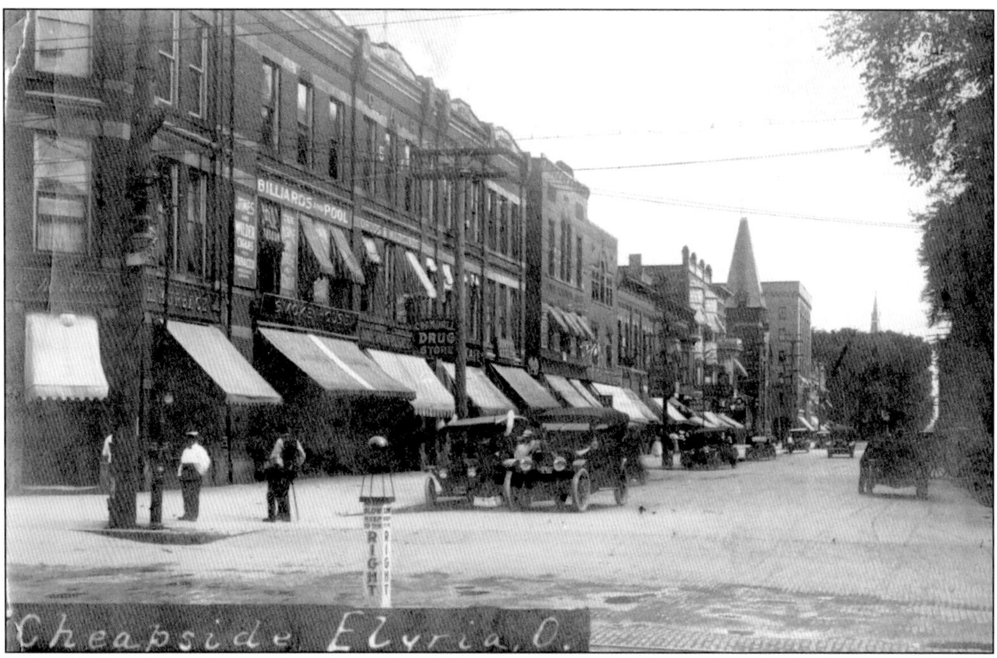

CLOSE-UP OF CHEAPSIDE. In this later shot, automobiles have replaced the horse and buggy, but the buildings are still very much the same. An early traffic regulator can be seen in the foreground. In the far distance, the spire of St. Mary's rises above the treetops.

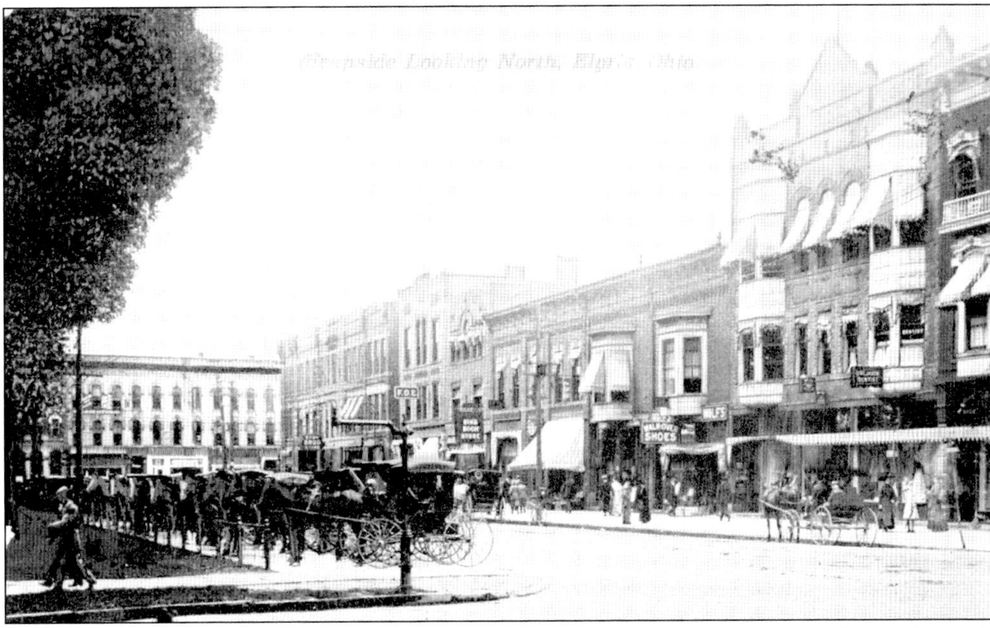

CHEAPSIDE LOOKING NORTH. On this warm summer's day, the awnings are out along Cheapside to protect the customers from the hot sun, while their horses wait in the shade of the trees in the square. This shot pre-dates the construction of the tall Lorain County Savings and Trust building.

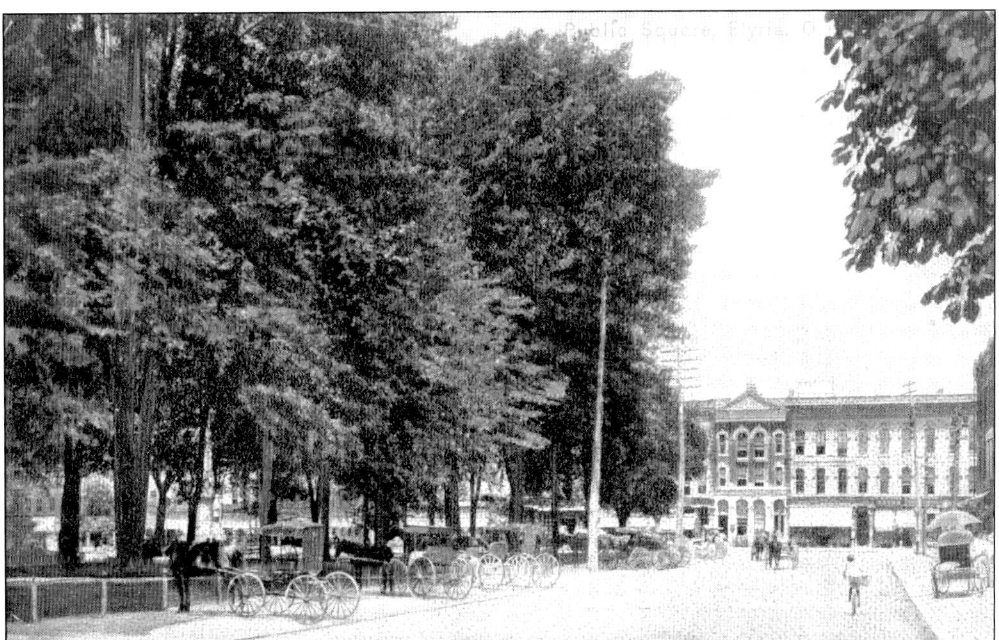

CHEAPSIDE LOOKING TOWARDS THE LIBRARY. In this shot looking down Cheapside, we can see the Elyria Public Library building where Cheapside meets Broad Street. The library was on the second floor of the building, which is recognizable by its white columns, brick façade, and pediment top.

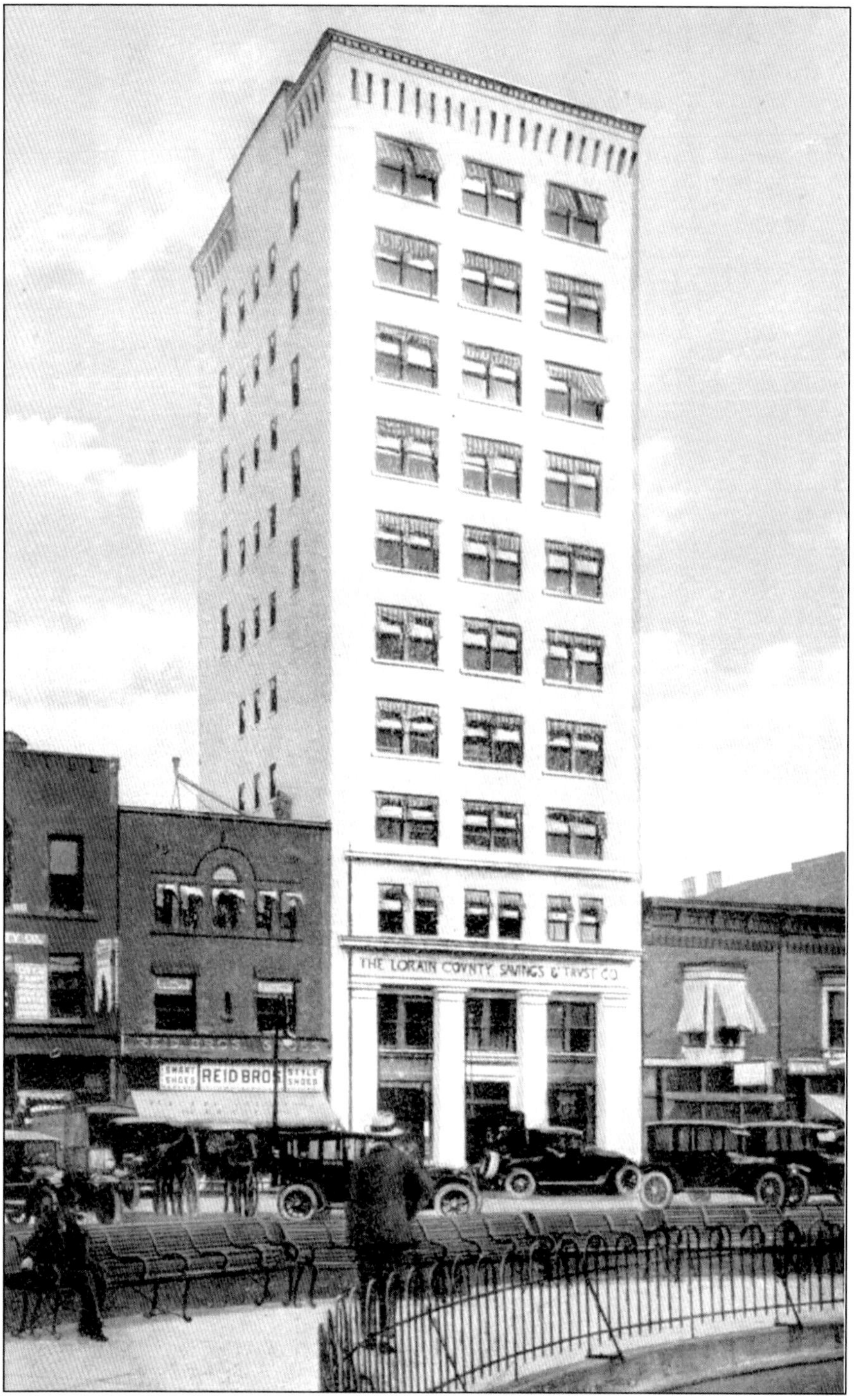

Lorain County Savings and Trust. When the Lorain County Banking Company moved from the Hotel Andwur into their new office building on Middle Avenue, they also changed their name and became known as Lorain County Savings and Trust (LCST). This was the tallest building in Elyria when it was completed in 1916 and remained so for many years.

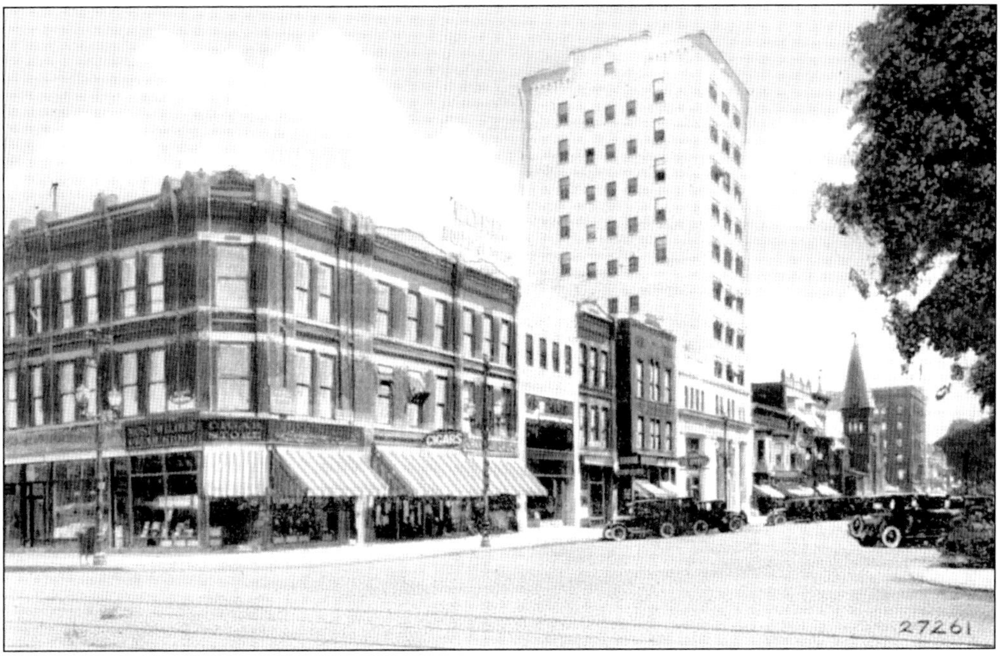

INTERSECTION OF BROAD STREET AND MIDDLE AVENUE. With the tall, new Lorain County Savings and Trust building anchoring the block and automobiles lining the street, Middle Avenue looks very prosperous in this view from the late 1920s.

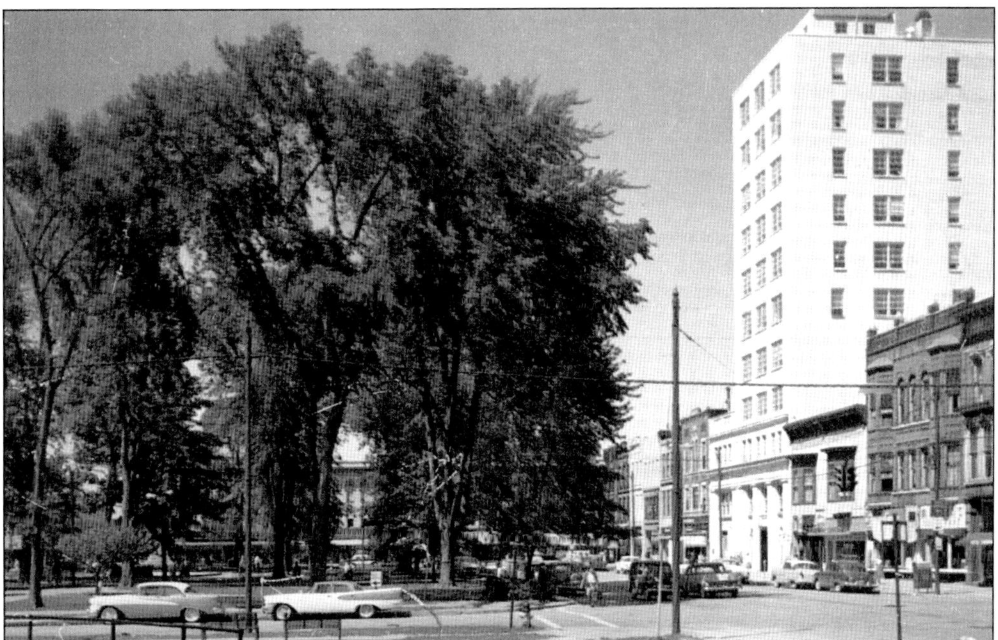

INTERSECTION OF MIDDLE AVENUE AND SECOND STREET. Looking north from the Court House steps, we see that Elyria was still a vital county seat in the 1960s. Offices, shops, and restaurants ringed the square to serve those who worked in the numerous county government buildings.

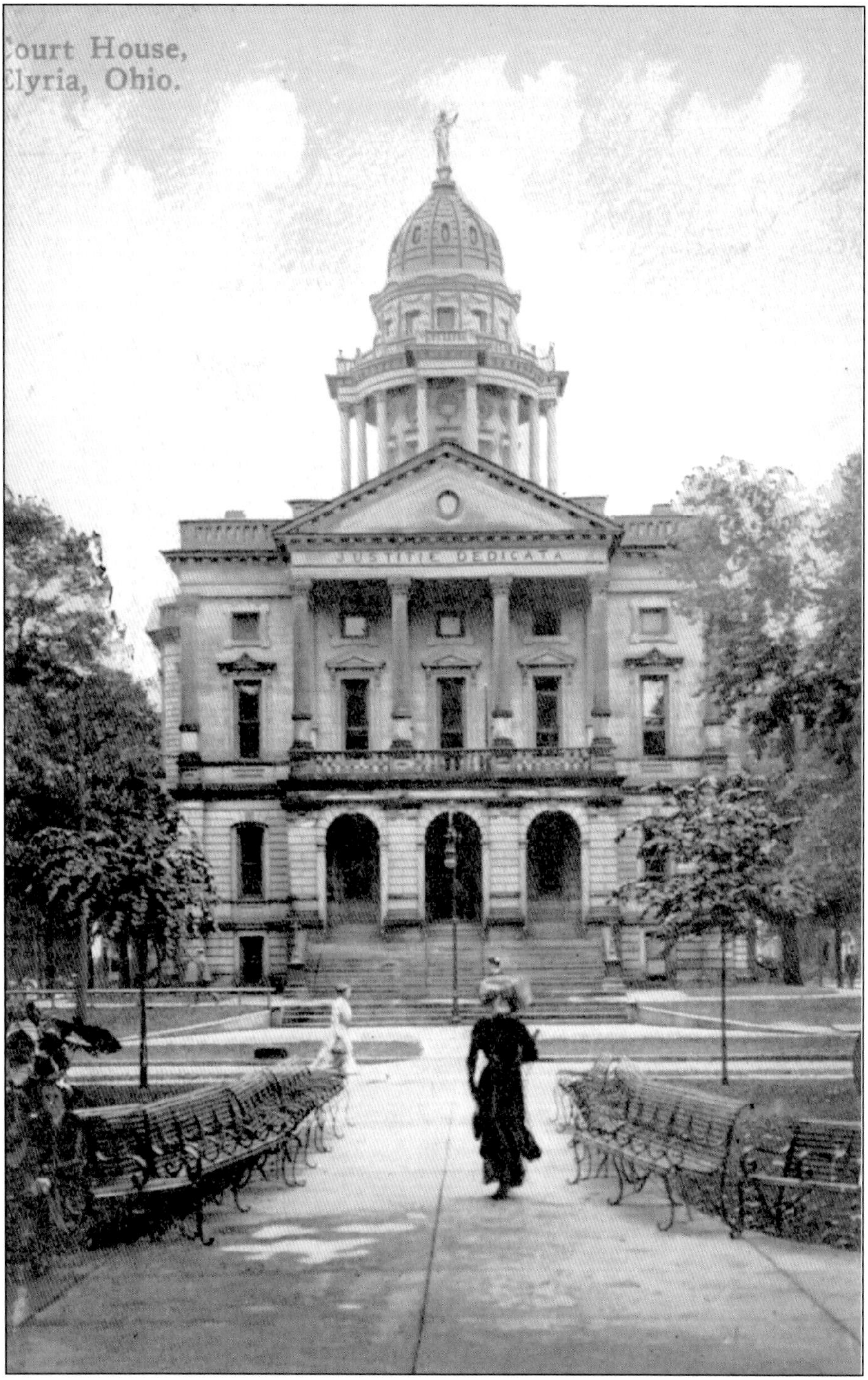

LORAIN COUNTY COURT HOUSE. The county court house in Elyria opened in 1881 and was the second court house located on this site. It was surmounted by a figure of Justice atop a large distinctive dome. The Court House has been in continuous use since its completion. This view shows the approach to the Court House from across Second Street in Ely Park in the early 1900s.

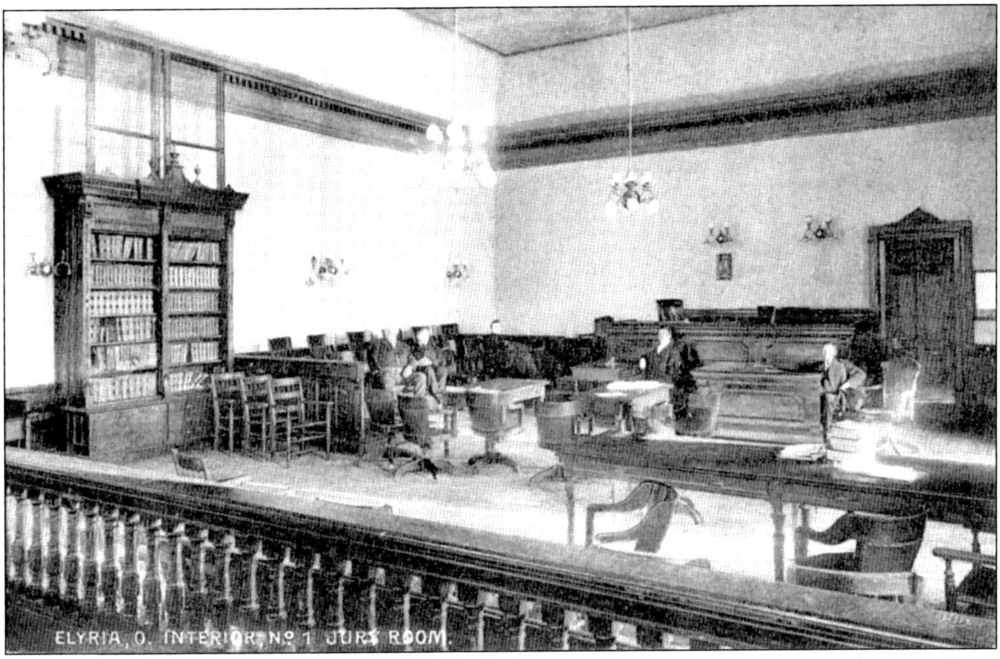

LORAIN COUNTY COURT HOUSE, INTERIOR. This unusual interior view shows a large courtroom from the spectators' seats as it appeared in the early 1910s. The occupied area at left center seems to be where the jury was seated during trials.

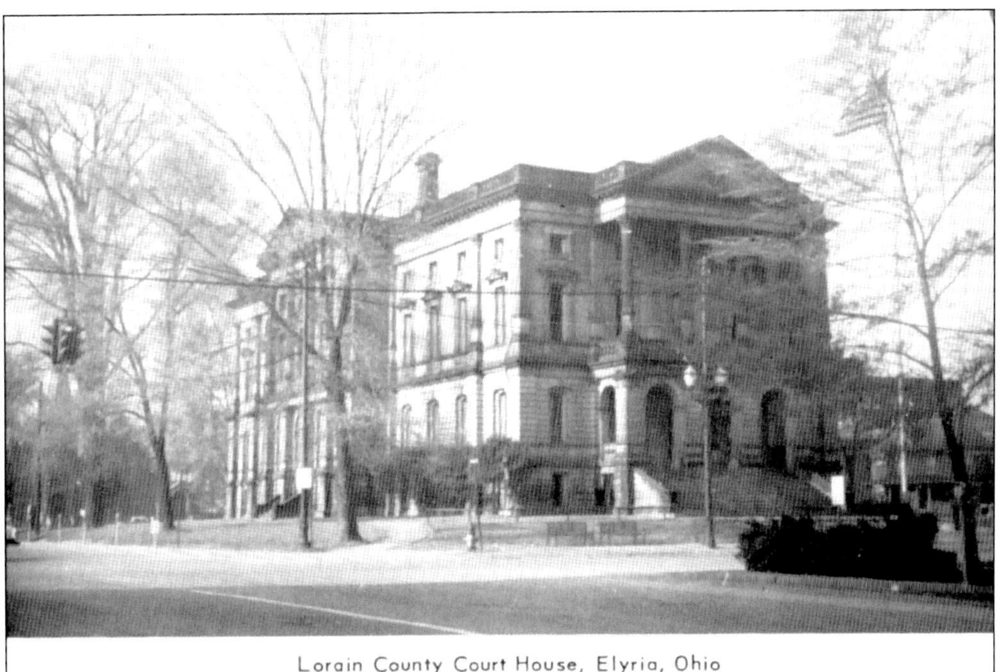

LORAIN COUNTY COURT HOUSE. In the early 1940s, the cupola and figure of Justice were removed from the Court House amid concerns that the badly deteriorated metal structures were likely to collapse. The Court House remains an imposing anchor at the south end of Ely Square.

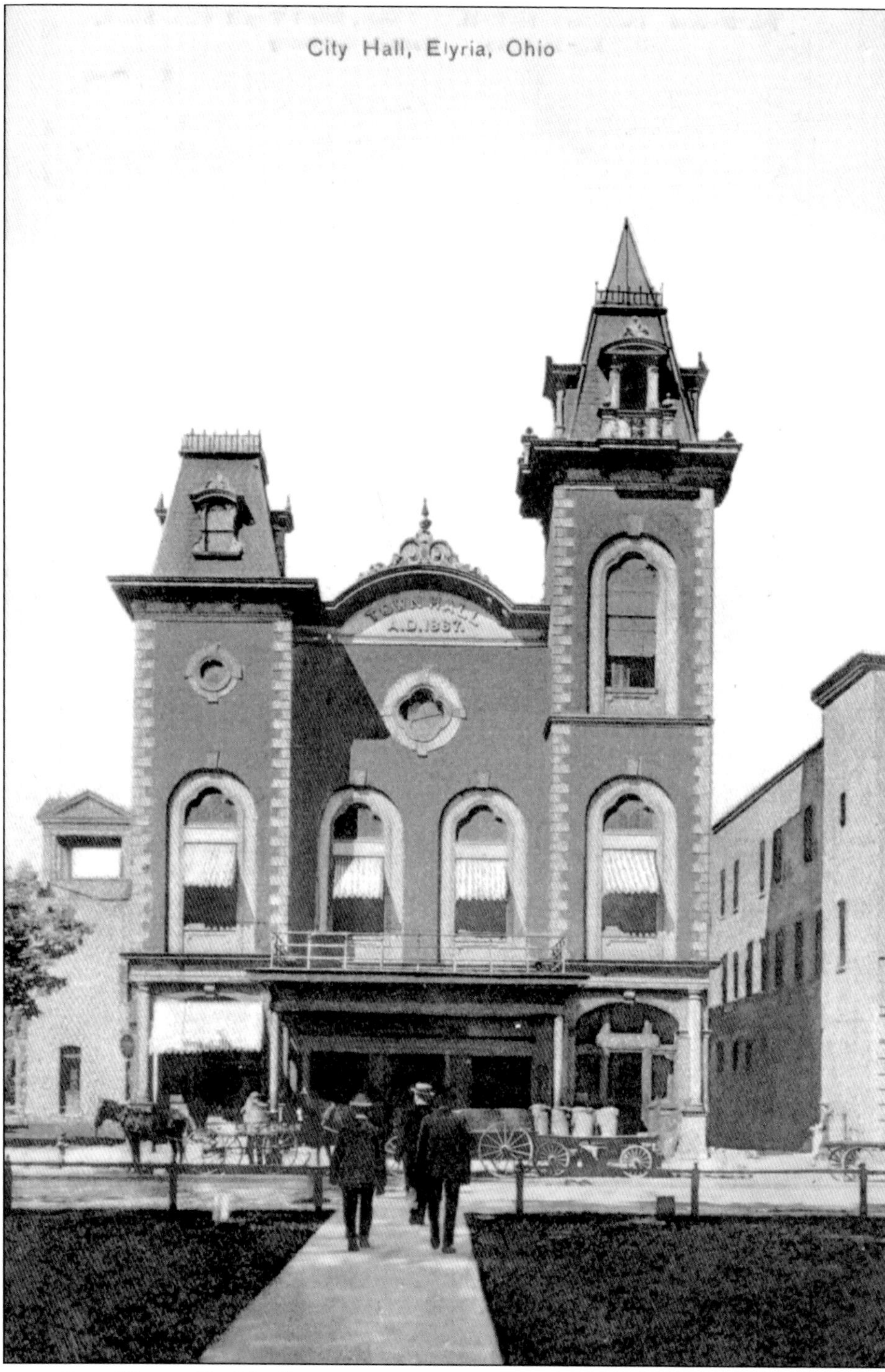

ELYRIA CITY HALL. Elyria's distinctive City Hall was built in 1867 on land purchased from Heman Ely, the town's founder. In 1878, during an extensive remodeling, the second floor was converted to an elegant opera house. The municipal fire department building can be seen at left rear.

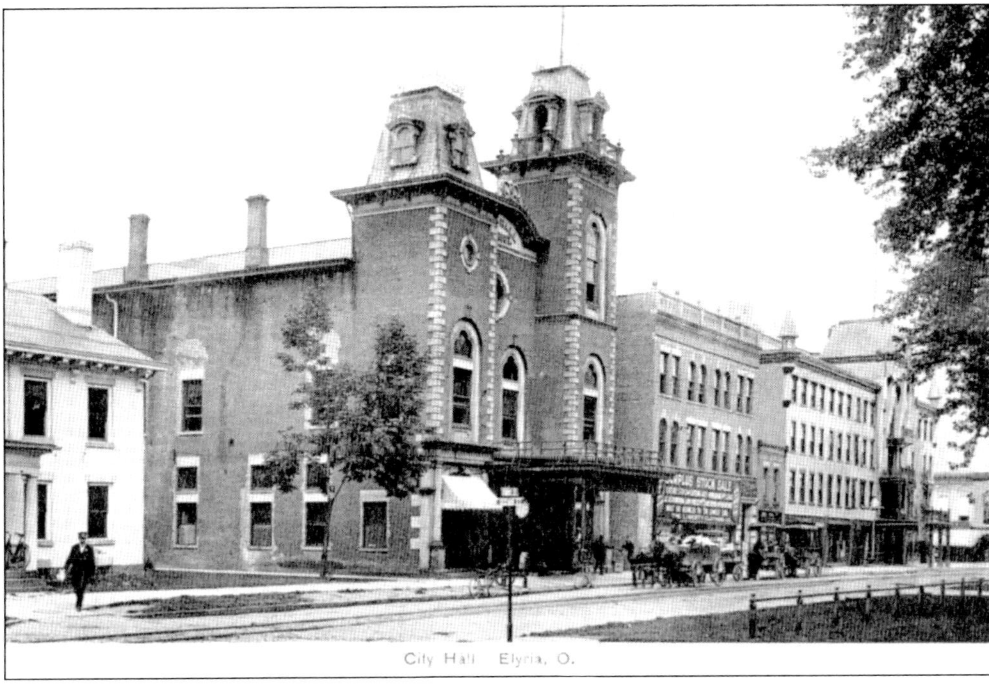

ELYRIA CITY HALL. The first block of Court Street included the William Cary residence, City Hall, the Turner Block, and the Hotel Andwur on the corner of Broad Street. In 1905, the opera house closed, and the space was converted to offices for city workers.

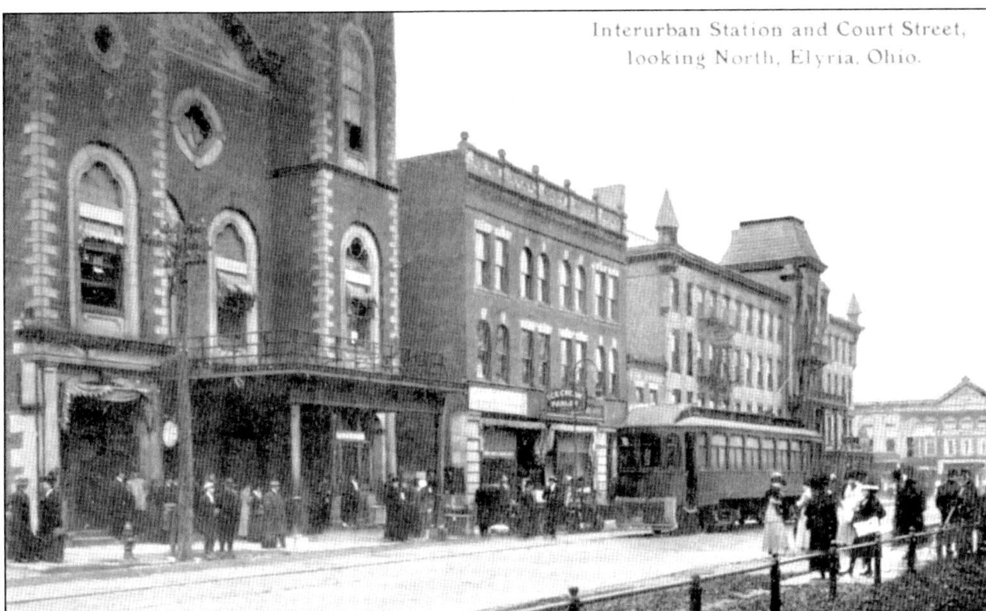

COURT STREET INTERURBAN STATION. A crowd of shoppers and travelers wait as a Green Line trolley approaches the Lake Shore Electric station on the first floor of City Hall. Passengers disembarking in Elyria found restaurants and a hotel nearby and the restful green space of the park across the street.

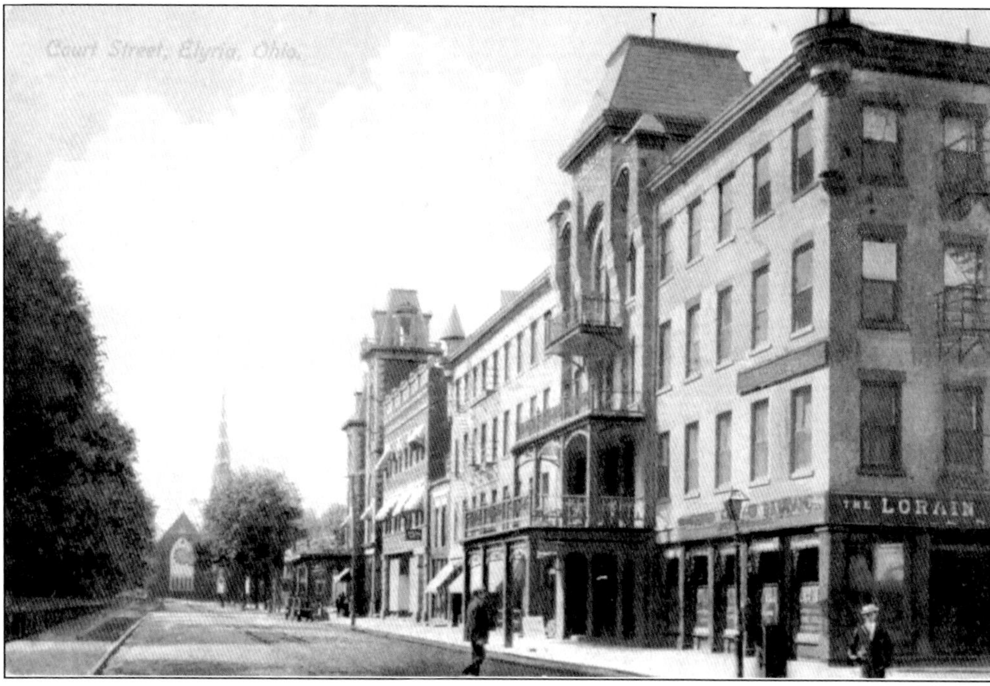

COURT STREET LOOKING SOUTH. The entire two-block length of Court Street, from the Hotel Andwur on Broad Street to the old Methodist Episcopal church on Third Street, can be seen here.

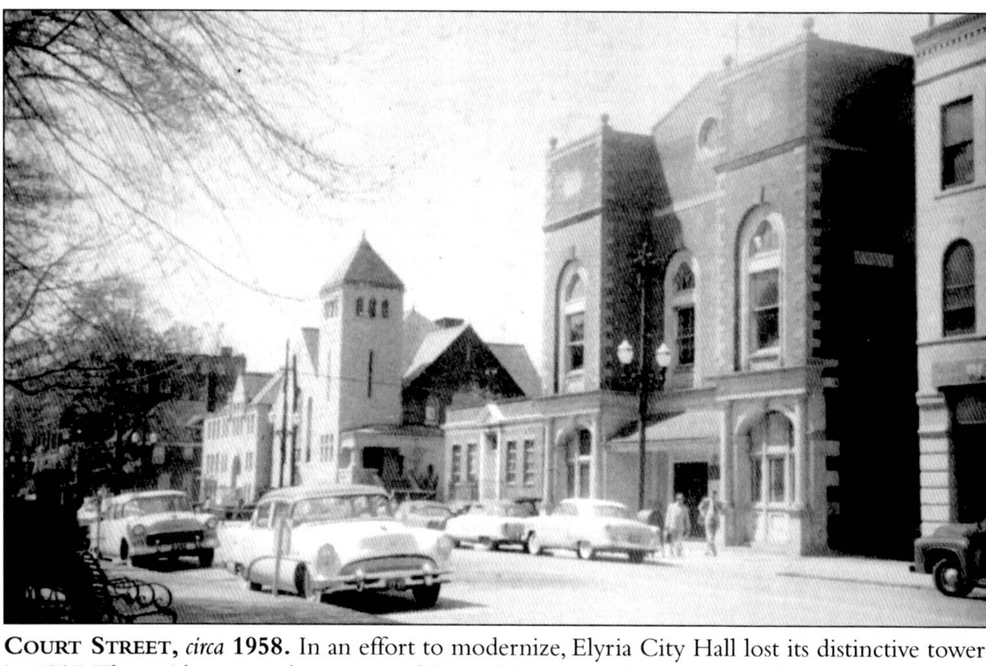

COURT STREET, *circa* **1958.** In an effort to modernize, Elyria City Hall lost its distinctive towers in 1937. The residence on the corner of Second Street had been replaced by a one-story brick building housing the Public Health Department. First Congregational Church and the YMCA occupied the second block of Court Street.

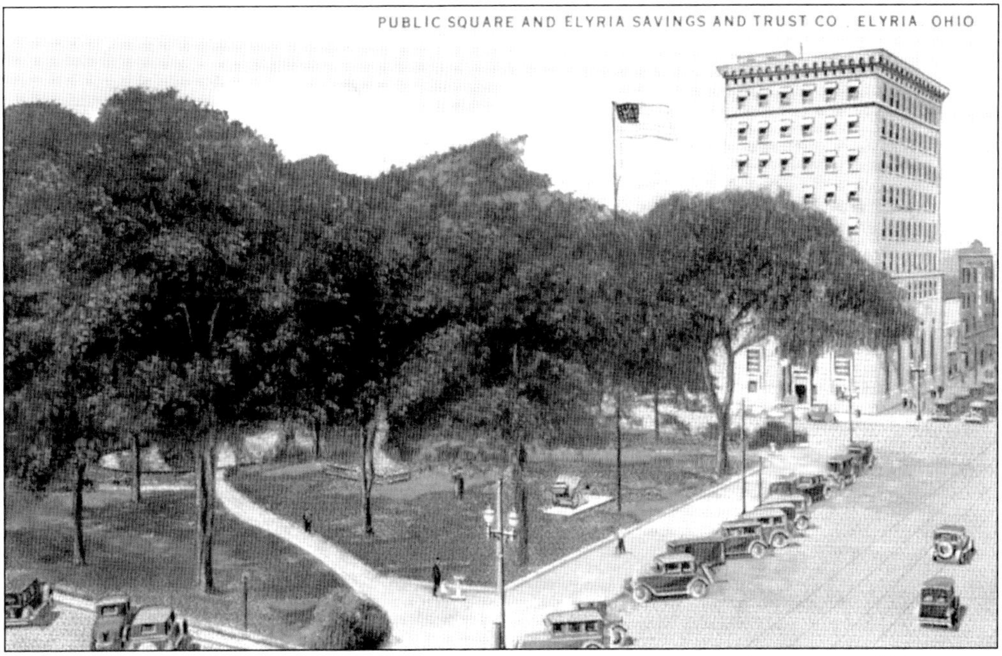

ELY PARK. Three of the four streets that border Ely Park can be seen in this view: Middle Avenue, Broad Street, and Court Street. The Elyria Savings and Trust Bank, built in 1923 on the site of the old Hotel Andwur, overlooks the park.

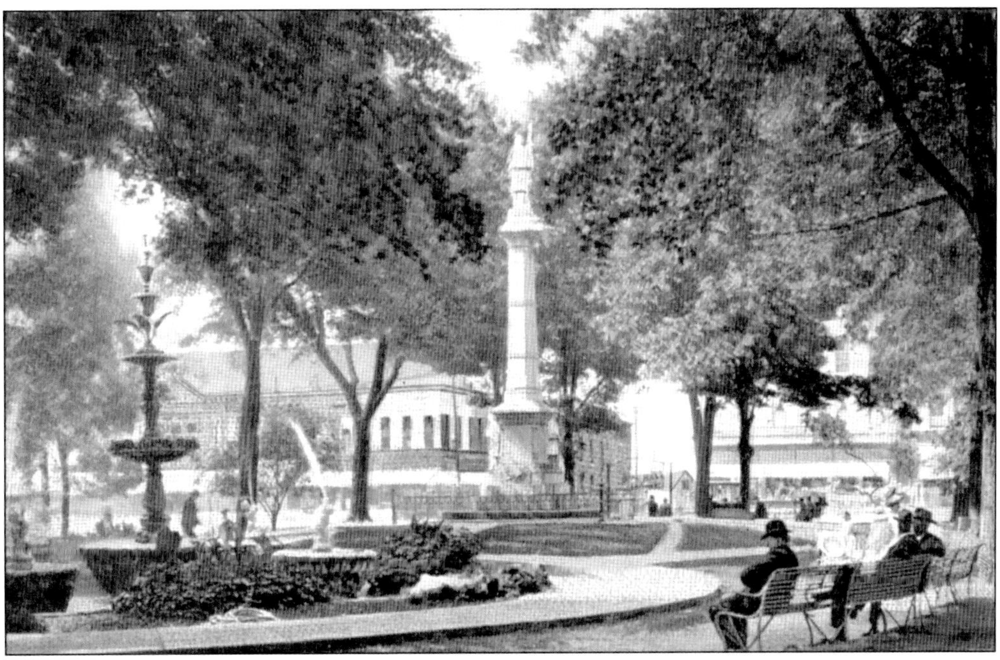

FOUNTAIN AND MONUMENT IN ELY PARK. A relaxing, shaded haven in the heart of Elyria's business district, Ely Park was the perfect spot to read, listen to the fountain, and watch the people go by. In this view to the north, the Mill Street (Lodi) intersection is just to the right of the monument.

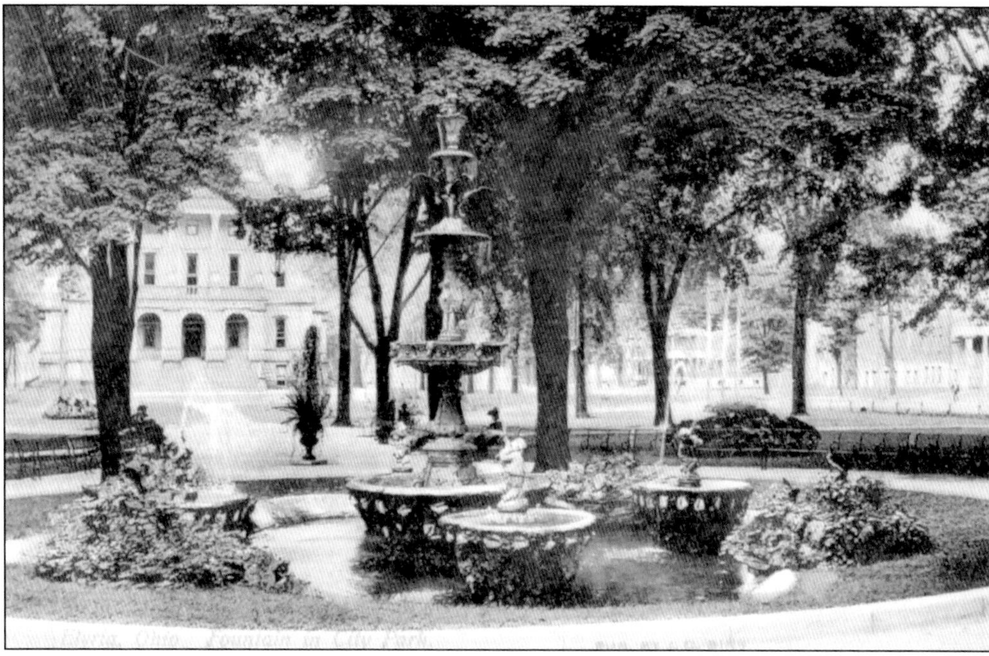

EARLY FOUNTAIN, ELY PARK. This graceful Victorian fountain dates to 1870, when it replaced the original fountain built on the same site in 1850. The Lorain County Court House can be seen in the background. Note the absence of fencing around the fountain.

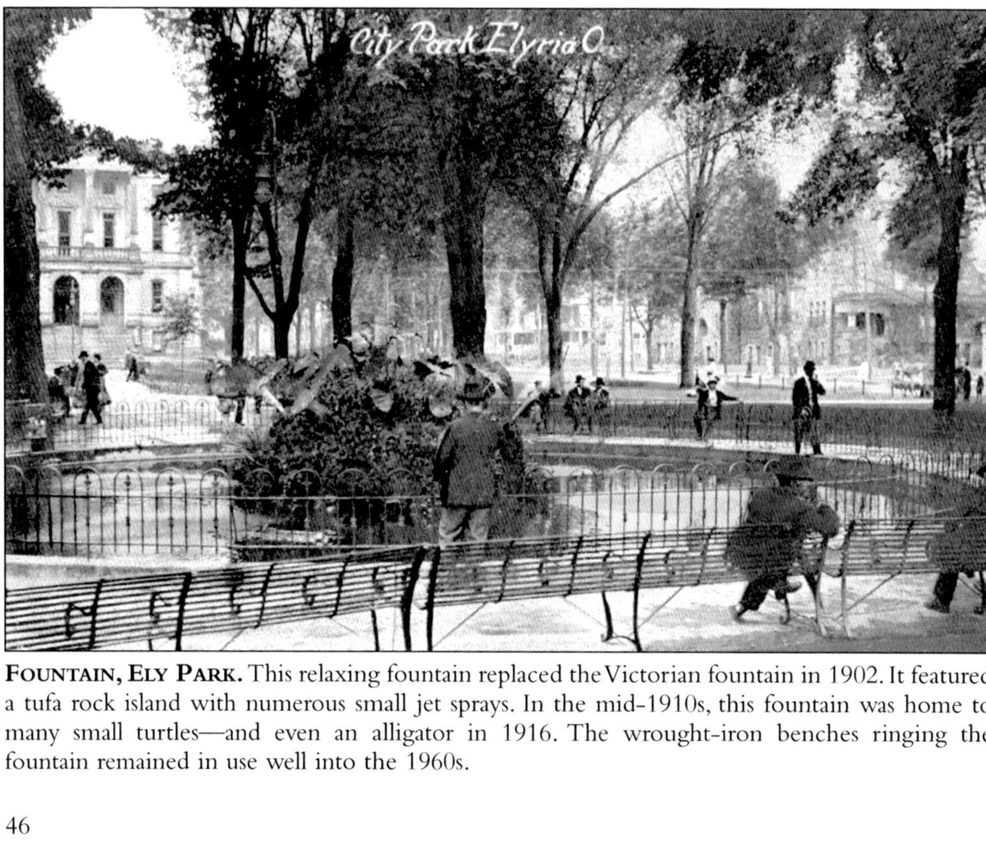

FOUNTAIN, ELY PARK. This relaxing fountain replaced the Victorian fountain in 1902. It featured a tufa rock island with numerous small jet sprays. In the mid-1910s, this fountain was home to many small turtles—and even an alligator in 1916. The wrought-iron benches ringing the fountain remained in use well into the 1960s.

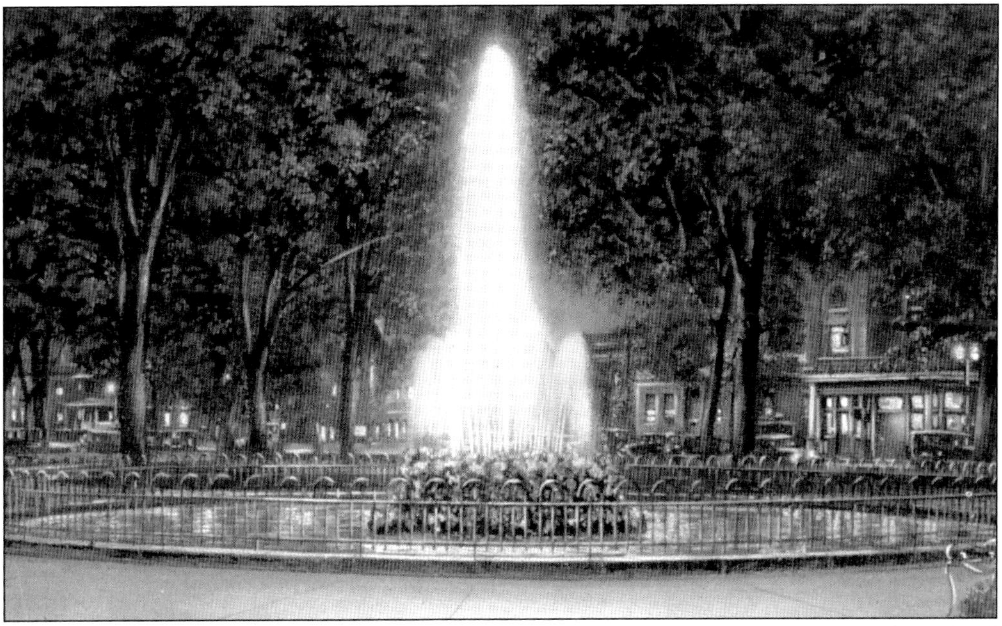

Electric Fountain, Ely Park. The 1930 remodeling of the fountain added multi-colored electric lighting and a strong vertical element. With its water changing colors at night, the electrified fountain attracted many out-of-town visitors.

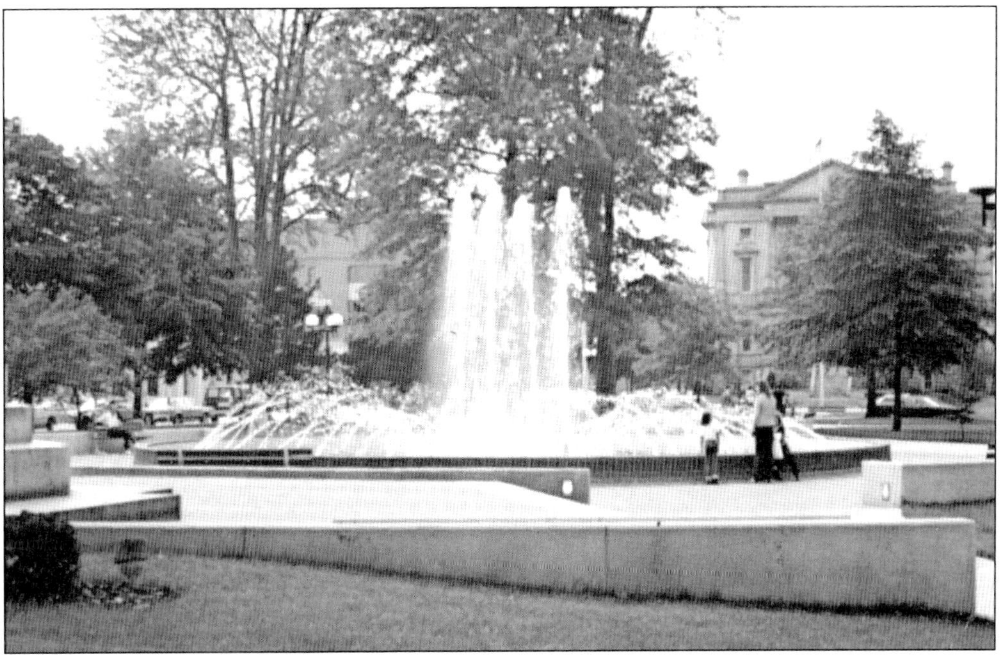

Ely Park Fountain, 1970s. In 1970, this modern fountain replaced the 1959 fountain with wrought iron fencing that many Elyrians remember. The fountain still serves as a focal point, drawing young and old to Ely Square. The Court House can be seen at right, minus its distinctive dome. In 1981, the fountain was remodeled again, this time with outward-spraying jets.

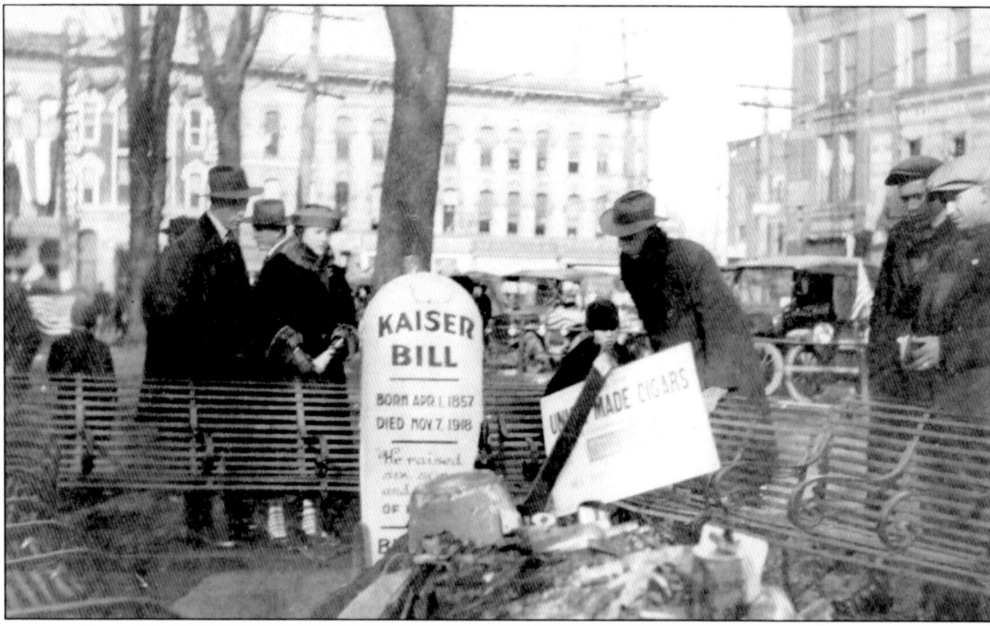

Ely Square, November 7, 1918. Thousands of Elyrians celebrated a premature end to World War I with the mock burial of Kaiser Wilhelm four days before the armistice was actually signed. The "burial" was preceded by a large procession through town, from the railroad station to the park.

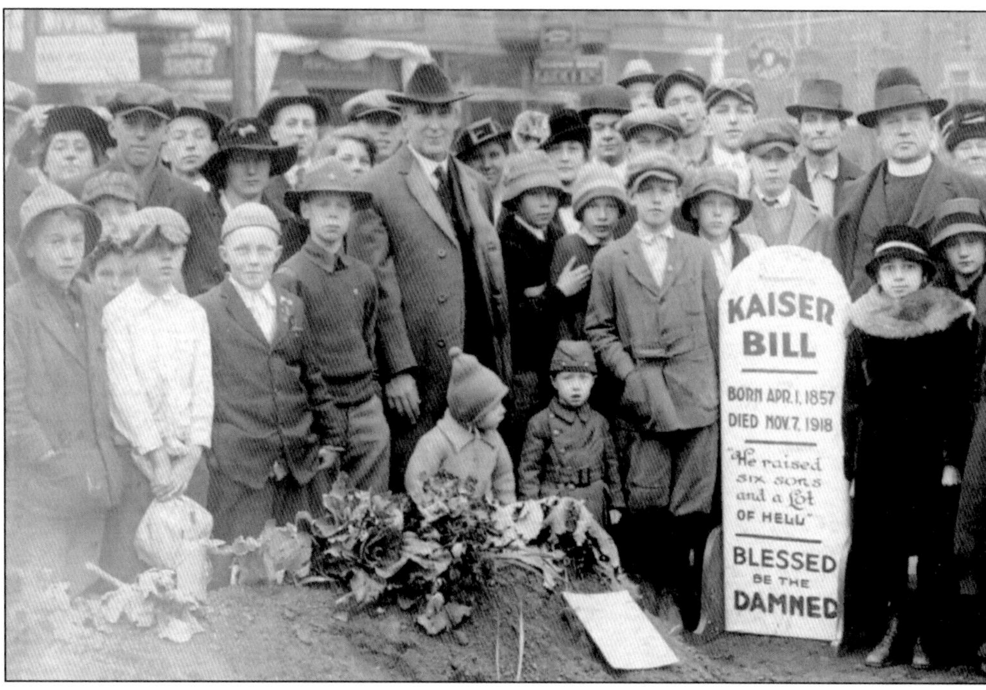

Ely Square, November 7, 1918. Elyria's mayor bowed to requests by townspeople for a celebration. Here, Elyrians cluster around the "gravesite" of Kaiser Bill. His "tombstone" reads, "He raised six sons and a lot of hell."

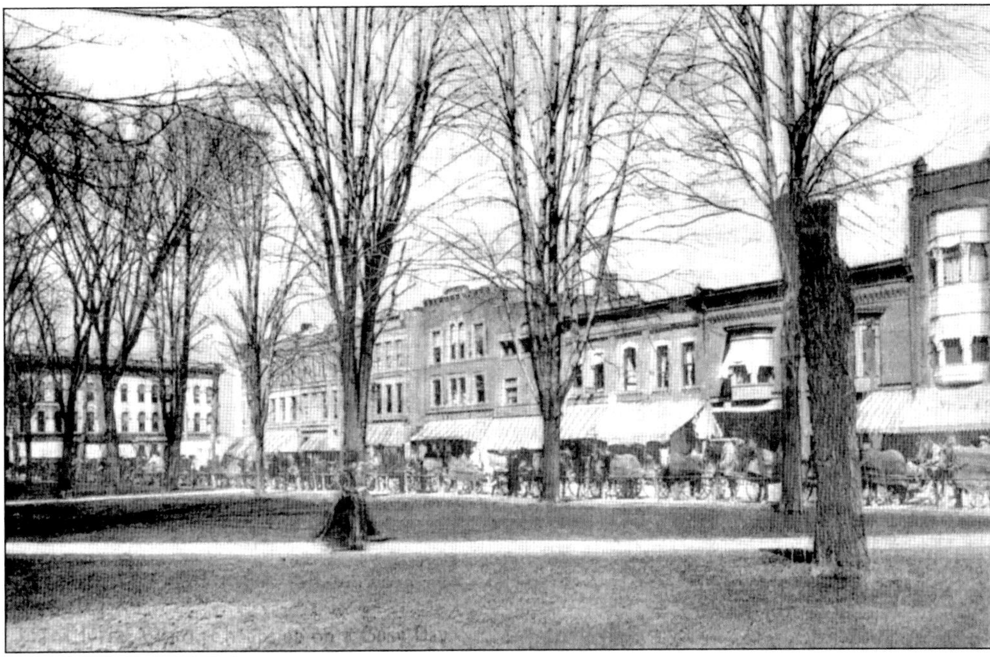

CHEAPSIDE SEEN FROM ELY PARK. The leafless trees of spring allow an unobstructed view of the Ely Block on Broad Street and the storefronts of Cheapside.

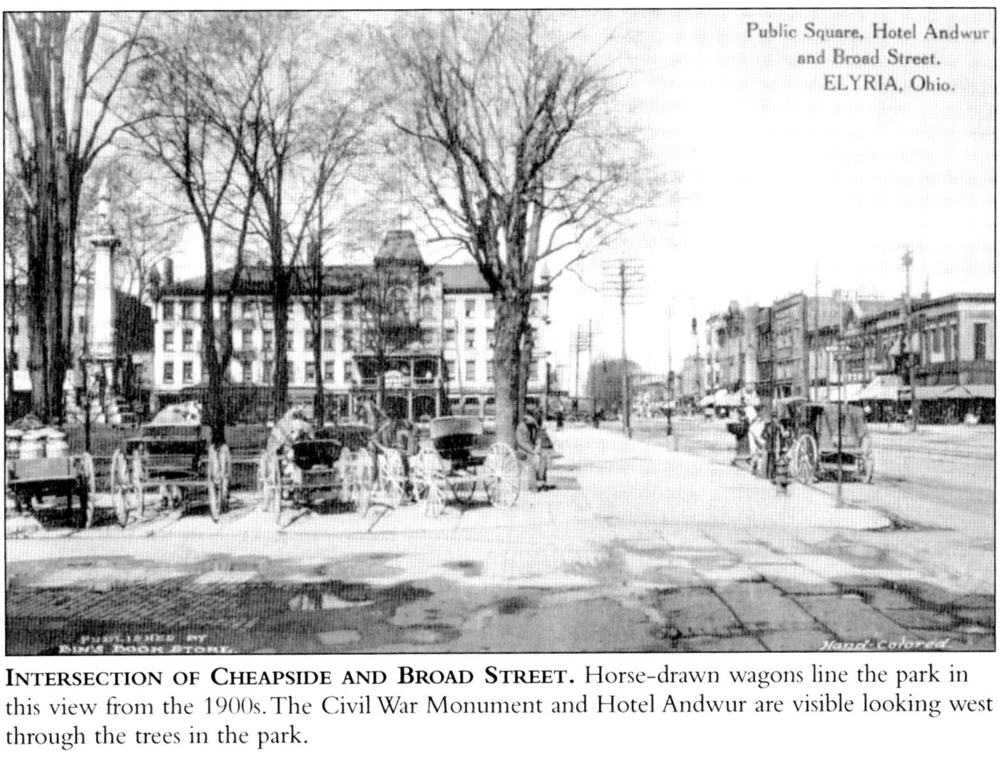

INTERSECTION OF CHEAPSIDE AND BROAD STREET. Horse-drawn wagons line the park in this view from the 1900s. The Civil War Monument and Hotel Andwur are visible looking west through the trees in the park.

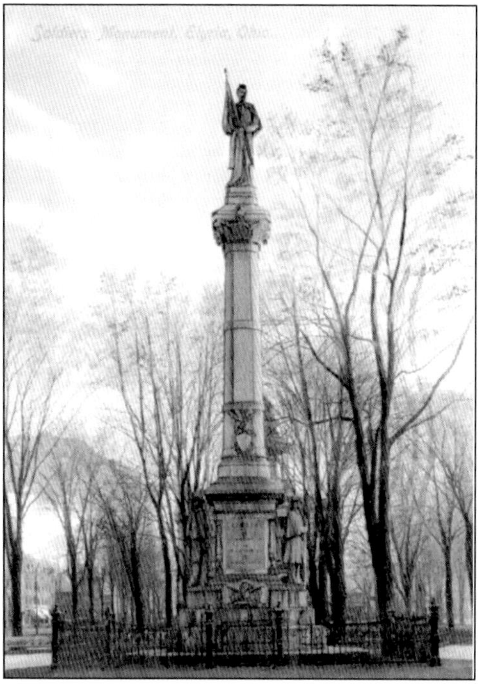

Soldier's Monument, Ely Park. This monument to Elyria's fallen Civil War heroes was erected in 1888 at the north end of the park. The inscription reads: "1861–1865—Elyria—To Her Heroes Who Fought and Her Martyrs Who Fell That the Republic Might Live."

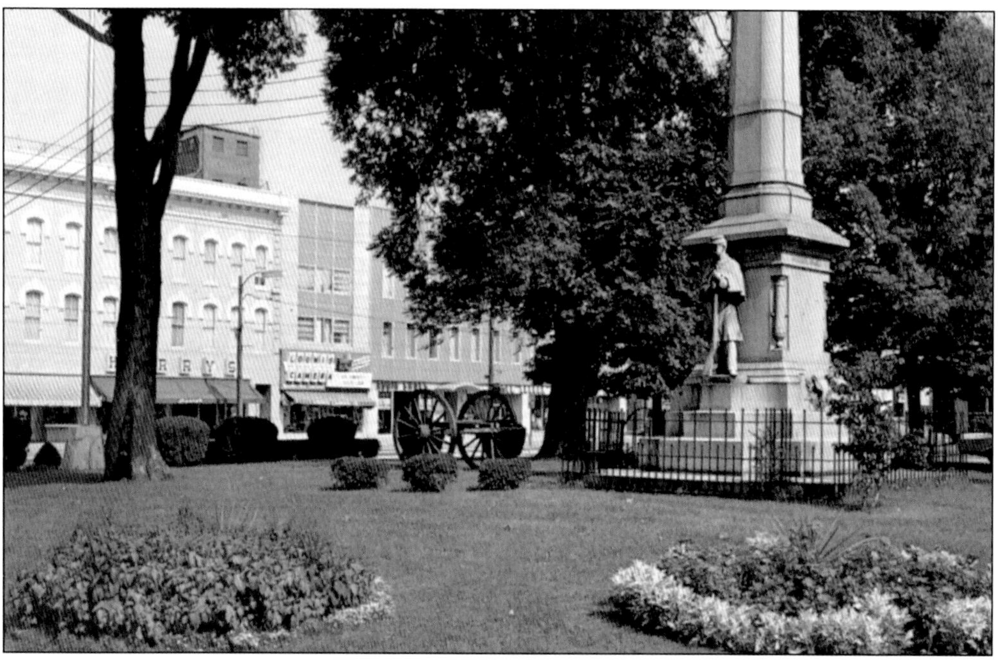

Ely Park Looking North. Visitors to the park in the 1970s had this view of the businesses on Broad Street, including Merthe's (far left), Harry's Men's Wear, and Loomis Camera. Generations of Elyrians owe a debt of gratitude to Heman Ely, who donated this land to the city in 1833.

Four

Schools, Churches, and Neighborhoods

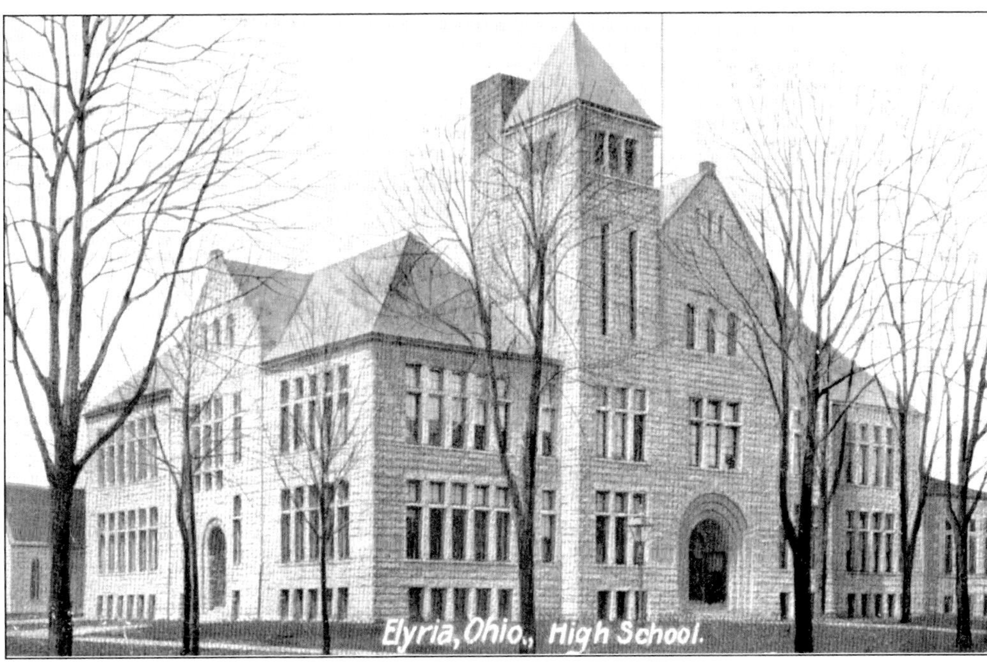

Washington Building. Elyria High School was the first high school chartered by the state of Ohio. This postcard shows the Washington Building, built in 1894. It stands on the northwest corner of Middle Avenue and 6th Street.

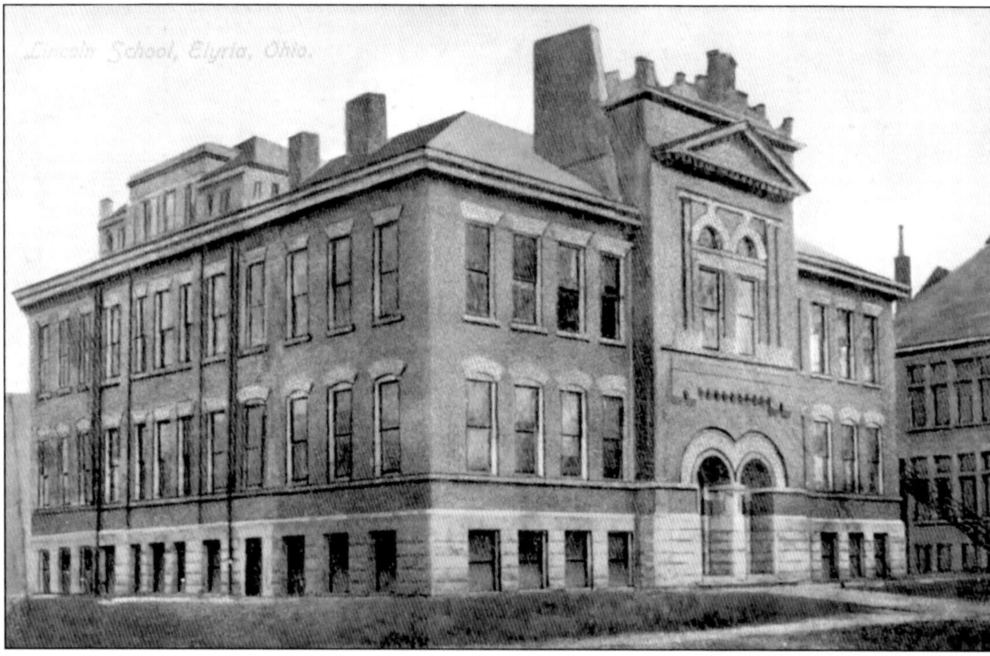

LINCOLN SCHOOL. Lincoln School was built immediately to the west of the Elyria High School on 6th Street in 1905. It was used as a middle school. The back of the high school, now known as the Washington Building, can be seen on the right in this postcard.

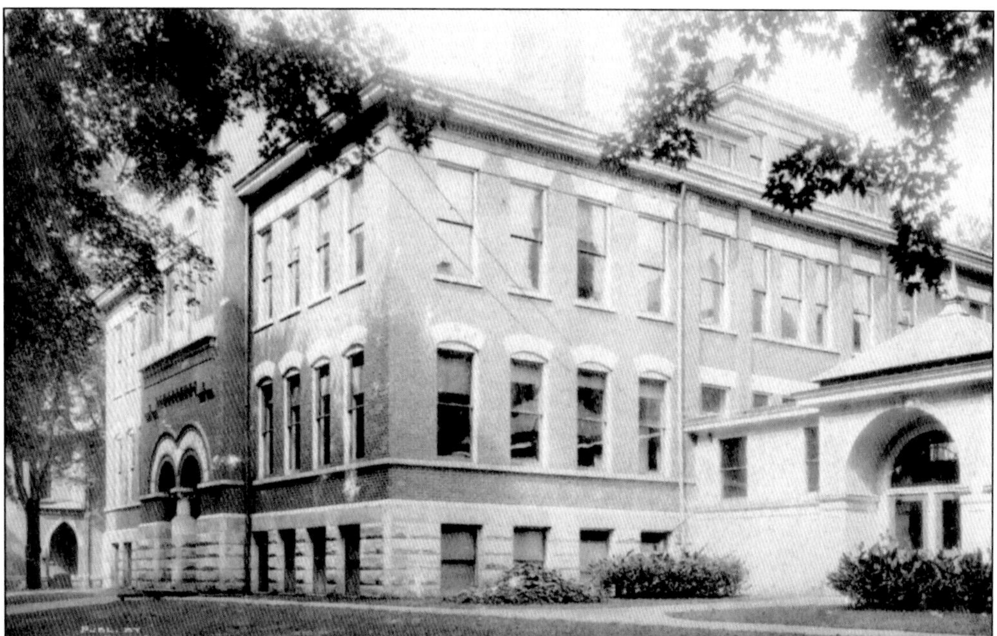

LINCOLN SCHOOL. Here is a later view of Lincoln School, now connected to the Washington Building. The old West Avenue School can be seen to the left. This building was demolished in 1954 to make way for a more modern building on the same site.

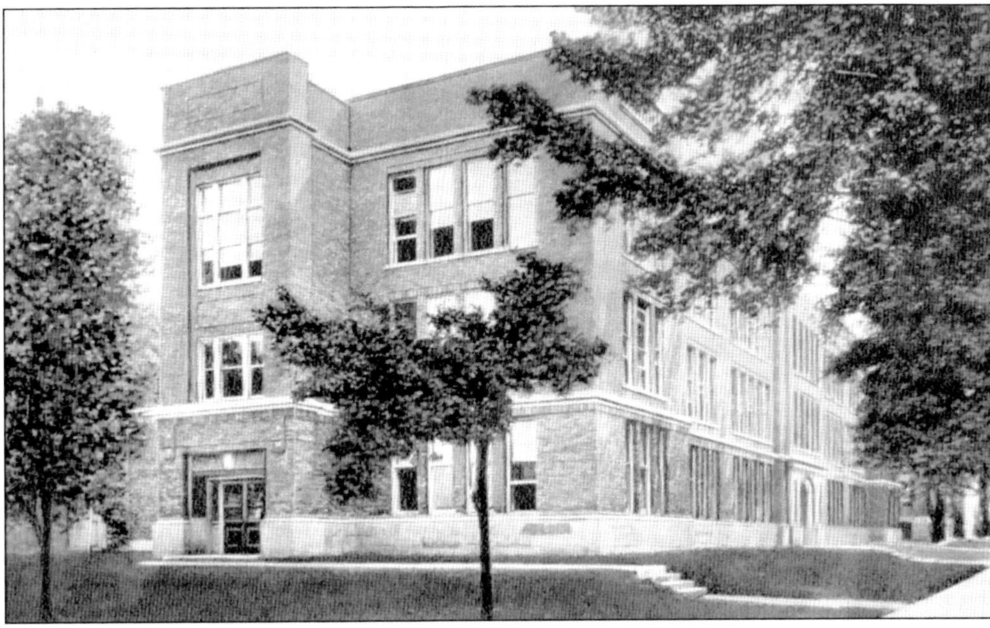

ELYRIA HIGH SCHOOL TECHNICAL BUILDING. The Technical Building was built in 1913. It was constructed west of Lincoln School on 6th Street. Current Elyria High students will recognize this building, but will have to imagine the auditorium/gymnasium building, since it was not added until the early 1950s.

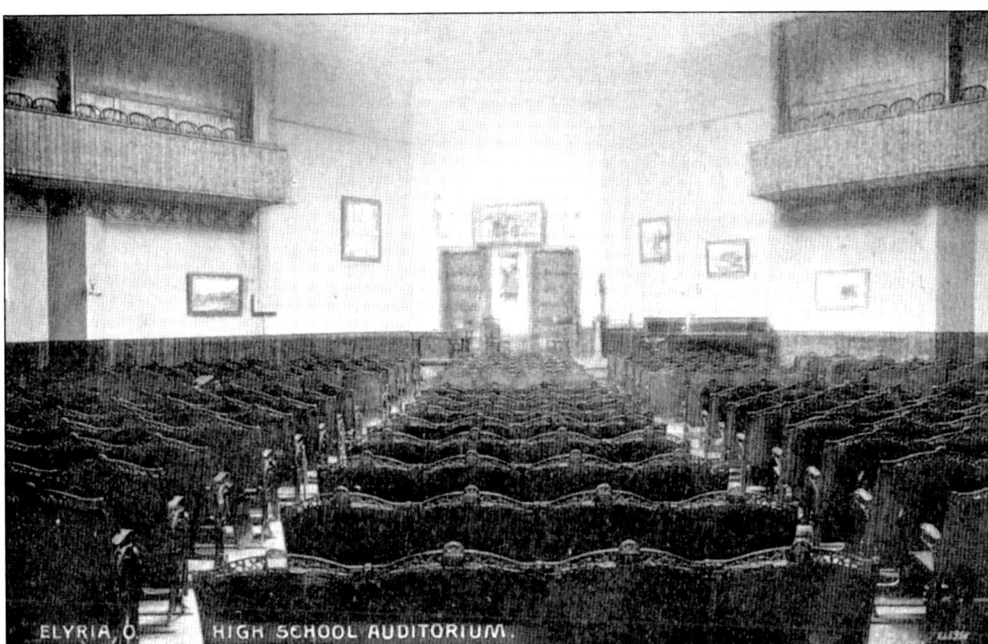

ELYRIA HIGH SCHOOL AUDITORIUM. This was the auditorium used by the high school until 1955 when the current gymnasium/auditorium building was completed.

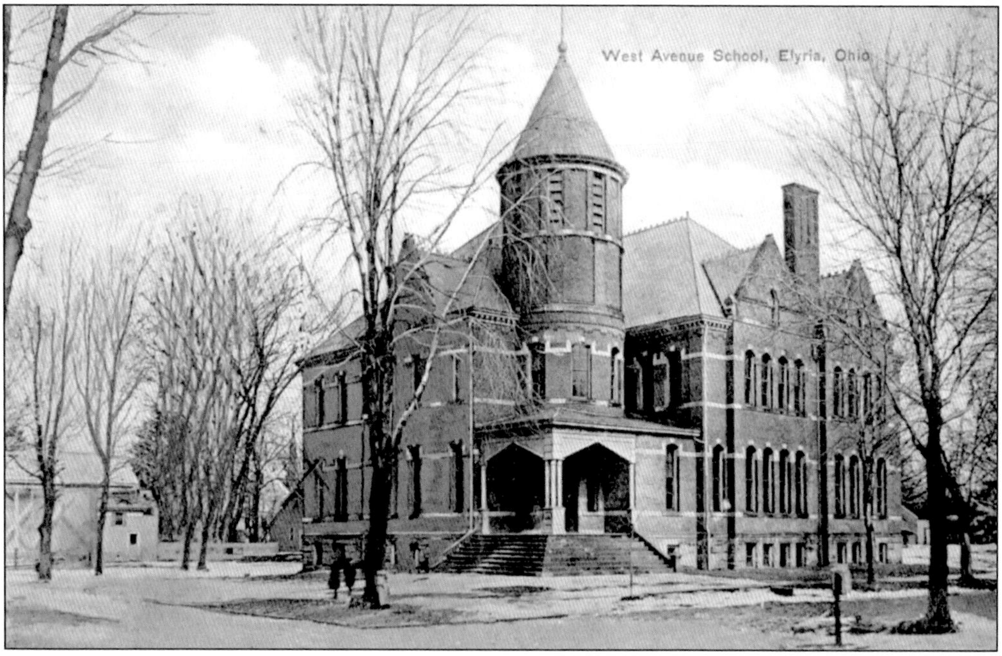

WEST AVENUE SCHOOL. West Avenue School, also known as "Franklin School," stood on the corner of West Avenue and 6th Street. It was torn down in the early 1950s to make way for an addition to the high school, which would house the auditorium and the gym. Students from the West Avenue School were re-located to the brand new Franklin Elementary School on West 11th Street.

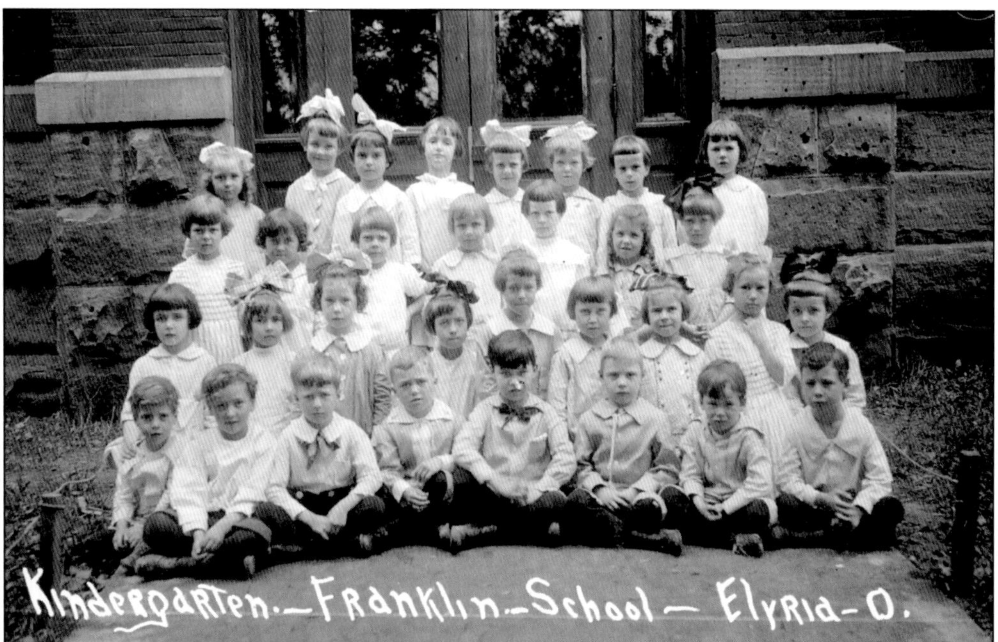

KINDERGARTEN CLASS, FRANKLIN SCHOOL. This postcard shows an early kindergarten class posed outside the old Franklin School on the corner of 6th Street and West Avenue.

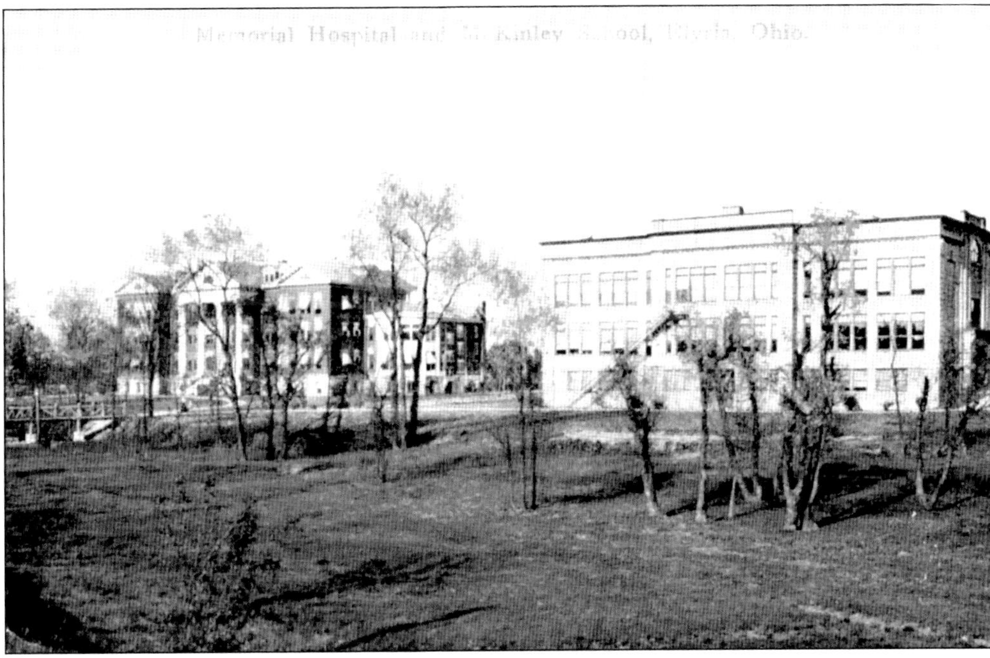

McKinley Elementary School. This early view shows McKinley Elementary School and its neighbor to the north, Elyria Memorial Hospital, side by side on East River Street. Today the foot bridge to the school is gone, and the road runs closer to both buildings.

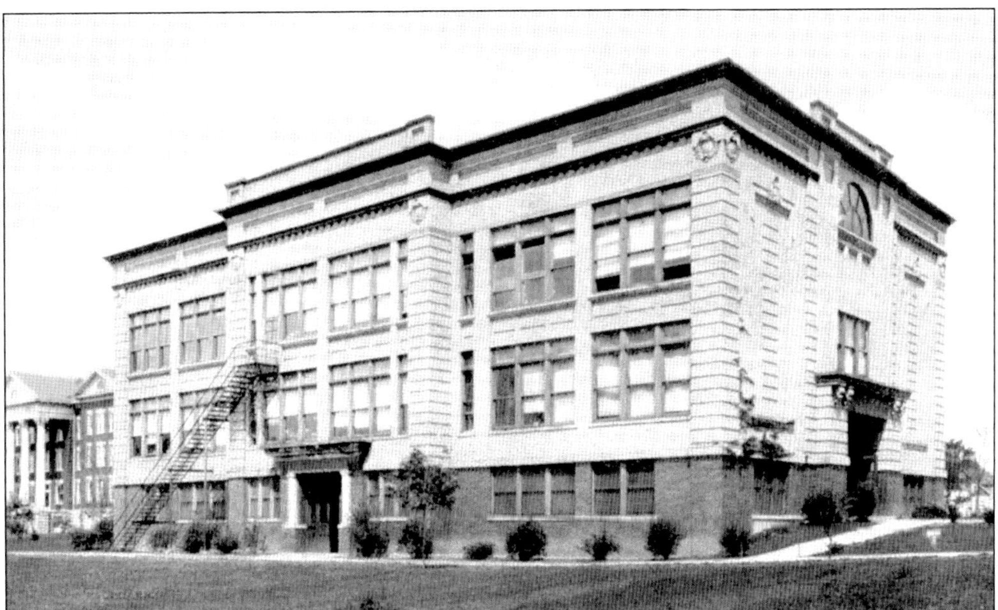

McKinley School. McKinley School is the oldest elementary school building still in use in Elyria. Built in 1908, generations of school children from the Eastern Heights neighborhood have walked to school here.

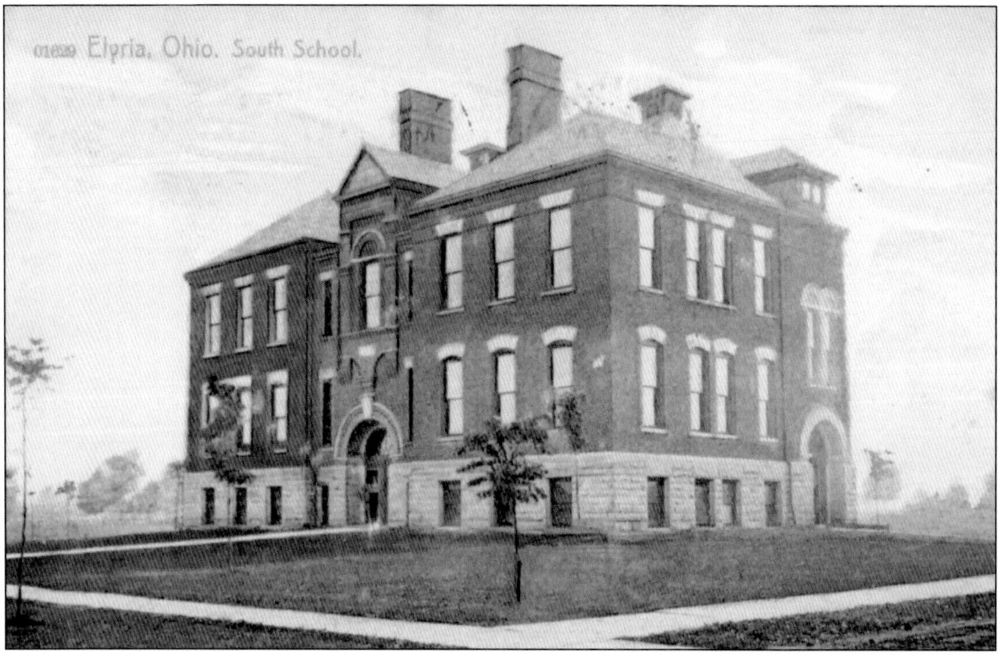

Hamilton Elementary School. Hamilton, also known as "South School," was built in 1900 on the corner of Middle Avenue and 13th Street. An addition was built in the 1960s and is the only part of the school that still remains. It serves today as a neighborhood center.

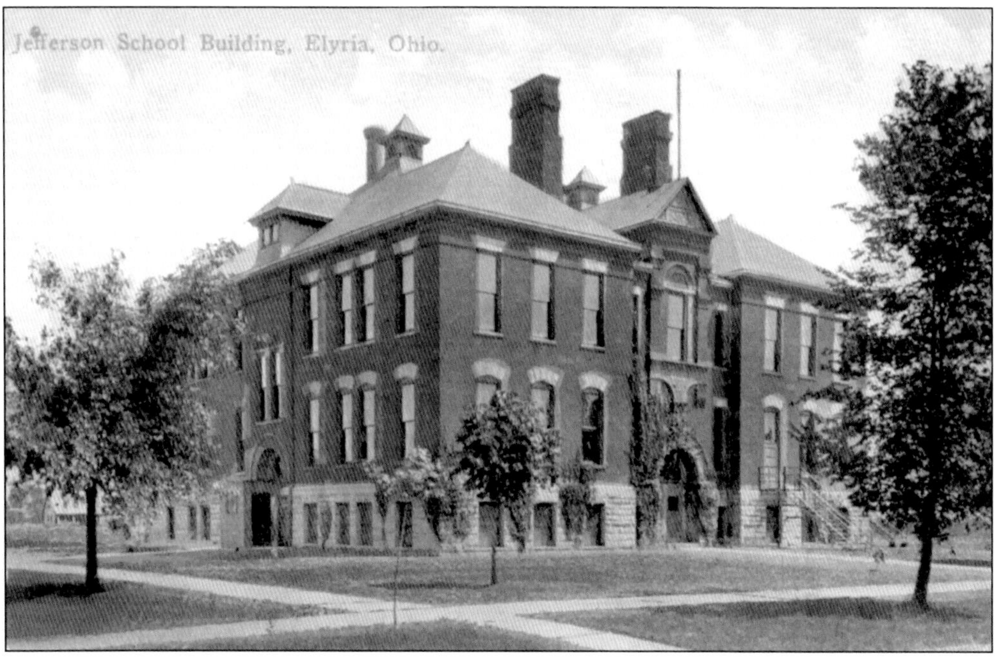

Jefferson School. Jefferson School was constructed in 1901, a year after Hamilton School was completed. Both buildings shared the same design and floor plan.

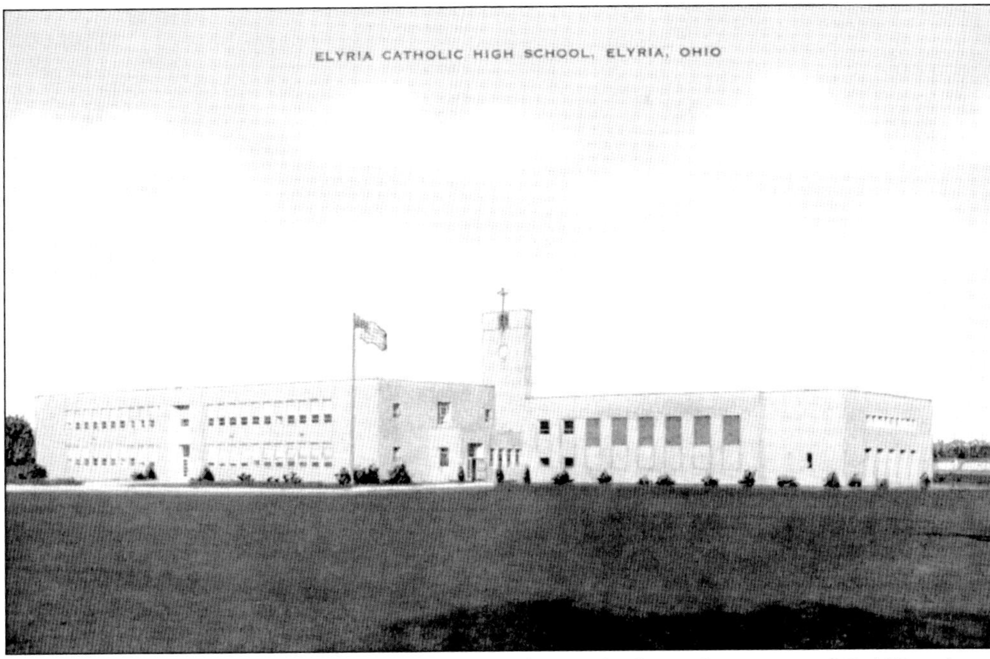

ELYRIA CATHOLIC HIGH SCHOOL. Elyria Catholic was built on the corner of Gulf Road and Poplar Street in 1949. This postcard shows the high school before the rotunda was added in 1965. Elyria Catholic, or "EC" as it is known, has traditionally drawn students from throughout Lorain County.

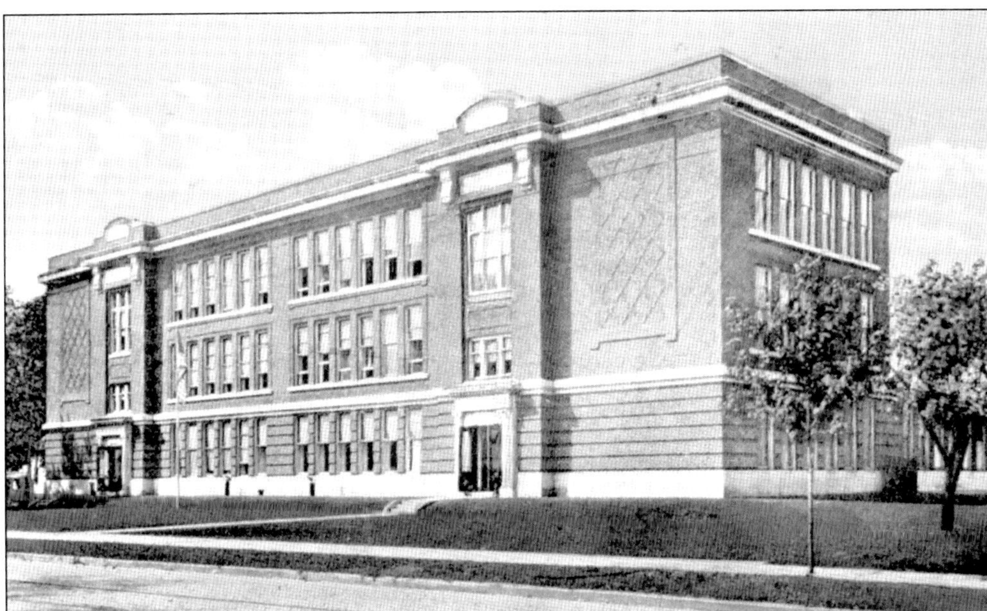

GATES ELEMENTARY SCHOOL. Gates School was built in 1913 to replace the Lake Avenue or School Street School. It stood on Lake Avenue and served the near west side of Elyria. It was the first elementary school in Elyria to have an auditorium that doubled as a gym.

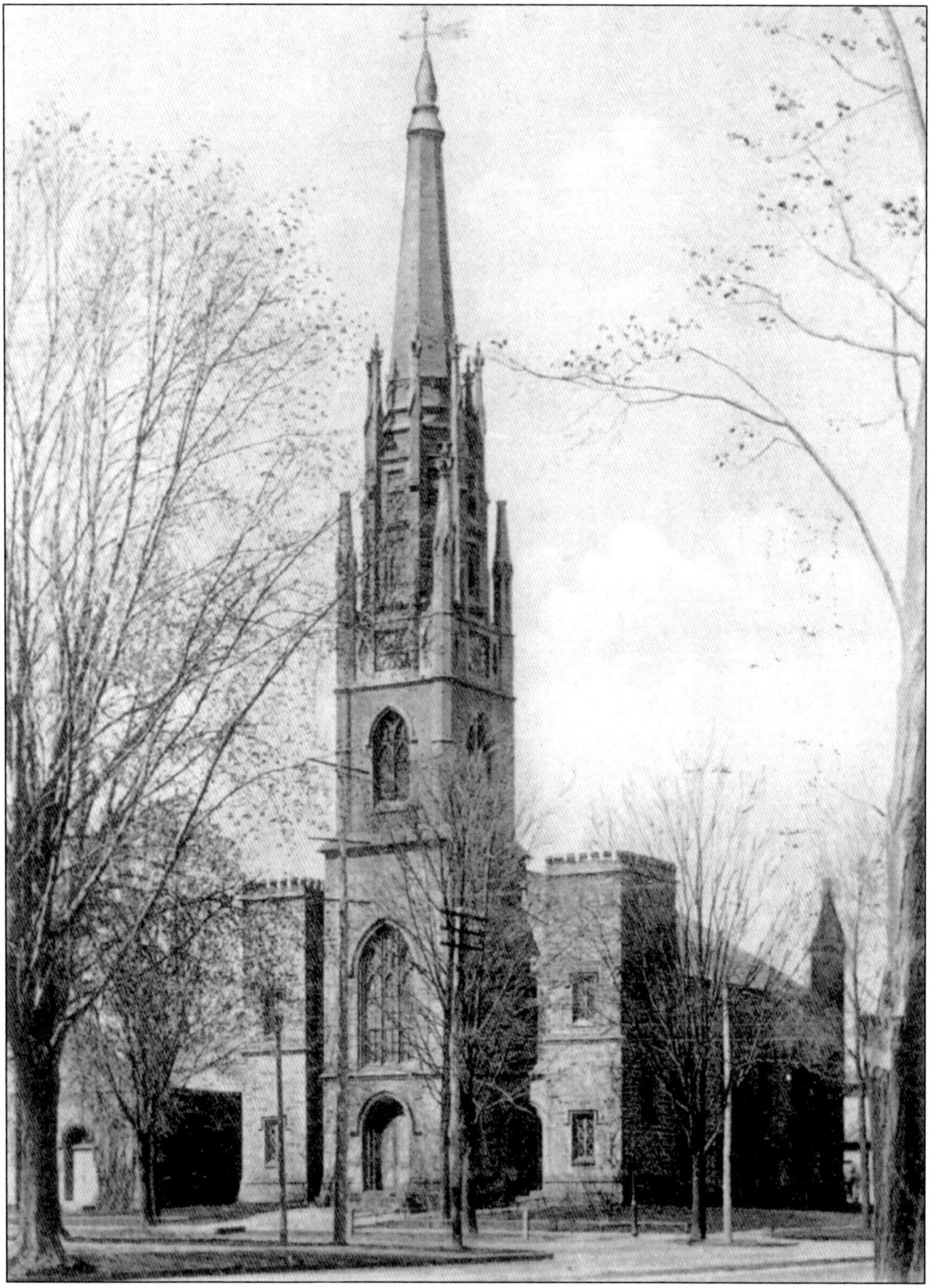

OLD FIRST CONGREGATIONAL CHURCH. When this beautiful gothic structure was built in 1848, it was known as the First Presbyterian Church of Elyria. It became the First Congregational Church in 1879 when the congregation left the Presbytery. The need for a new building became evident after falling spire sections resulted in several near-accidents. This church was torn down in 1898.

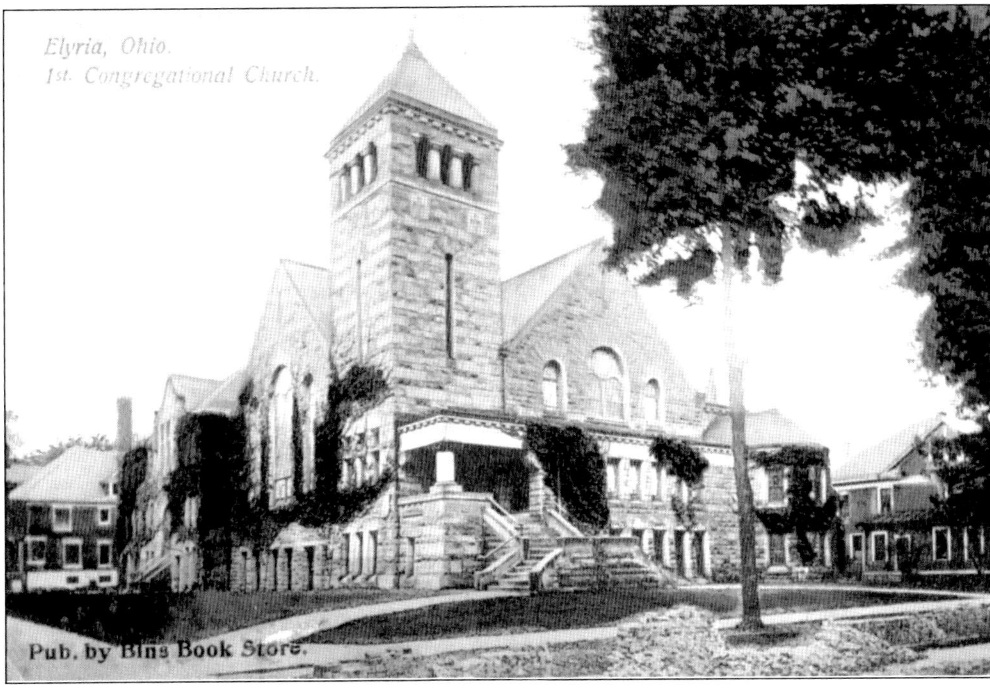

FIRST CONGREGATIONAL CHURCH. In 1898, the current church was built on the same site at a cost of $55,000. Additions were built on the west side around 1967 and on the east side around 1982. This beautiful sandstone church is now dwarfed by the new Lorain County Justice Center, which looms just behind it.

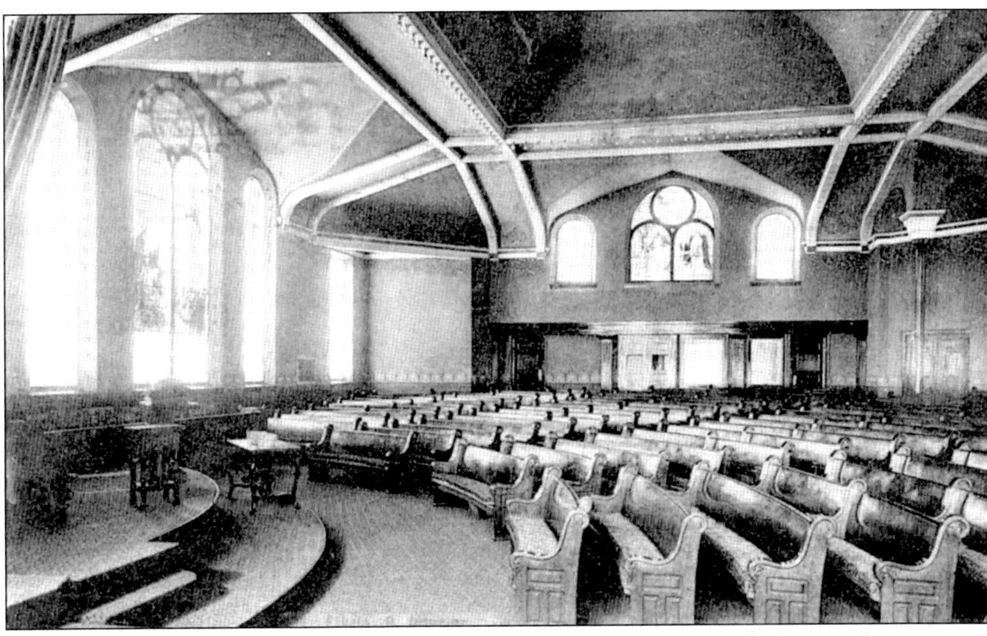

FIRST CONGREGATIONAL CHURCH, INTERIOR. The beautiful stained glass windows, created and installed by the Louis Comfort Tiffany Company, can be seen in this view of the interior of the church. Through several remodelings, the sanctuary remains much the same today.

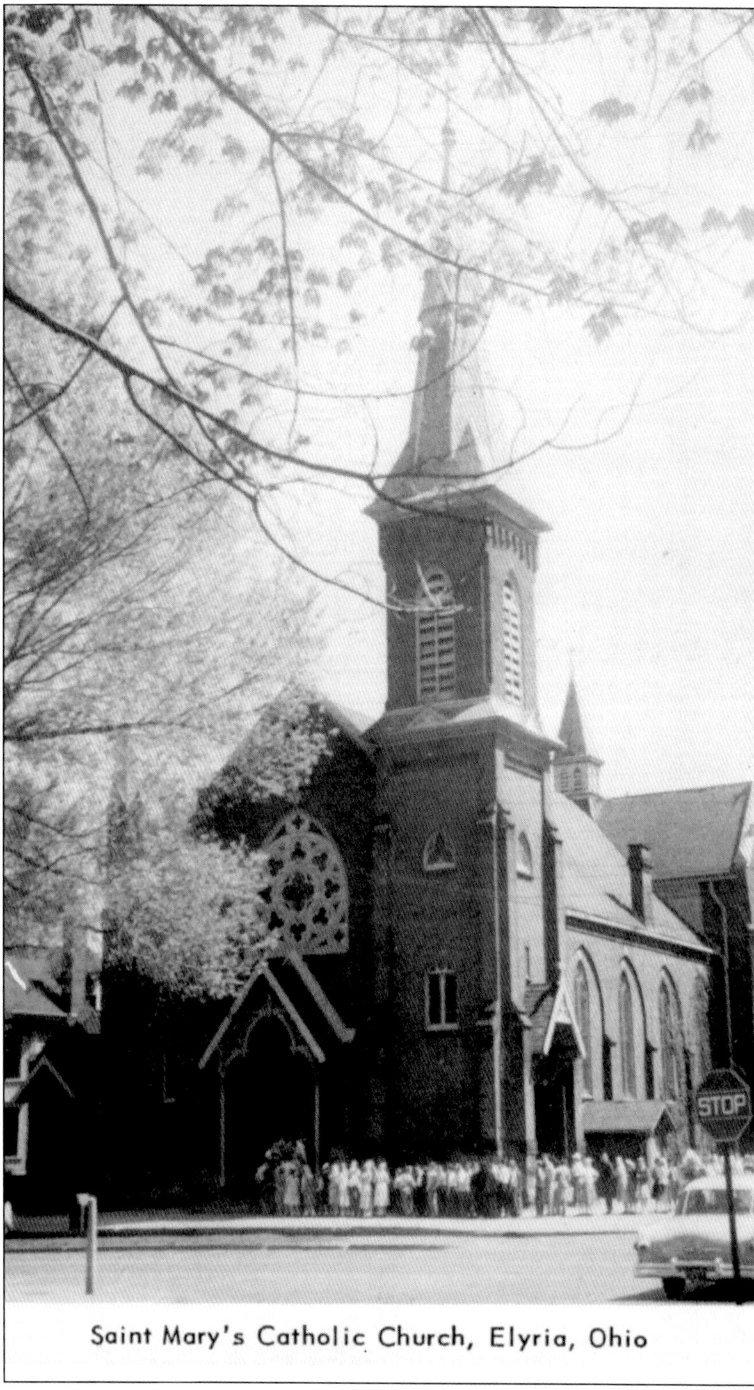

Saint Mary's Catholic Church, Elyria, Ohio

SAINT MARY'S CATHOLIC CHURCH. Saint Mary's parish started out in 1845 in a small wooden church on the southwest corner of Middle Avenue and Fourth Street. After the Civil War, land was purchased on the northeast corner for the construction of the present church shown here. It was the only Catholic Church in Elyria until 1914 when Saint Agnes Parish was established.

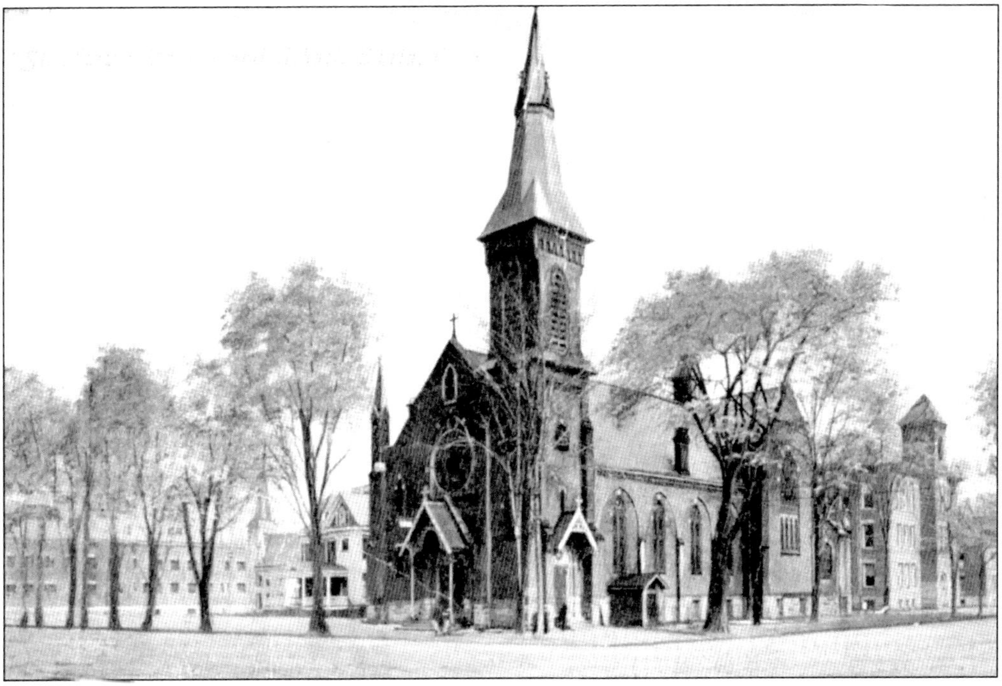

SAINT MARY'S CATHOLIC CHURCH AND SCHOOL. This view shows most of the St. Mary's buildings, including the Rectory to the church's left and the school and Convent at right. The Lorain County Jail on Middle Avenue can be seen at far left. The Rectory has been gone for some years, and the Convent was torn down in 2003 to make room for school expansion.

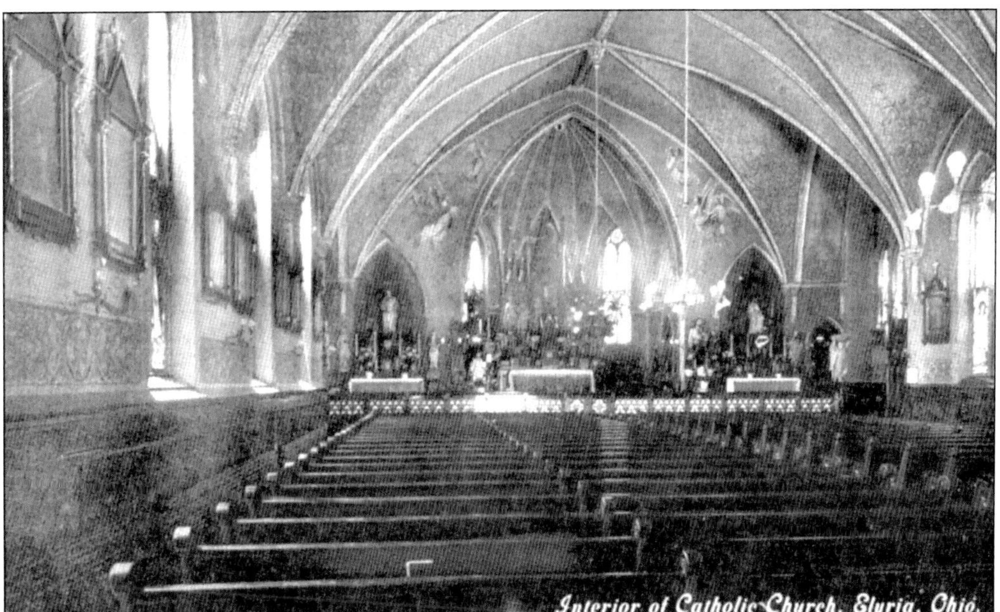

SAINT MARY'S, INTERIOR. The church's tall windows and airy, vaulted ceilings were designed to lift ones eyes and thoughts heavenward. Though much of the ornamentation was removed in the late 1960s following Vatican II, the church retains its serene beauty.

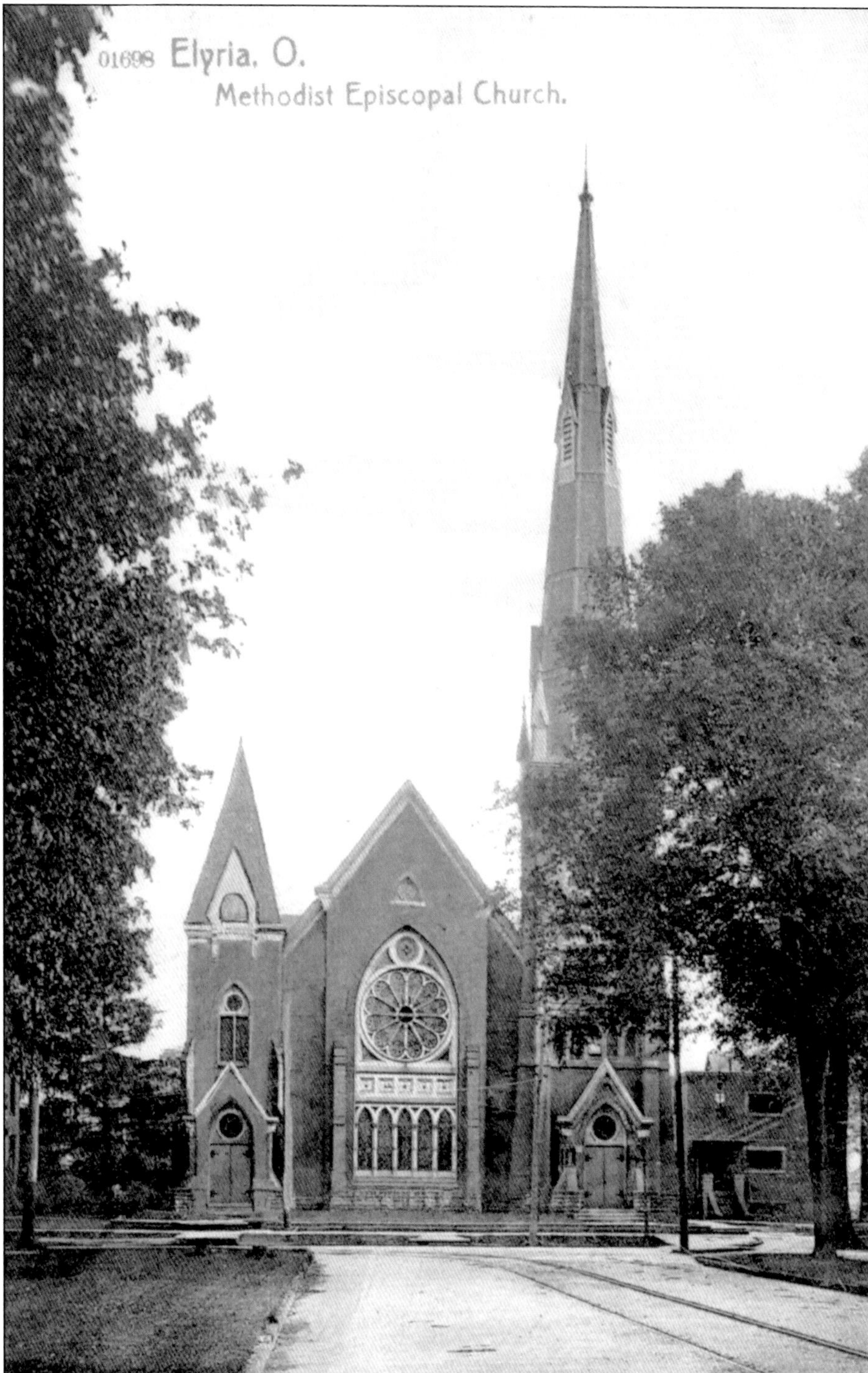

METHODIST EPISCOPAL CHURCH. The graceful Methodist Episcopal Church shown here was built on Third Street at the end of Court Street in 1881. It had to be torn down in 1925 due to crumbling brick. The present Methodist Church stands on this same site.

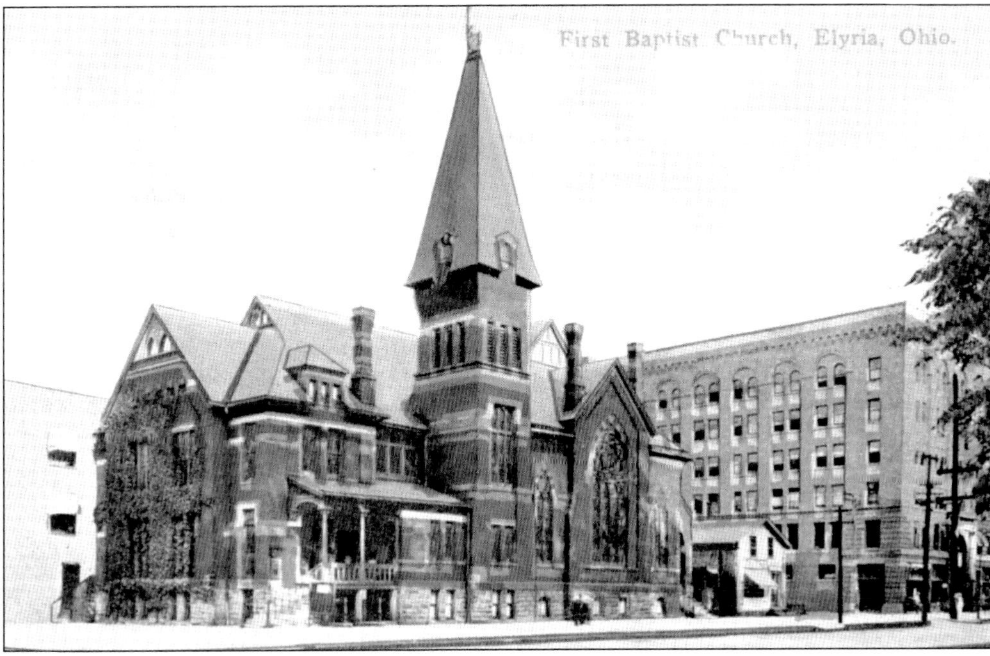

FIRST BAPTIST CHURCH. Elyria's First Baptist Church was built on the corner of Second Street and Middle Avenue in 1883. The old Masonic Temple can be seen at right with a small gas station located in between on Temple Court.

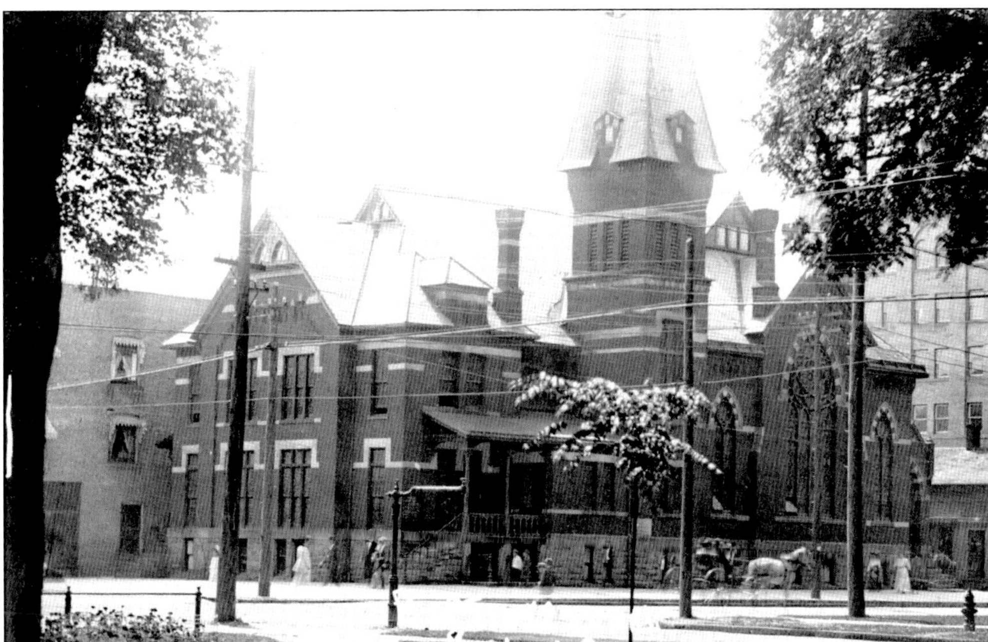

FIRST BAPTIST CHURCH, CLOSE-UP. The First Baptist Church was demolished in 1951 after the congregation moved to 276 Washington Avenue. Northern Savings and Loan occupies this site today.

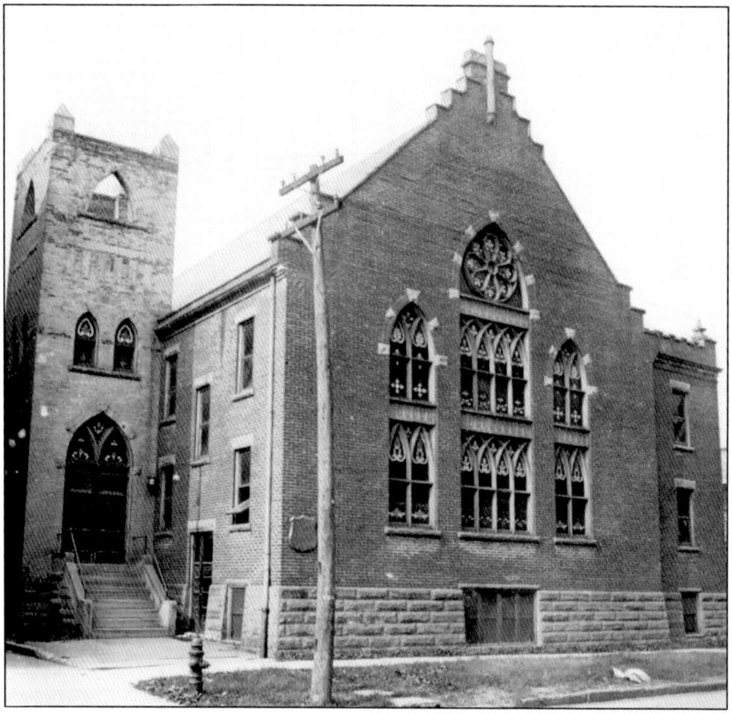

CHURCH OF CHRIST. The Church of Christ was built on East Second Street in 1881. The nearby alley connecting Second with Broad Street was known as Chapel Court, and the Rialto Theater was located next door. In 1952, the congregation moved their church to its present building at 301 Washington Avenue.

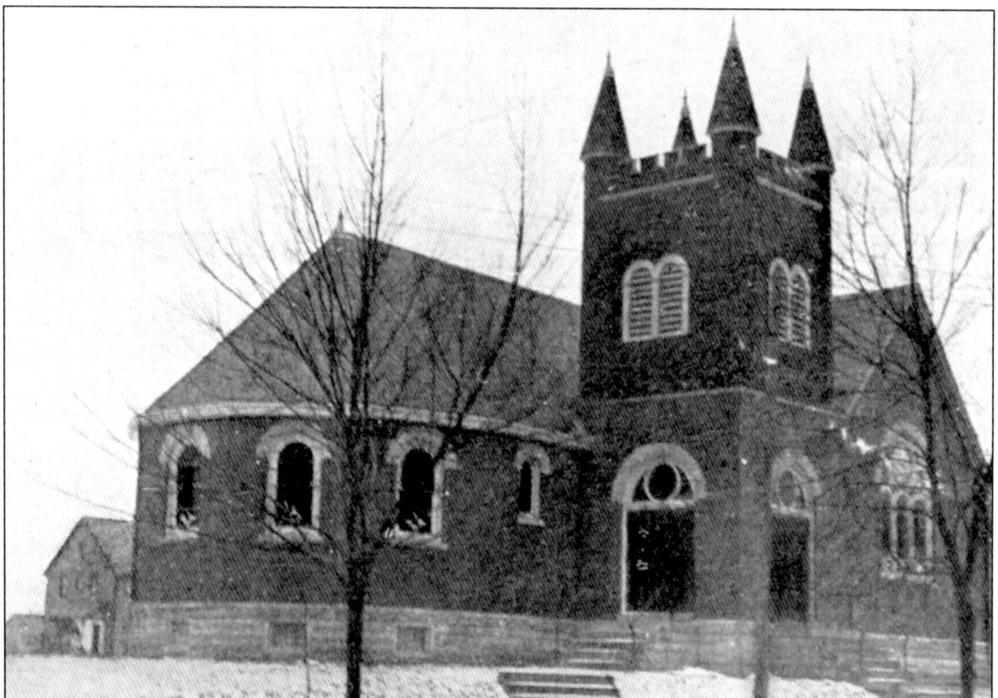

GRACE LUTHERAN CHURCH. Grace Lutheran was built in 1907 at 720 East River Street. In 1968, the congregation moved to a new church farther out on East River. This church is currently the home of the New Life Baptist Church.

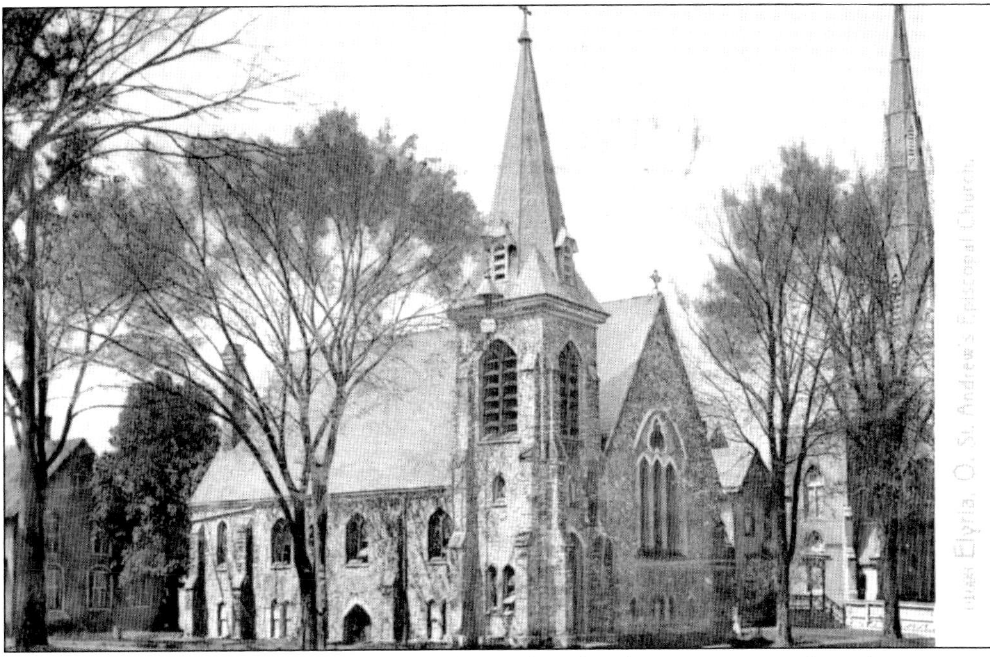

SAINT ANDREW'S EPISCOPAL CHURCH. This gothic church was constructed on the corner of Third Street and Middle Avenue in 1875. Additions were later made to the back of the church along Middle Avenue. The tall spire of the old Methodist Episcopal Church can be seen at right.

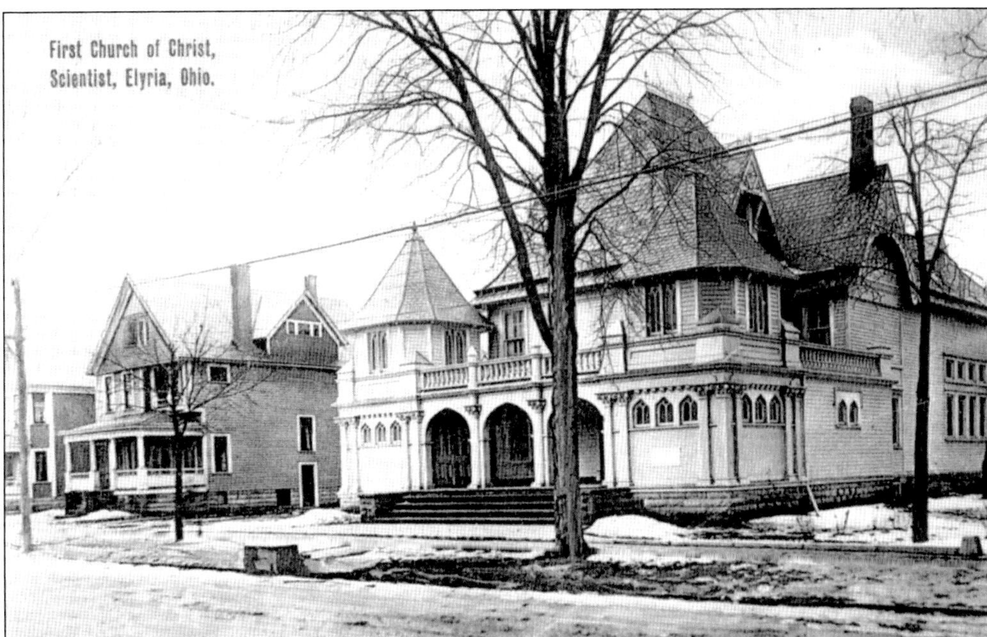

FIRST CHURCH OF CHRIST, SCIENTIST. In 1906, the Elyria congregation moved into the former home of Charles Johnson located at 309 East Avenue, shown here. The house was split in two, with an auditorium, dome, and front porch built between the halves.

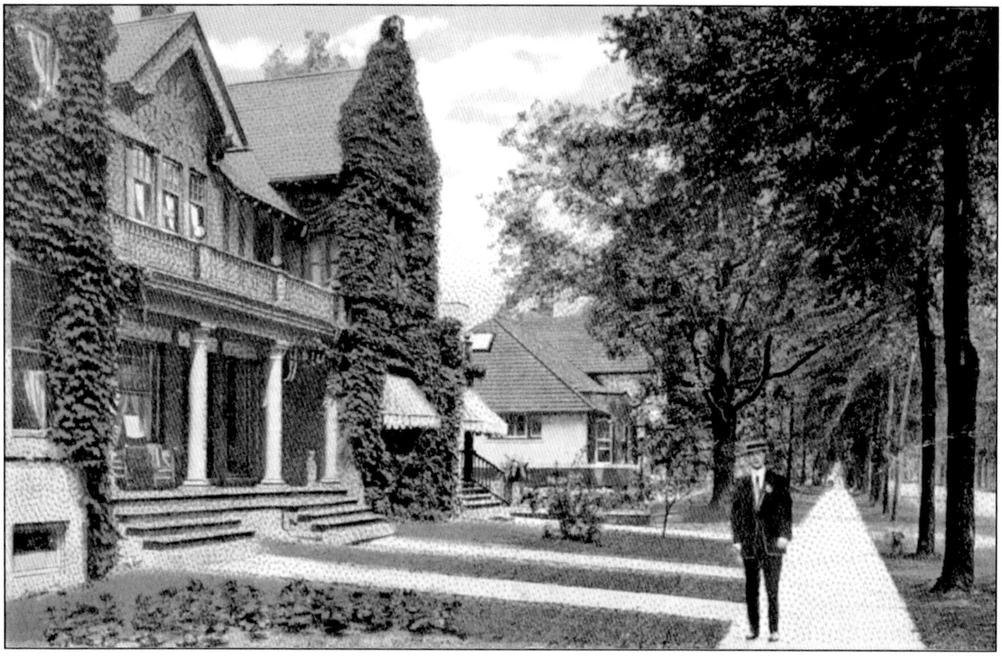

WASHINGTON TERRACE APARTMENTS. This apartment building was built overlooking the East Falls of the Black River and serves as a gateway to Washington Avenue even today. The distinctive tile roof of the Katz residence can be seen beyond.

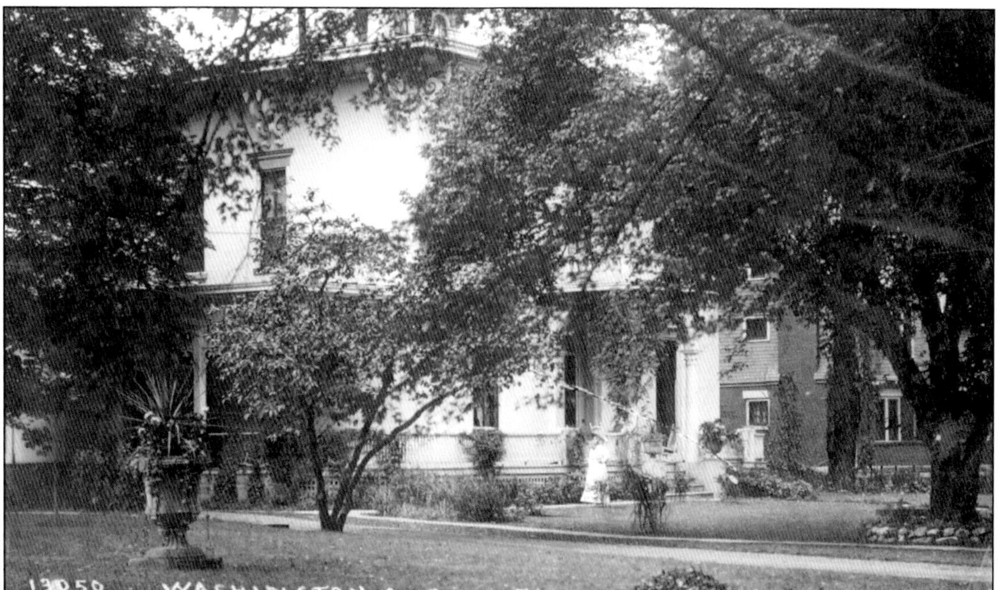

WASHINGTON AVENUE HOME. This home's cupola identifies it as the house later incorporated into part of the First Baptist Church when the congregation moved to Washington Avenue in 1951.

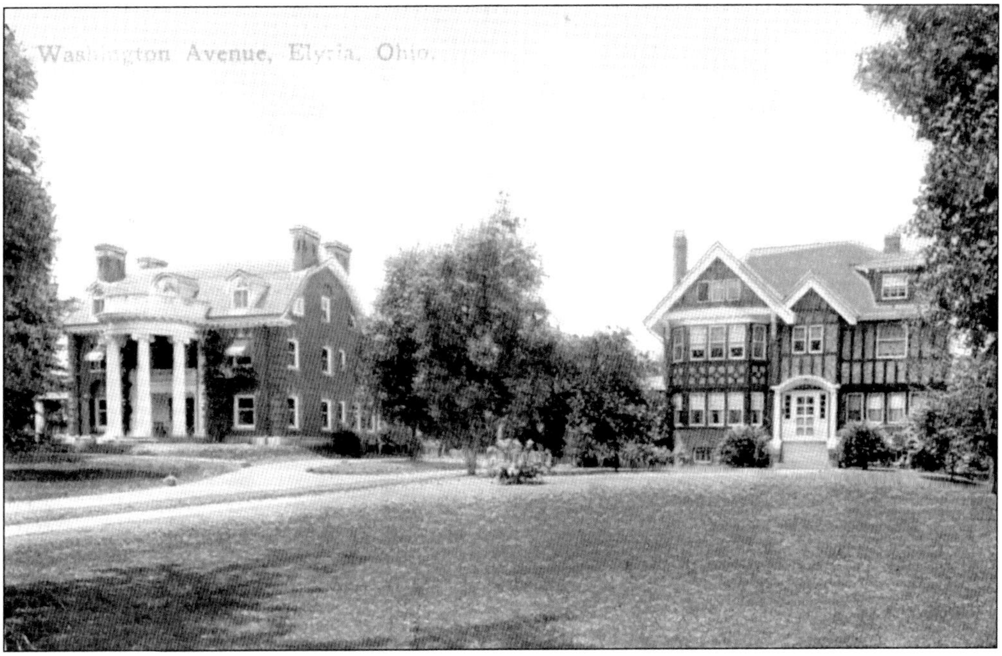

WASHINGTON AVENUE HOMES. These lovely brick homes on Washington Avenue were long ago torn down to make way for more modern, but less attractive buildings. The large, gracious lawns were a hallmark of Washington Avenue homes.

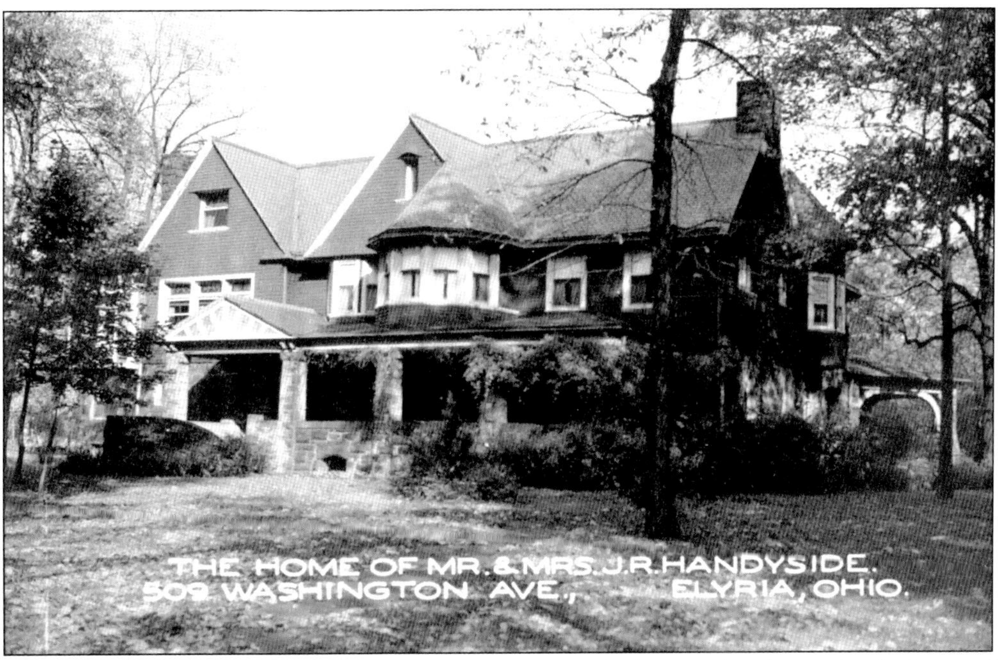

"THE HICKORIES." This stately mansion was originally the home of Arthur L. Garford, one of Elyria's most prominent industrialists. It is currently the headquarters of the Lorain County Historical Society.

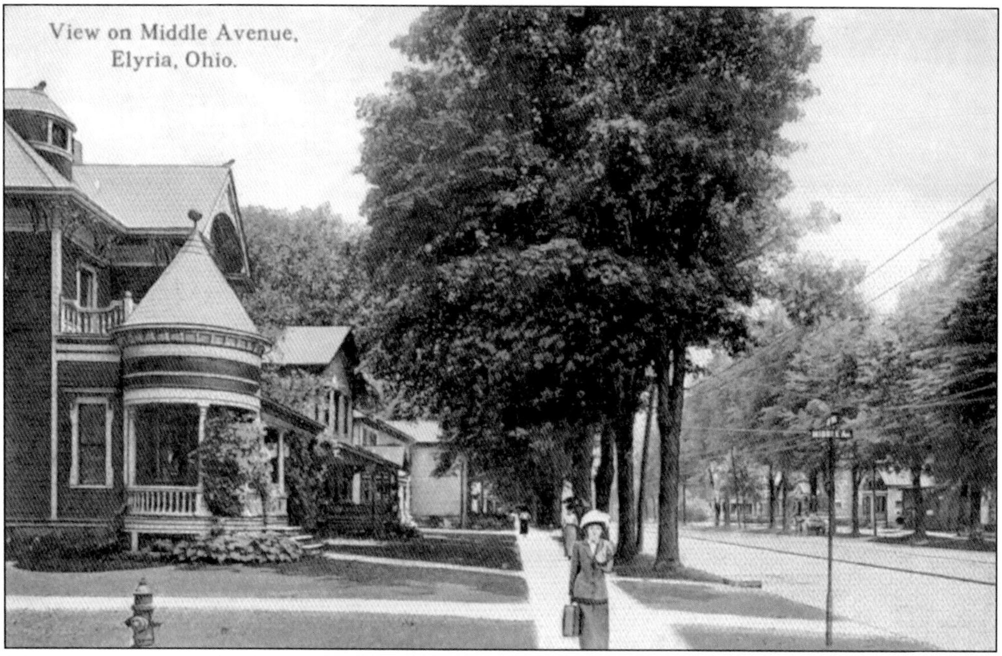

MIDDLE AVENUE. This large distinctive home on the corner of Middle Avenue and Fourth Street still stands across the street from St. Mary's Catholic Church. It is easily recognizable by the round tower on the corner of the porch.

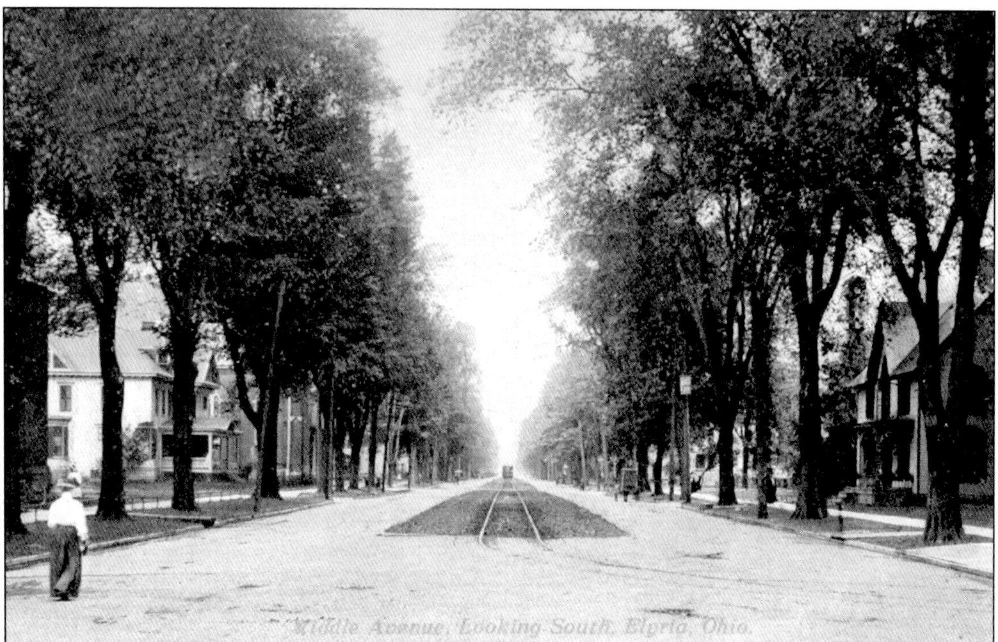

MIDDLE AVENUE, LOOKING SOUTH. A trolley approaches downtown Elyria on the tracks running down the middle of the street through this quiet residential area. When the trolley tracks were removed, pedestrian islands replaced them.

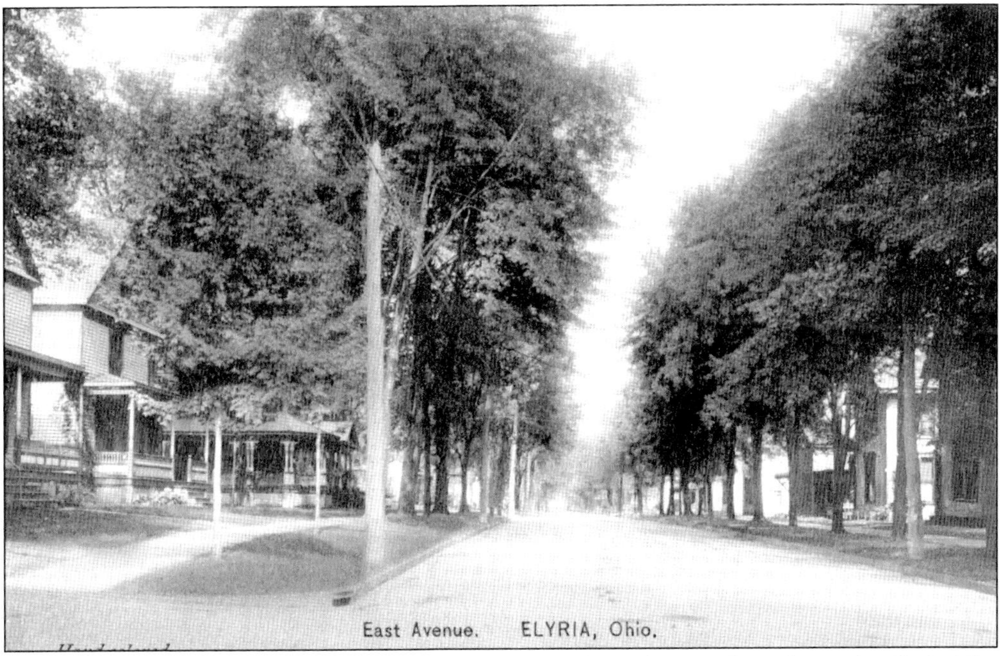

EAST AVENUE. This quiet, tree-lined avenue is one of the oldest residential areas in Elyria. The street runs along the east branch of the Black River, and some older residents may remember rowing across the river to play in the fields that became Eastern Heights.

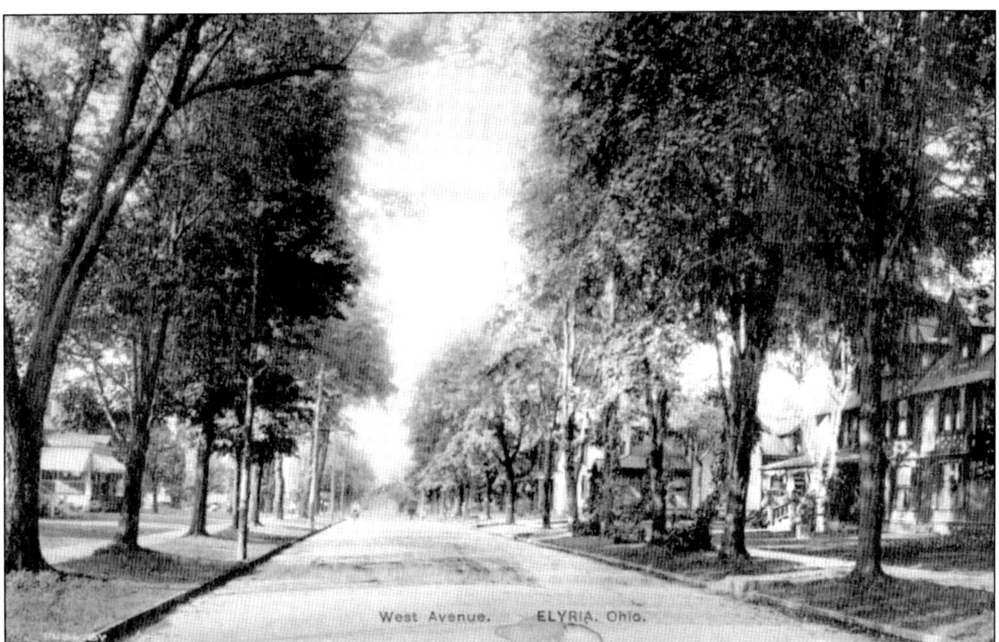

WEST AVENUE, LOOKING NORTH. Following the west branch of the Black River, the properties on the left-hand side of the street in this view extend back to the river. Seen from the intersection of Fourth Street and West Avenue looking towards Broad Street, the YWCA building is at far right.

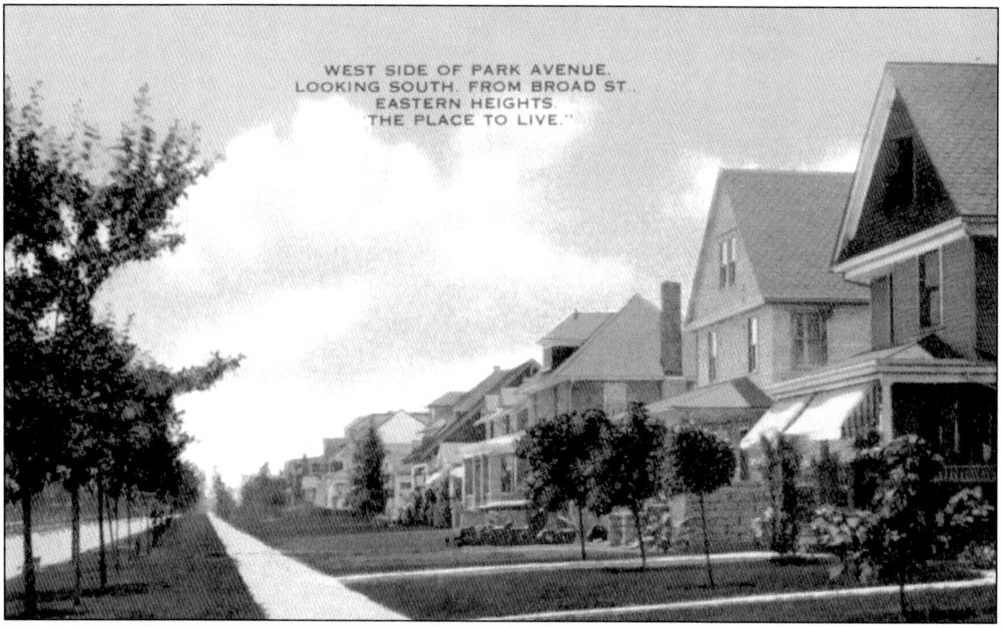

EASTERN HEIGHTS, PARK AVENUE. The houses in this postcard have been torn down to make way for expansions to Elyria Memorial Hospital, but they once stood as a gateway to the Eastern Heights neighborhood, "the place to live" in Elyria.

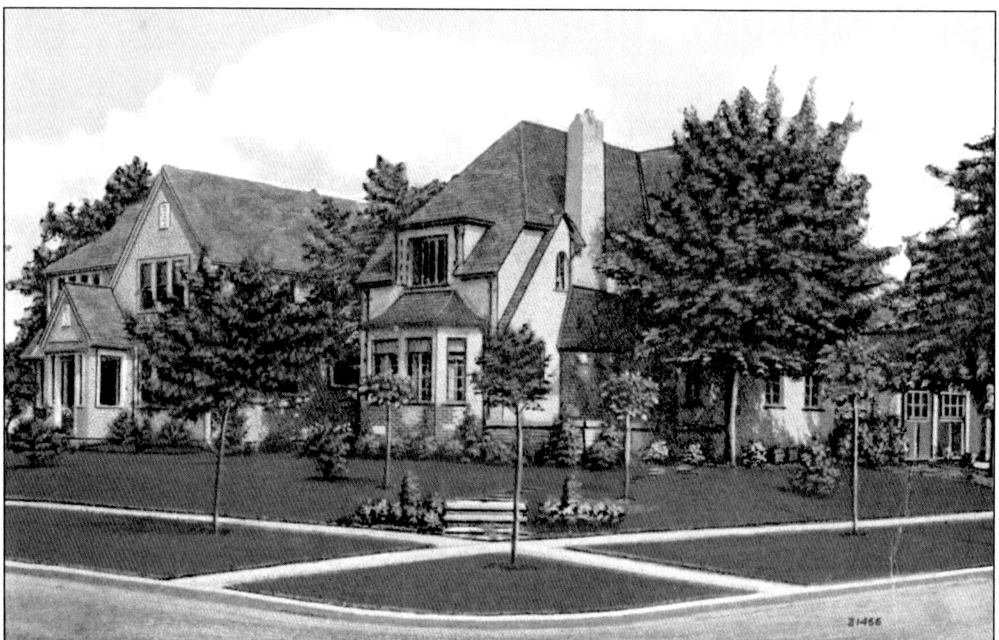

EASTERN HEIGHTS, CORNELL AVENUE. The styles of the houses in Eastern Heights were varied and included this stucco home, which still stands on the northwest corner of Garford and Cornell Avenues.

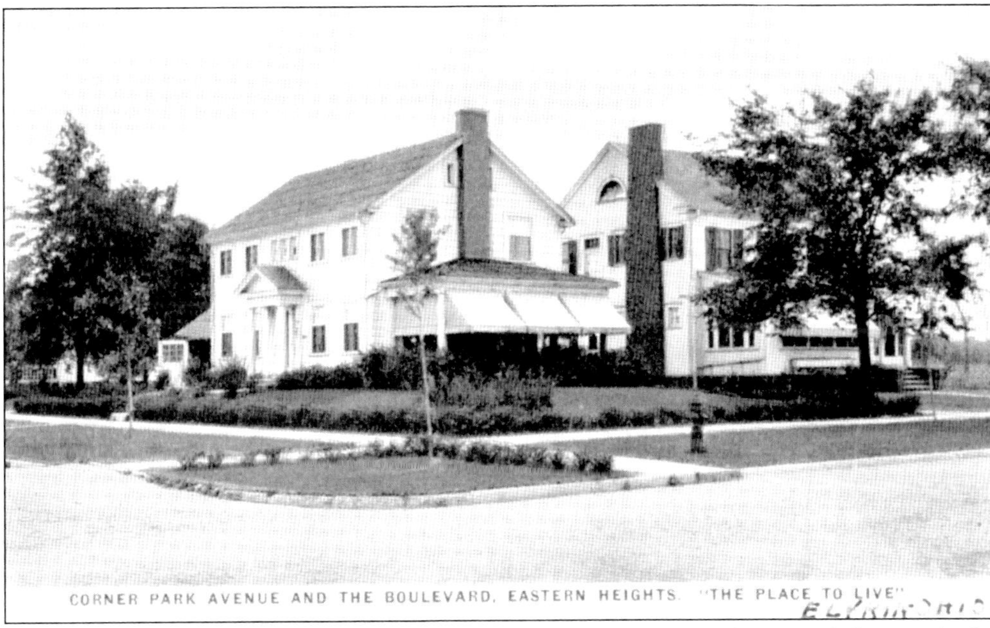

EASTERN HEIGHTS, EASTERN HEIGHTS BOULEVARD. This corner home and the one in the postcard below should be familiar to Elyrians, as they still stand across the street from each other at the corners of Park Avenue and Eastern Heights Boulevard, the heart of the Eastern Heights neighborhood.

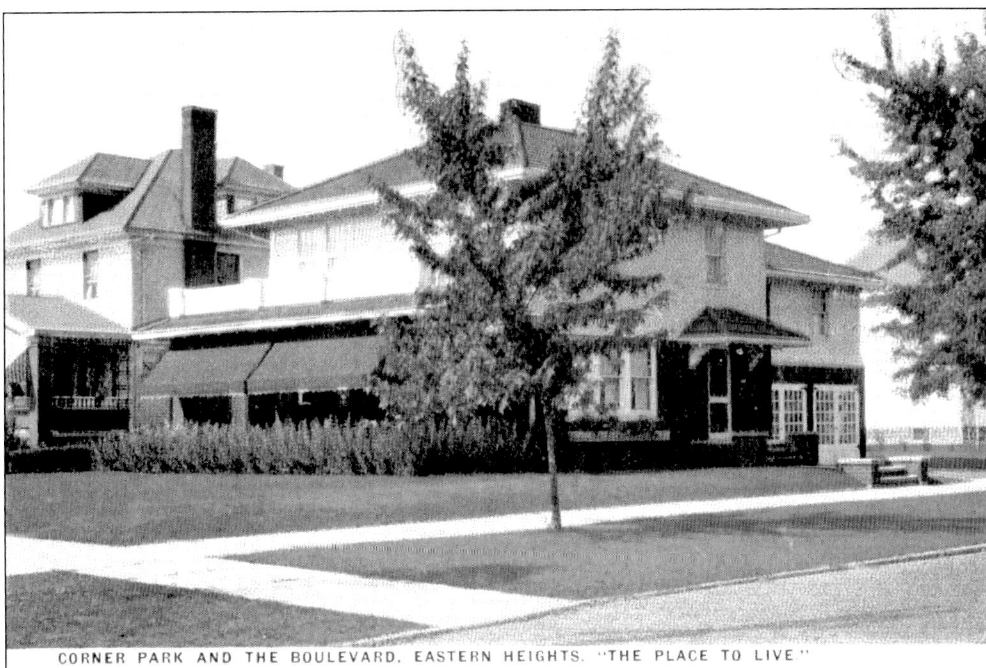

EASTERN HEIGHTS, EASTERN HEIGHTS BOULEVARD. This southwest corner of the intersection is a familiar stop for neighborhood residents, as a mailbox has been located here for many years.

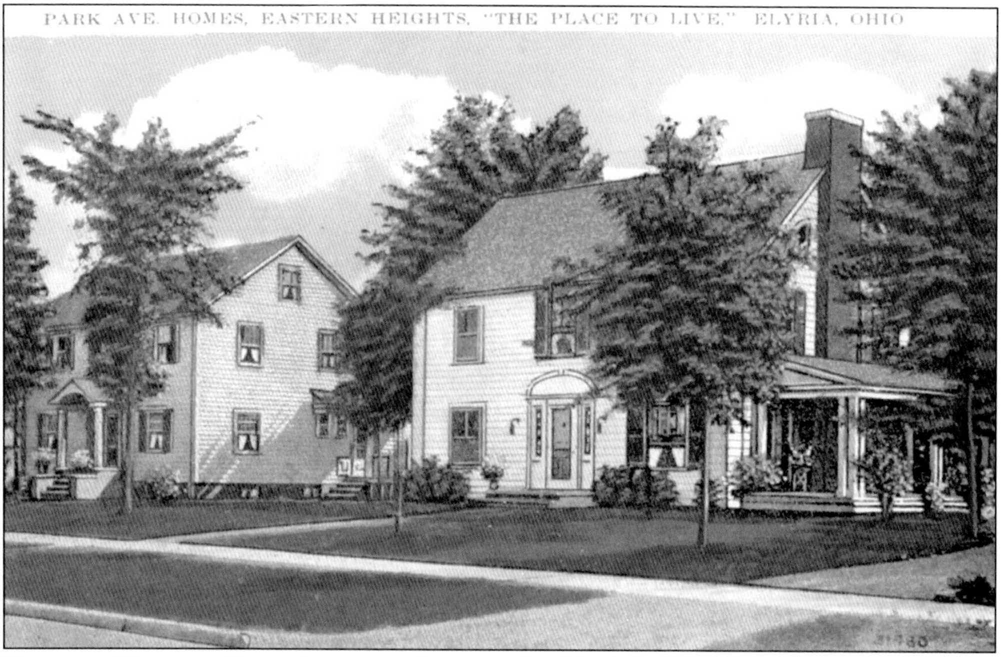

EASTERN HEIGHTS, PARK AVENUE. These comfortable frame houses are typical of those that line Park Avenue, the main north-south artery through Eastern Heights. The large shade trees that are today a hallmark of this neighborhood have not yet matured.

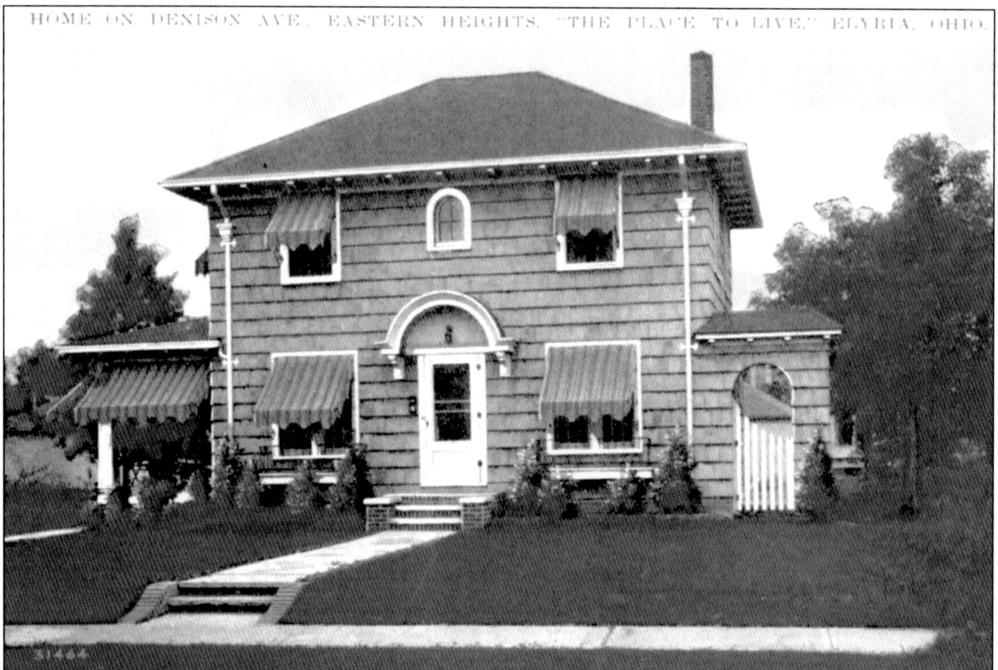

EASTERN HEIGHTS, DENISON AVENUE. This shingled house on the north side of the 300 block of Denison Avenue today looks much as it did when this postcard was printed. Awnings protect the south-facing front windows to shade the house from the hot summer sun.

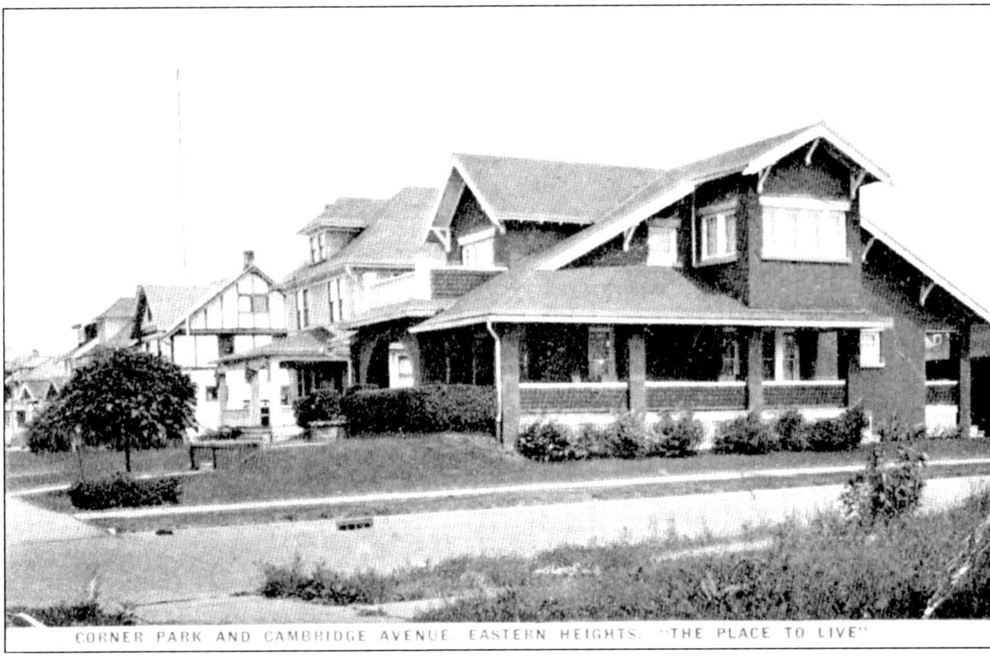

EASTERN HEIGHTS, CAMBRIDGE AVENUE. This large brick home on the northeast corner of Park and Cambridge Avenues looks virtually unchanged today. In this view, the lot on the southeast corner has not yet been developed.

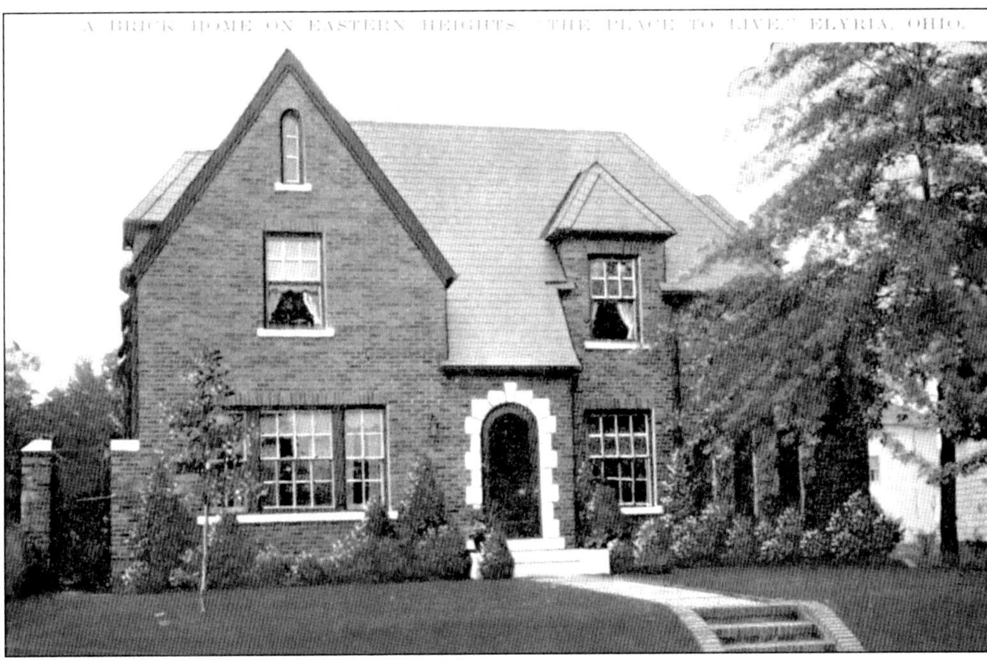

EASTERN HEIGHTS NEIGHBORHOOD. Many variations of these "place to live" postcards were sent out by realtors, hoping to interest prospective buyers in the Eastern Heights neighborhood. This handsome, well-landscaped brick home would have been an appealing advertisement for the area.

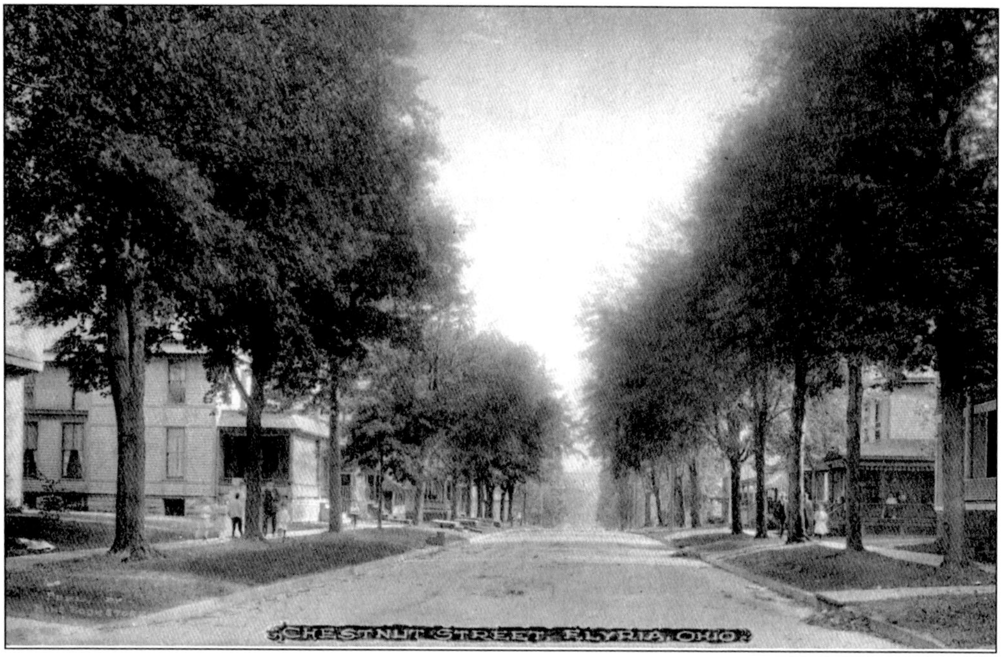

CHESTNUT STREET. In one of the first residential areas in Elyria, even the modest homes on Chestnut Street featured the wide porches and shaded lawns that were a hallmark of houses built near the turn of the century.

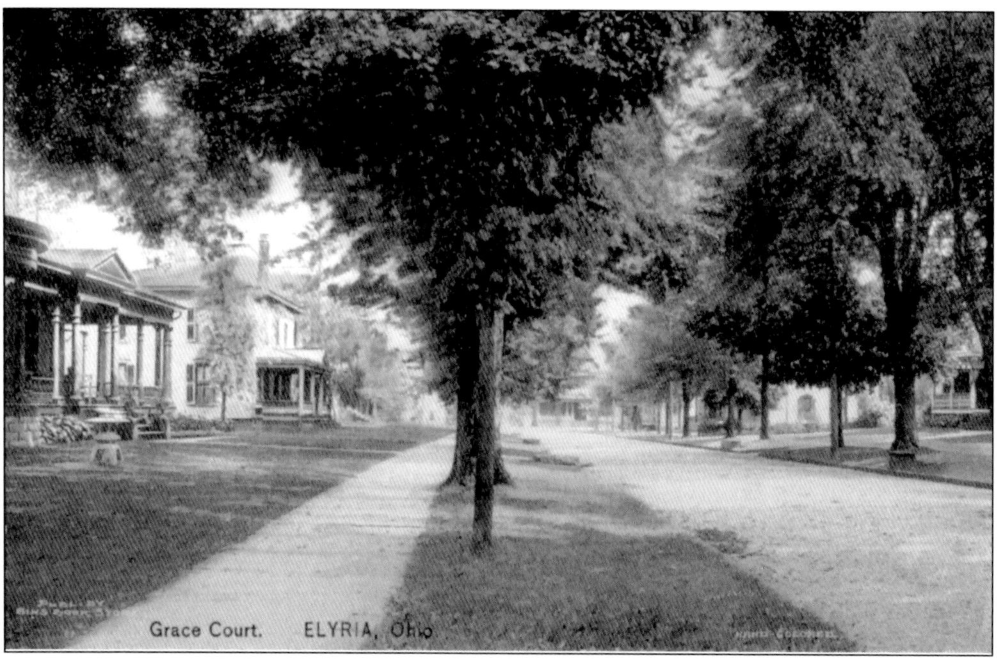

GRACE COURT. Second Street between East Avenue and Cedar Street was once a dead-end street known as Grace Court. At that time, Cedar Street did not extend south of Broad Street. A house can be seen in the distance where Grace Court ended.

Five

Bridges, Trains, and Industry

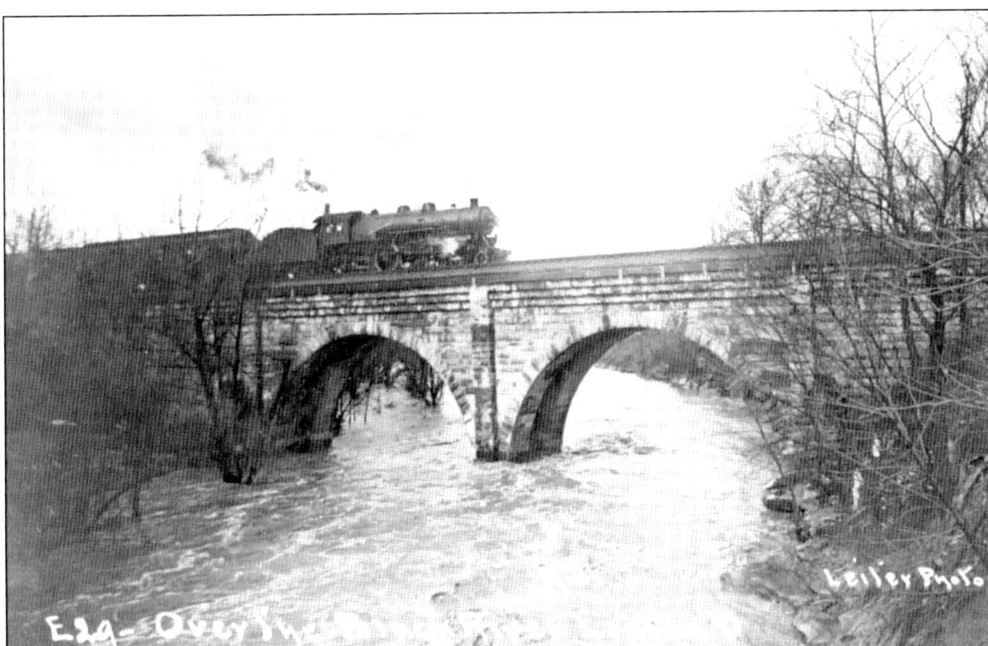

Lake Shore and Michigan Southern Railroad Bridge. This bridge was located just west of the East Bridge Street Bridge. A similar bridge was located near West Bridge Street over the West Branch of the Black River. The LS and MS Railroad was formed through an 1869 merger and survived until the establishment in 1914 of the New York Central Railroad.

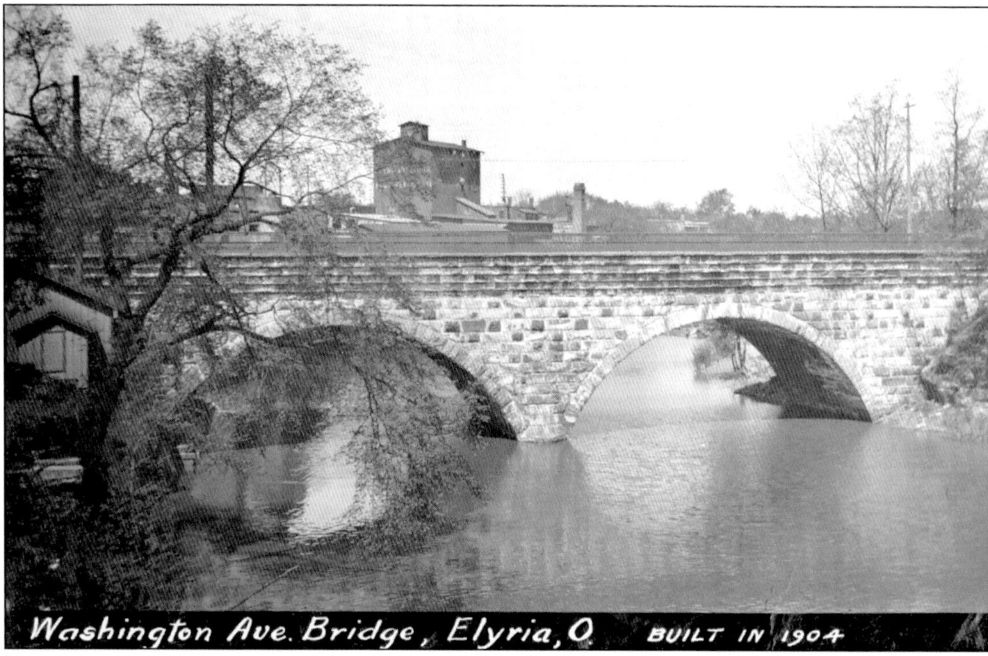

WASHINGTON AVENUE BRIDGE, STONE. In 1904, this beautiful double-arch sandstone bridge replaced an old iron bridge at Washington Avenue dating back to 1872. This new bridge could better accommodate two-way automobile traffic. The Red Mill, standing near the East Falls, can be seen in this west-facing view. This proud new bridge would last only seven years.

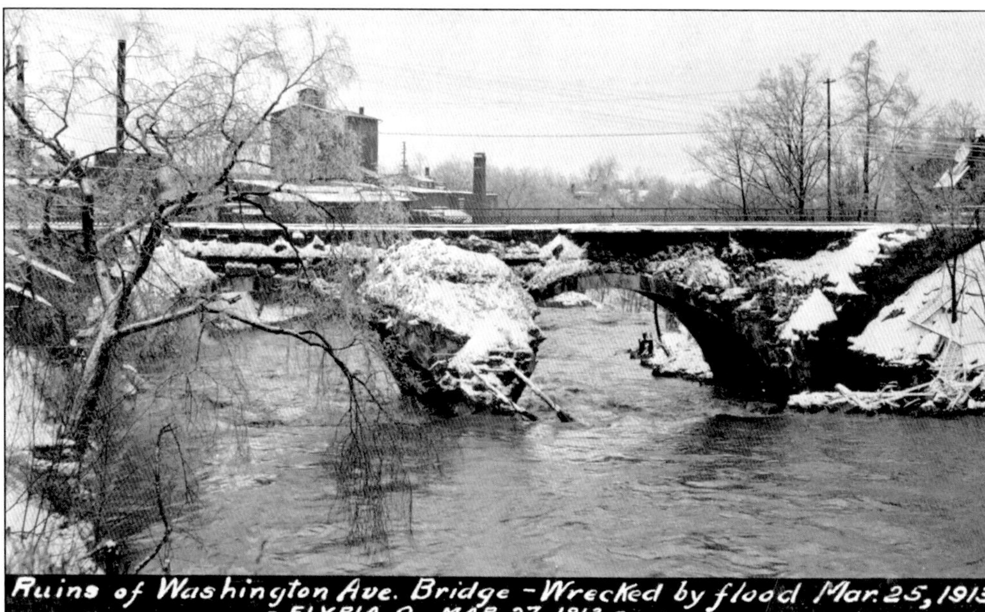

WASHINGTON AVENUE BRIDGE, RUINS. In 1913, several days of heavy rains and melting snow produced widespread flooding all across Ohio. The relatively new stone bridge across the east branch of the Black River succumbed to flood waters that, for many hours, nearly reached the surface of the road. In this view, only the southbound lane of the bridge is still intact.

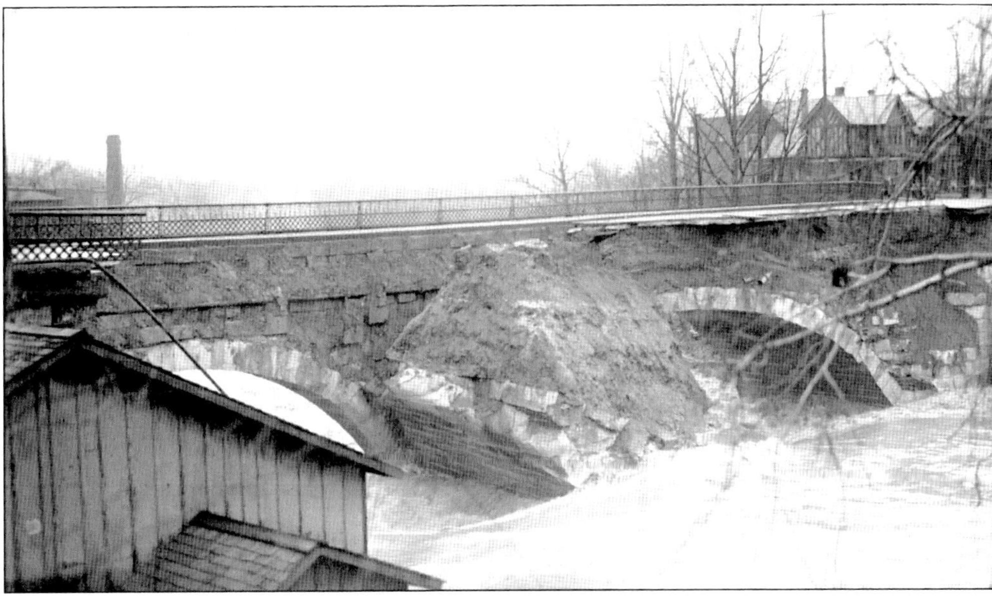

WASHINGTON AVENUE BRIDGE, RUINS. As the spring flood waters receded, the extent of damage to the bridge became evident. Efforts to clear the ruins began almost at once. The massive sandstone blocks, weighing two to three tons each, were sold for $1 per load, provided the new owner would haul them away. Many were cut up and used to build home foundations around town.

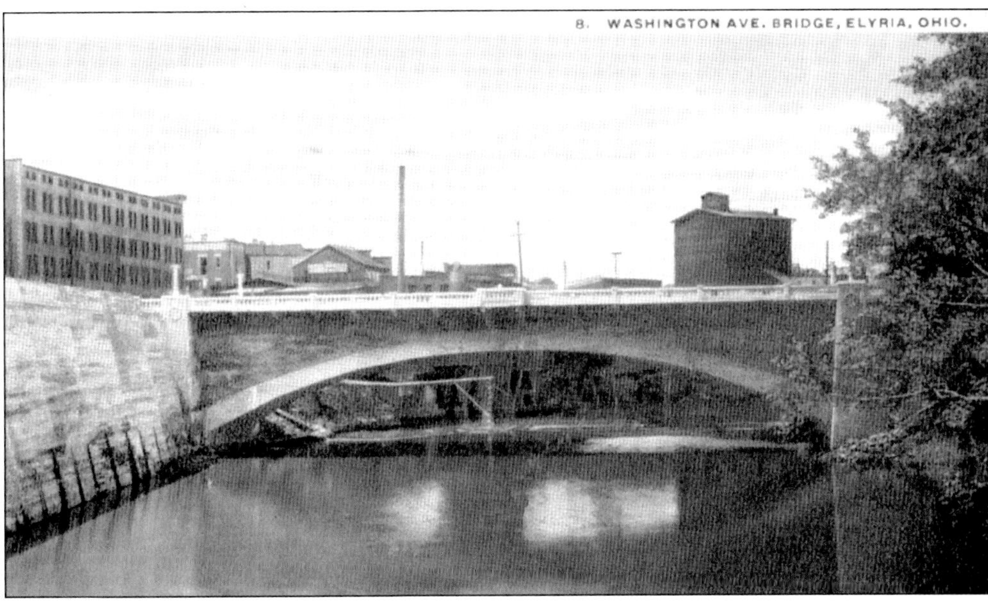

WASHINGTON AVENUE BRIDGE, CONCRETE. By the fall of 1914, a modern concrete bridge was ready for traffic across the Black River. This new single-arch design was better able to withstand the force of spring flood waters and lasted over 75 years. It was remodeled in 1959 and finally replaced with the present bridge in 1991. Note that the New York Central tracks, crossing Washington Avenue on the left in this view, had not yet been elevated—the tracks running along the concrete wall are on street level.

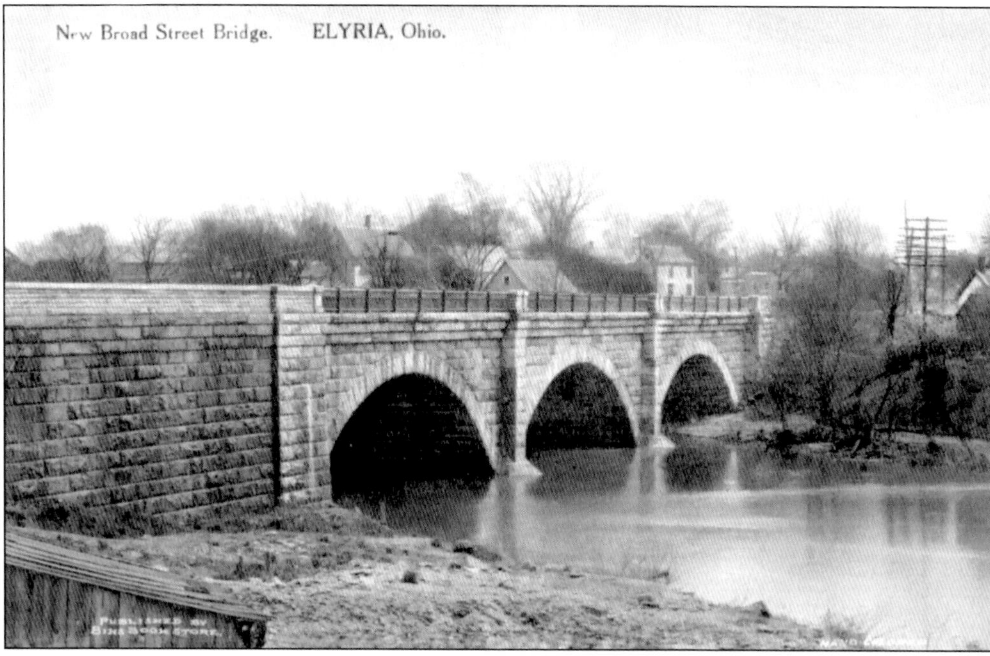

BROAD STREET BRIDGE. This stone bridge built in 1907 extended East Broad Street out to East River Street. Together with an improved bridge at Fourth Street, this construction helped accelerate development of the Eastern Heights residential district. This bridge is still in use today, nearly 100 years later.

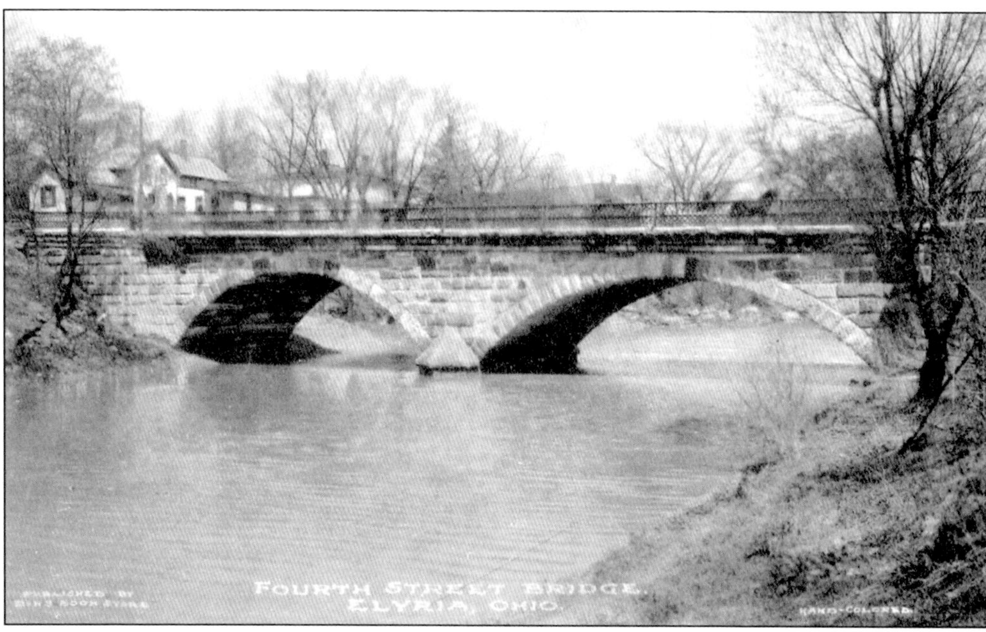

FOURTH STREET BRIDGE. This stone bridge built in 1907 replaced a 33-year old iron bridge at the same location. The bridge connected downtown Elyria with Eastern Heights Boulevard, at the heart of the new Eastern Heights residential development. It lasted for over 90 years before being replaced by the present concrete bridge in 1998.

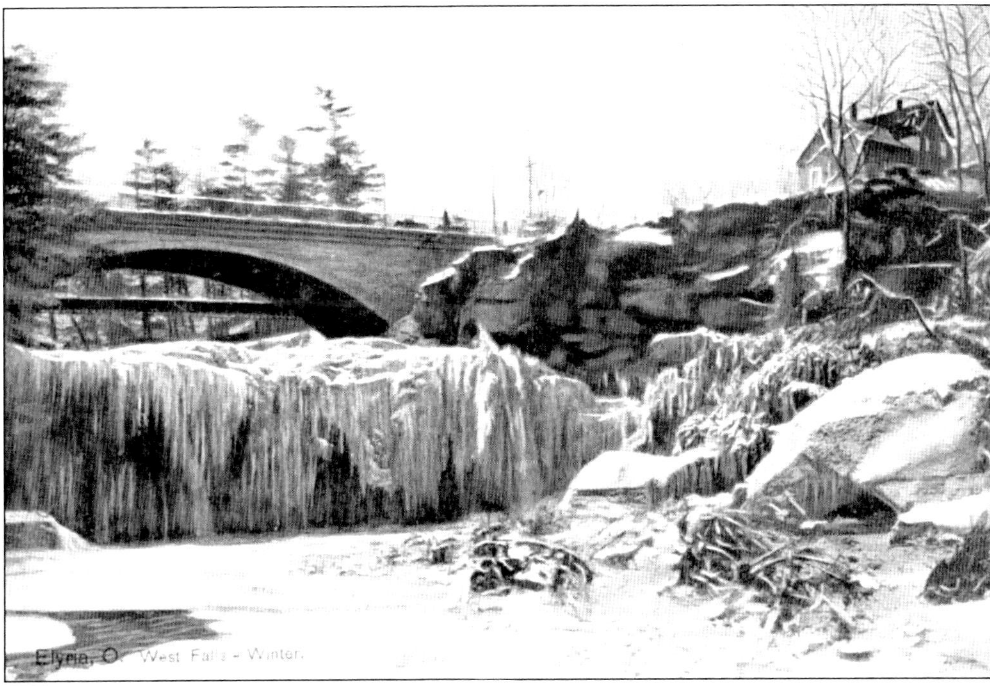

LODI STREET BRIDGES, WINTER. The sandstone bridge seen here (and on back cover) was preceded by an iron bridge dating to 1869. In this view, the old iron bridge can still be seen behind the new sandstone one. The iron bridge was later relocated and served for many years as the Ford Road Bridge.

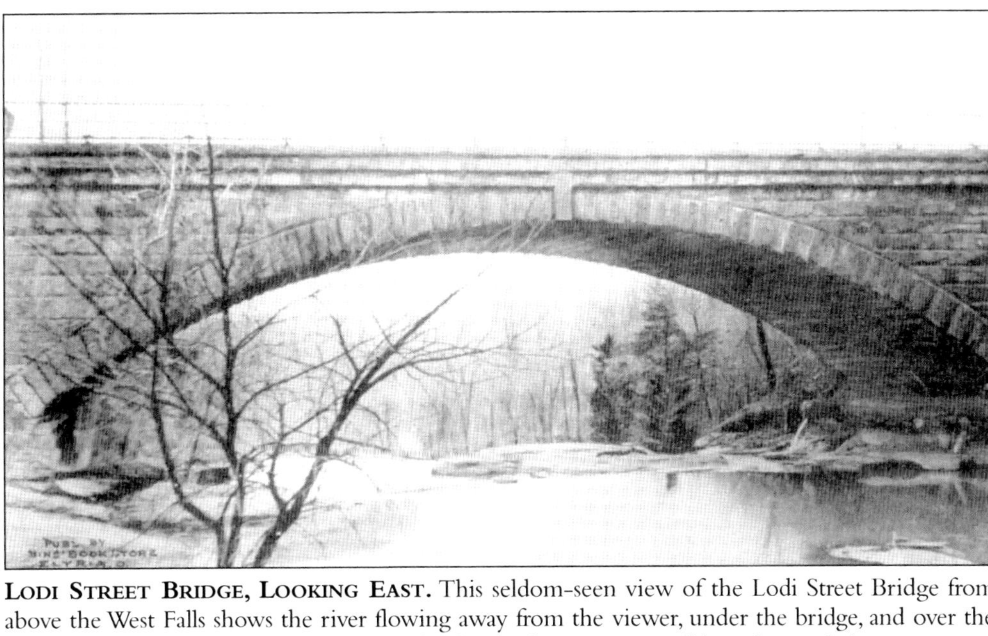

LODI STREET BRIDGE, LOOKING EAST. This seldom-seen view of the Lodi Street Bridge from above the West Falls shows the river flowing away from the viewer, under the bridge, and over the falls. Cascade Park is in the distance. This bridge, built in 1894, is still heavily traveled.

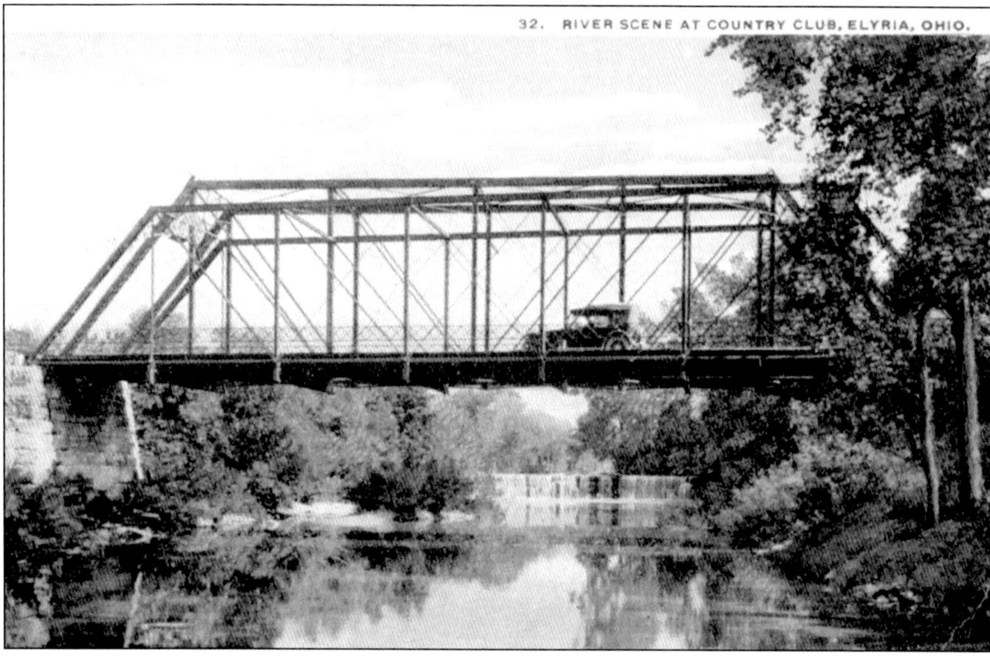

OBERLIN ROAD BRIDGE. This picturesque span was located just south of Elyria as Ohio Route 20 headed west past the Elyria Country Club towards Oberlin. Cottesbrook Dam can be seen in the distance.

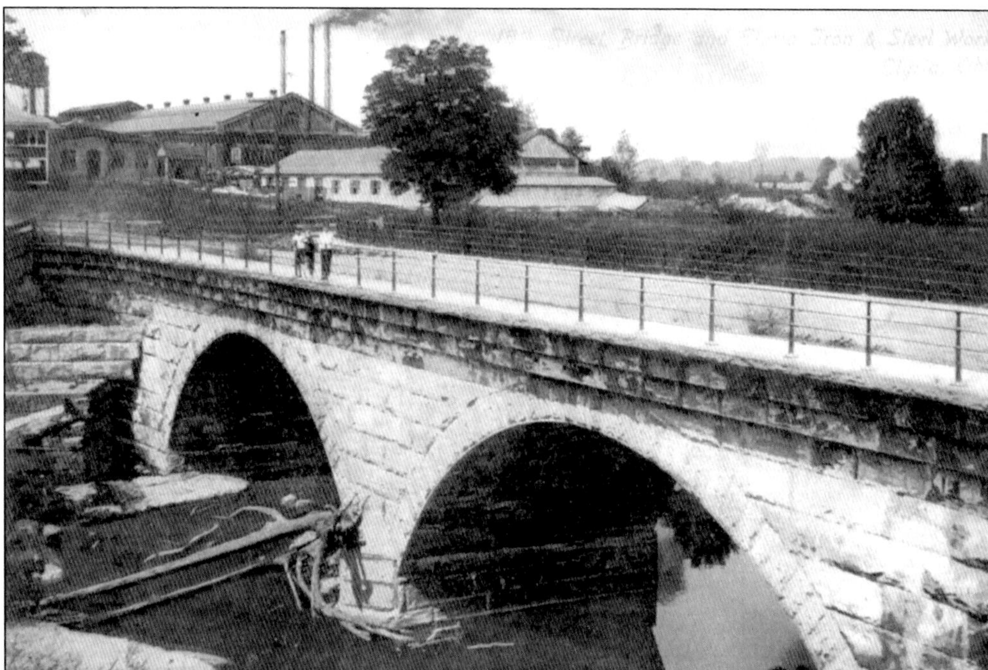

MUSSEY AVENUE BRIDGE. The 15th (then 13th) Street Bridge was built about 1904 to accommodate traffic for the new Elyria Iron and Steel Company, seen here in the background. Sandstone for this bridge was taken from the nearby Mussey quarry.

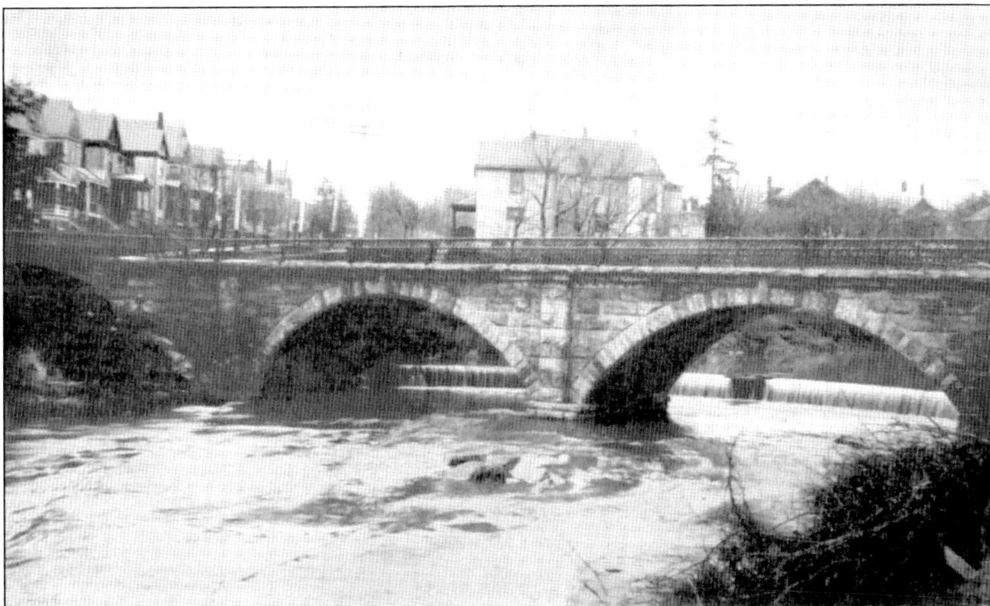

WEST THIRD STREET BRIDGE. The first bridge erected here was made of iron. It was built in 1867 to accommodate visitors to the new Lorain County Fairgrounds, then located in Elyria on the west side of the Black River. The sandstone bridge shown here replaced that bridge and was itself replaced with a concrete span in 1975 to encourage development of an industrial park west of town.

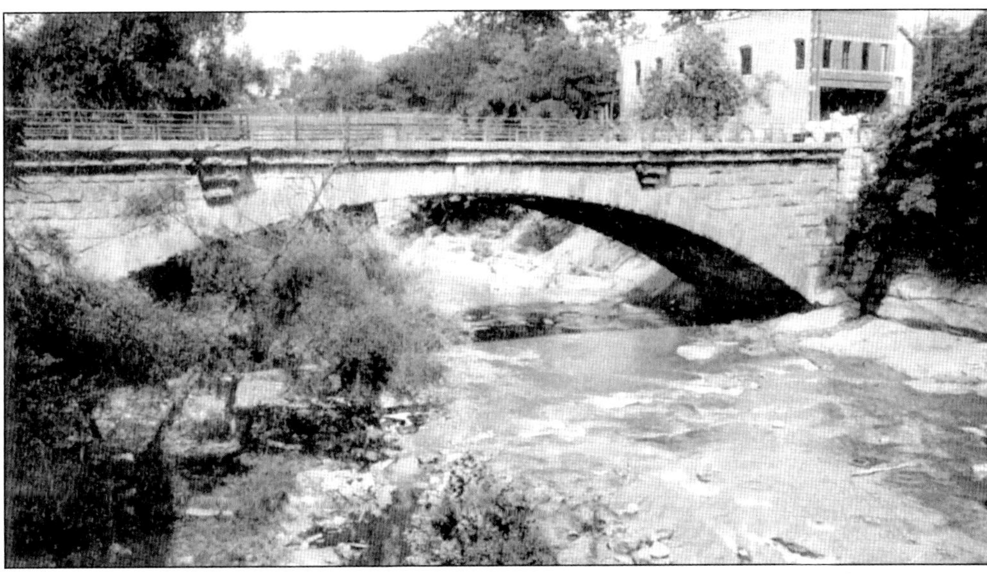

EAST BRIDGE STREET BRIDGE. This was likely the site of Elyria's first bridge, dating to 1817. The sandstone bridge shown here replaced several wooden structures. It was built in 1886 of stone from the Weller Quarry in Cascade Park. At that time, it was actually the second flattest bridge in the world—a span over the Danube at Ulm was slightly flatter. This bridge was replaced in 1999.

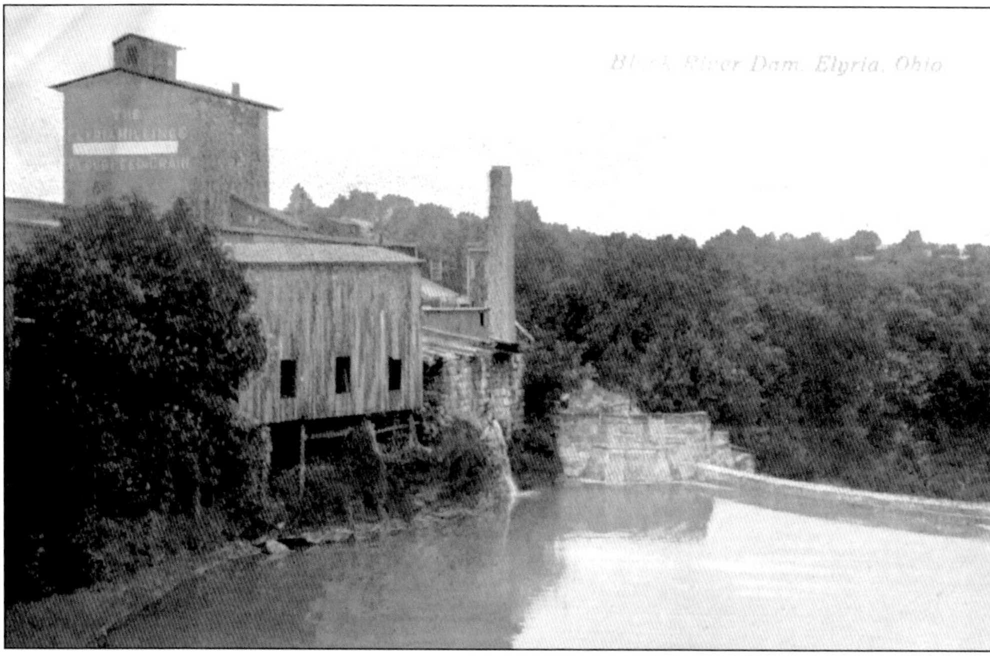

Elyria Milling Company. The Red Mill, as it was known around town, was a grist mill built on the site of Elyria's second-oldest mill—the 1824 "Old Red Mill." In this view from the Washington Avenue Bridge, we see the mill buildings and the dam above the East Falls. This company later dabbled in hydroelectric power generation, using dynamos located in a building below the falls. (See the Cascade Park section of this book.)

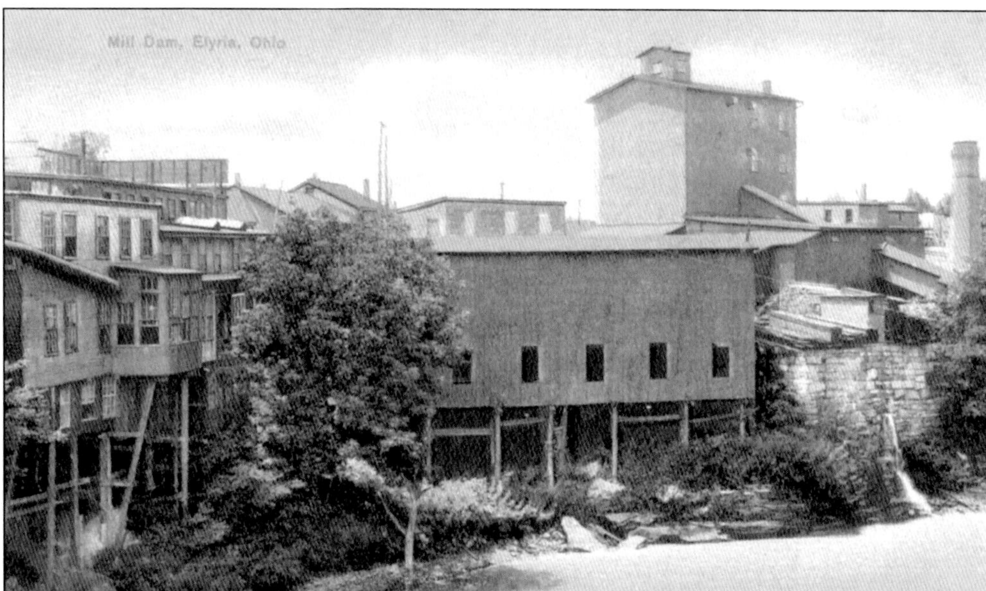

Parsch Planing Mill. This mill was established above the East Falls in 1873 by Christian Parsch on what was then Mill Street, later Lodi Street. It evolved into Parsch Lumber, a major local supplier of lumber and coal. The Red Mill can be seen behind the Parsch buildings.

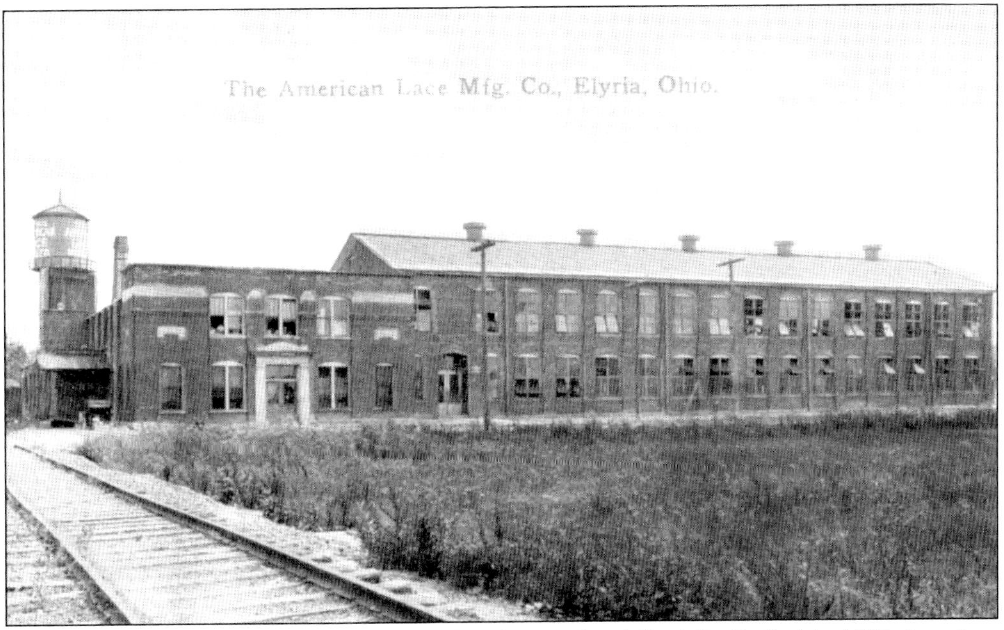

American Lace Company. Co-founded by Elyria industrialist A.L. Garford in 1907, American Lace produced world-class hand-woven lace products at this plant on Taylor Street. It later expanded to production of wool, cotton, and rayon goods and during World War II, made parachutes and camouflage netting. The buildings today are owned by the Parker-Hannifin Corporation.

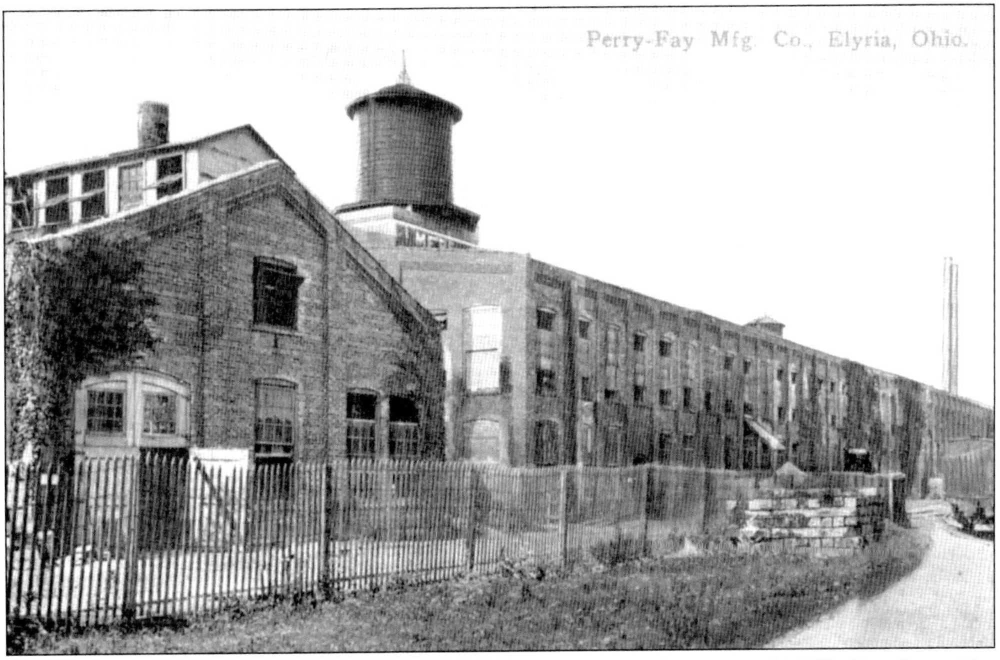

Perry-Fay Company. Founded in 1906 by Elyrians Richard Perry and Willis Fay, Perry-Fay manufactured valves and machine screw products for many years at this plant at 200 Perry Court. Today, the company is a division of the Parker-Hannifin Corporation.

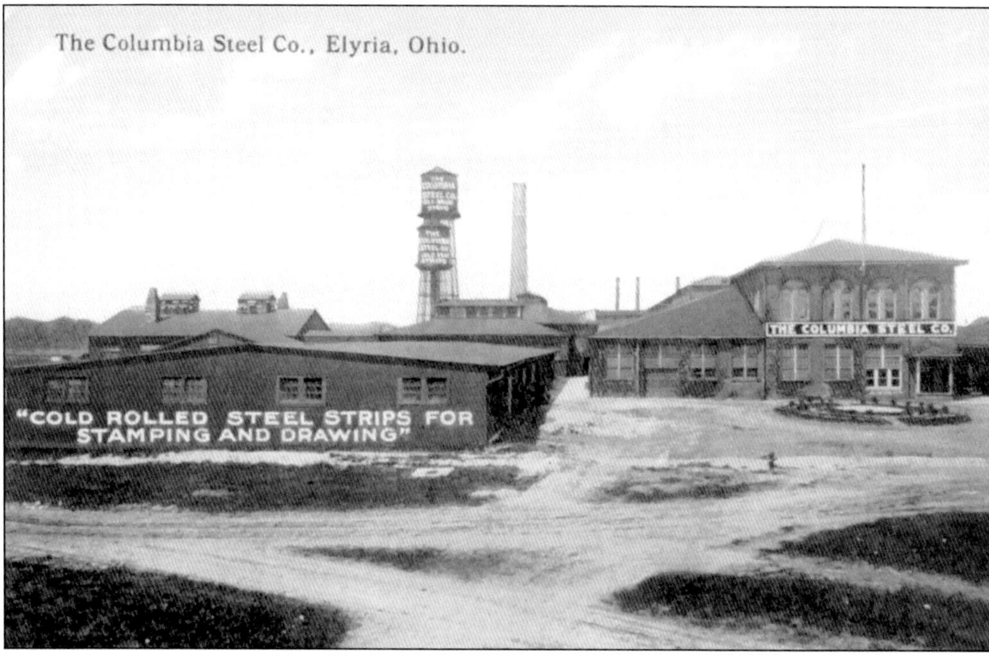

COLUMBIA STEEL COMPANY. Situated on Elyria's near-west side, Columbia Steel began operations in 1903 near the north-south B & O Railroad. It produced rolled steel, which was shipped across the country by rail and truck.

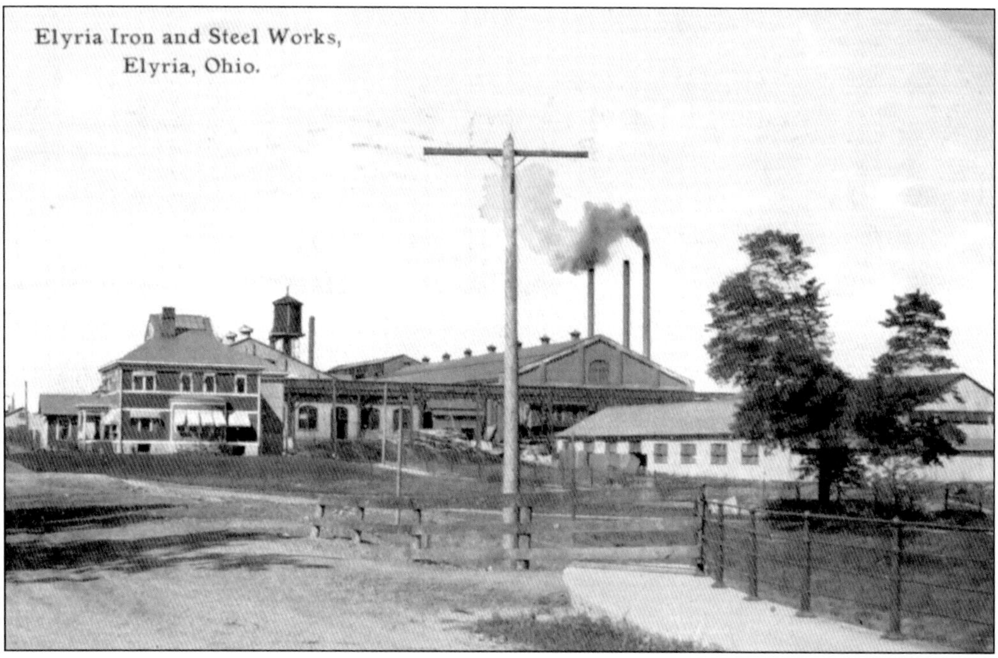

ELYRIA IRON AND STEEL COMPANY. This pipe mill was built on Mussey Avenue in 1902. In 1926, the plant became Steel and Tubes, Inc., which pioneered the use of electrical welding methods for high carbon steel. The plant is still in production and still uses Elyria's original water storage tank across the street from these buildings.

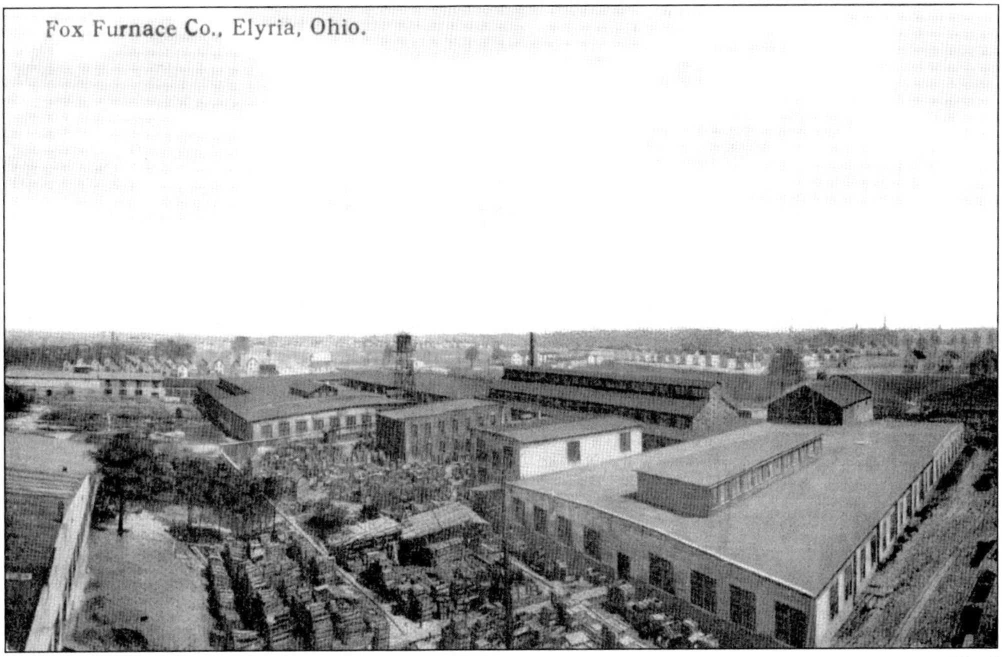

FOX FURNACE COMPANY. Another of Elyria's west side factories, Fox Furnace on Woodford Avenue was a Cleveland company until 1915 The company made heating furnaces and later, air conditioners for residential and commercial customers. Later known as American Standard and then the Tappan Company, the plant closed in the 1970s.

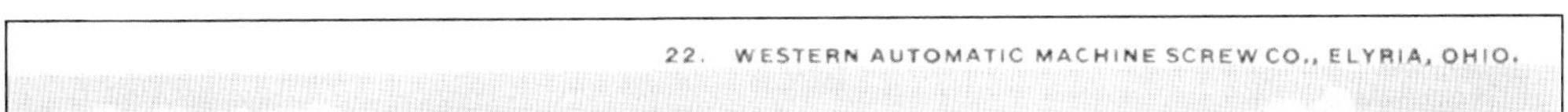

WESTERN AUTOMATIC MACHINE SCREW. One of Elyria's oldest businesses, Western Automatic was incorporated in 1882. It manufactured a wide range of screws, nuts, fasteners, taps, and related screw machine products at this plant on Woodland Avenue on Elyria's near-west side. Western Automatic eventually became Stanadyne and is today known as Moen, Inc., well-known manufacturer of sink faucets.

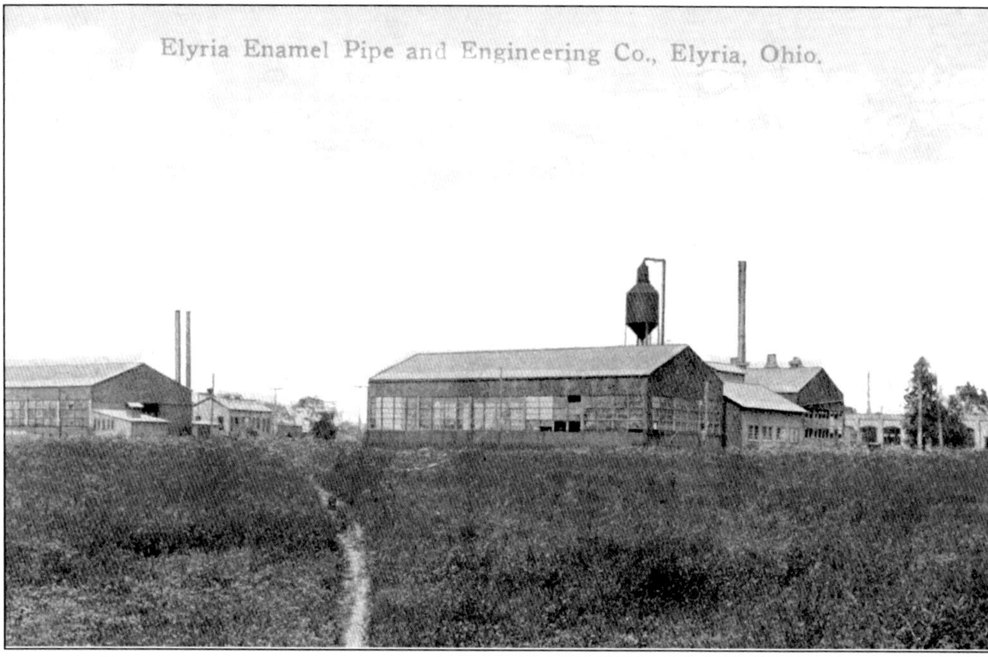

Enamel Pipe and Engineering Company. This Taylor Street company was formed in 1908 and manufactured high-tech glass lined tanks for use in the chemical and food-processing industries. Later known as Pfaudler, Ritter-Pfaudler, and finally Sybron, the plant ceased operations in 1981.

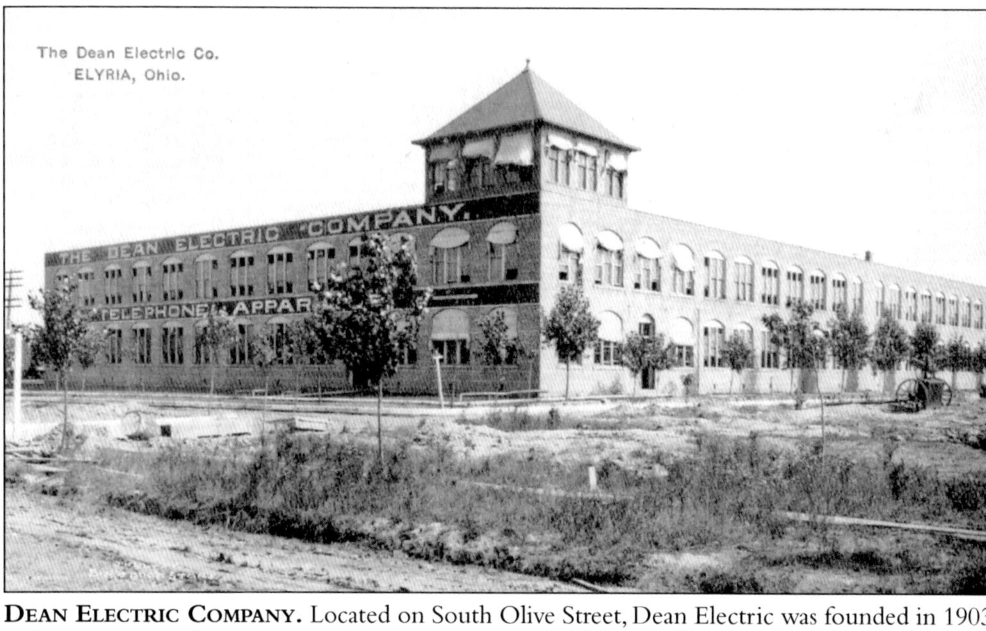

Dean Electric Company. Located on South Olive Street, Dean Electric was founded in 1903 and became one of the country's largest suppliers of telephones and related equipment. When this part of the business was sold to Stromberg-Carlson, the company became known as General Phonograph. After further diversification, the company was called General Industries and is today known as Industrial General Corporation.

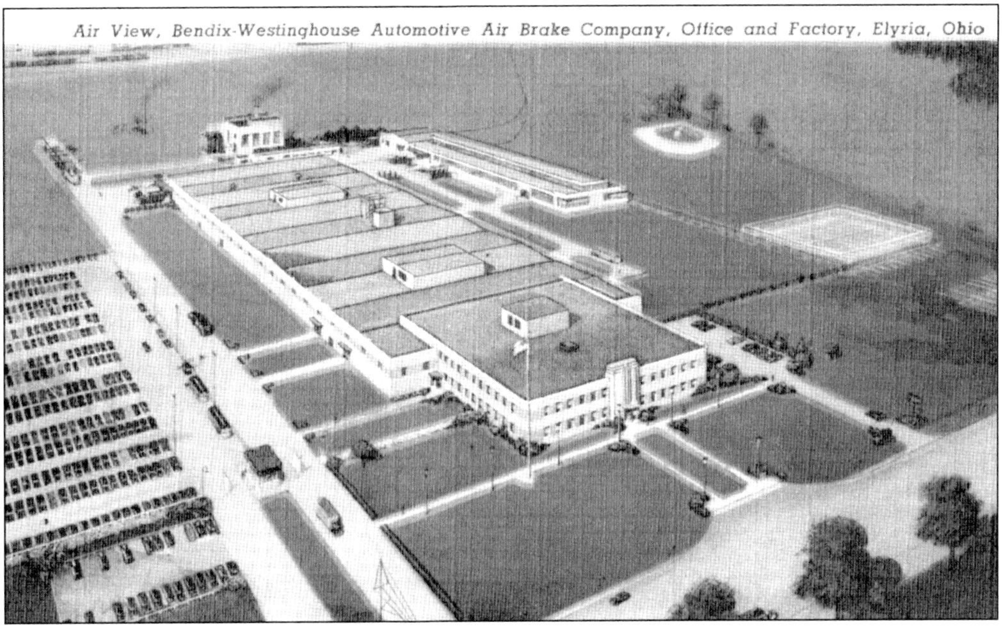

BENDIX-WESTINGHOUSE. Bendix-Westinghouse started production in Elyria in 1941. This complex on Ohio Route 20 (Cleveland Street) dates to the early 1950s. The company eventually employed 1,500 in the manufacture of Bendix, Fram, and Autolite brand spring and air brakes for cars, trucks, and buses. Bendix left in 1983, and Allied-Signal, Inc. and Invacare Corporation have used the buildings since then.

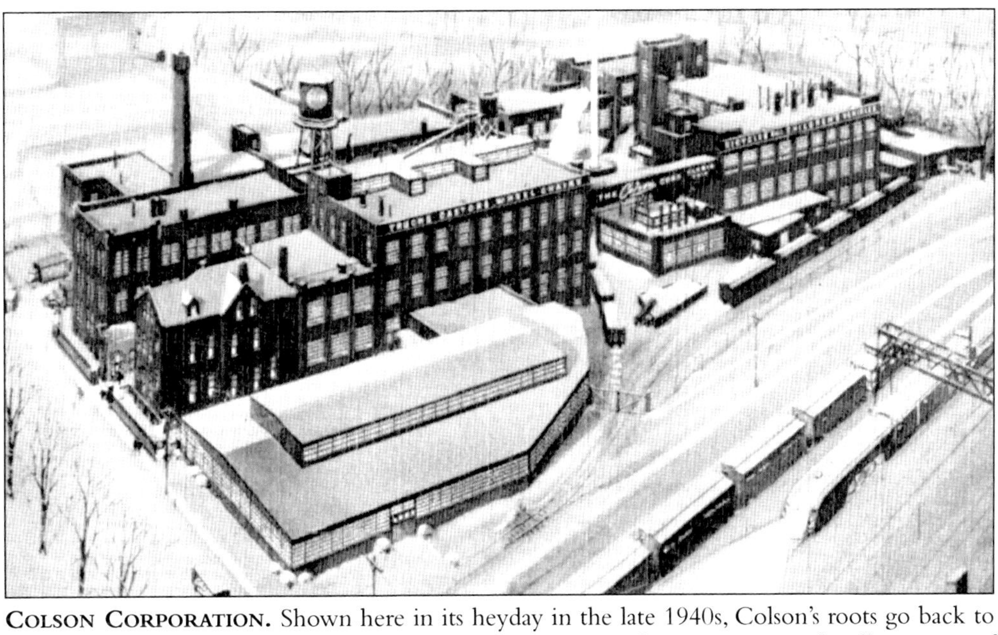

COLSON CORPORATION. Shown here in its heyday in the late 1940s, Colson's roots go back to the 1885 founding of the Fay Manufacturing Company. The company made all manner of tricycles, bicycles, wagons, "invalid chairs," casters, and related parts. It was one of Elyria's best employers until it moved to Jonesboro, Arkansas, in 1958. The nearby Harshaw Chemical Company purchased the buildings.

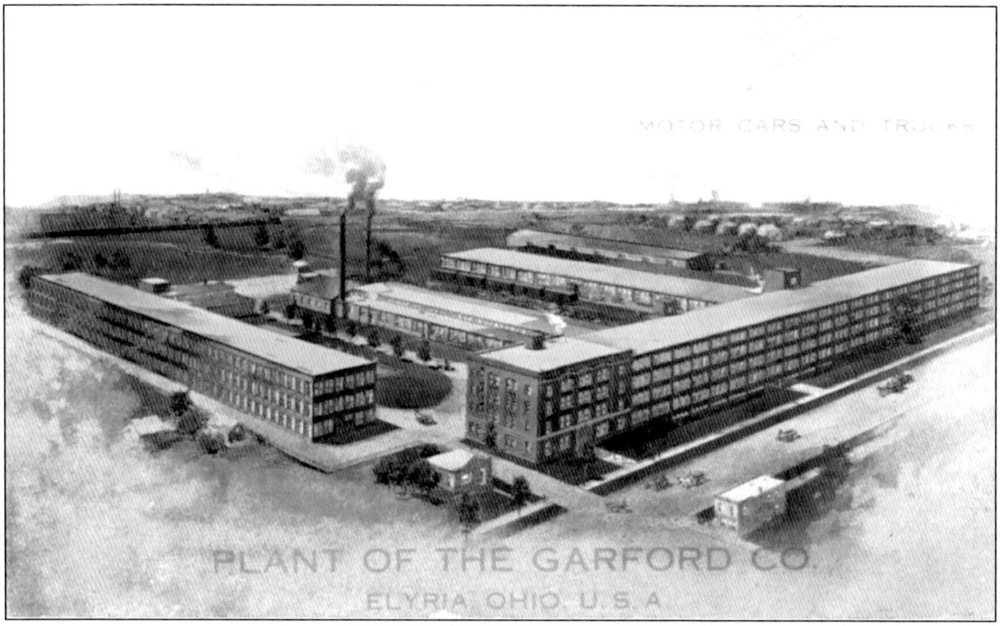

GARFORD COMPANY, BIRDS-EYE VIEW. Founded in 1905 by Arthur L. Garford, this large complex on Clark Street turned out elegant, high-end automobile chassis in partnership with Studebaker. The business was sold off after only seven years, following the success of Ford's mass-produced Model T.

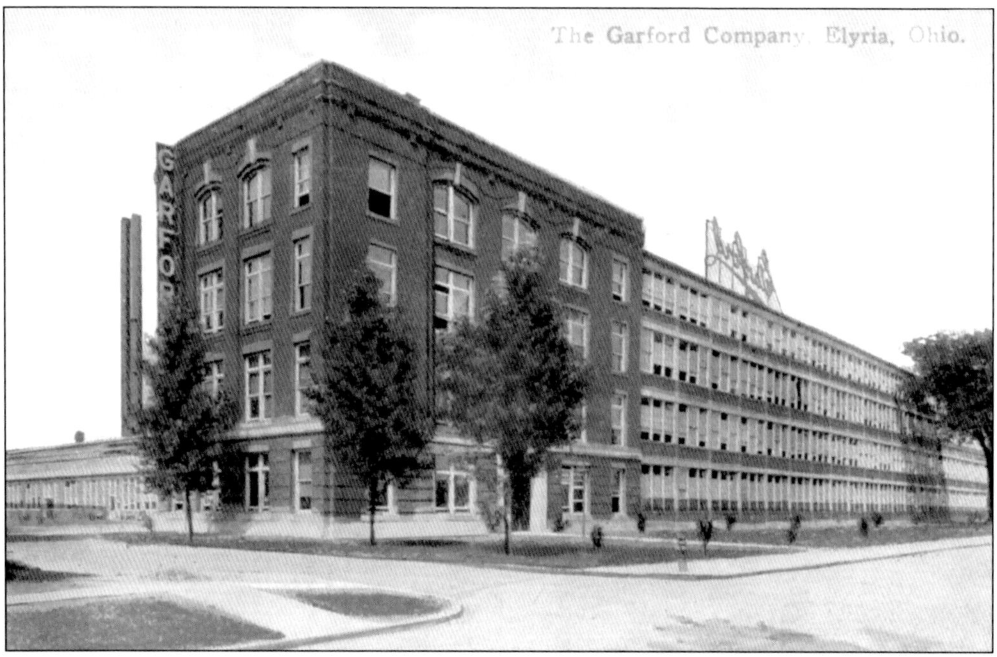

GARFORD COMPANY, STREET-LEVEL VIEW. The Garford plant was sold in 1912 to the Willys-Overland Company and in 1927, to Falcon Motors Corporation. Today, these buildings are home to Elyria's own Ridge Tool Company, producing the Ridgid brand of industrial hand tools.

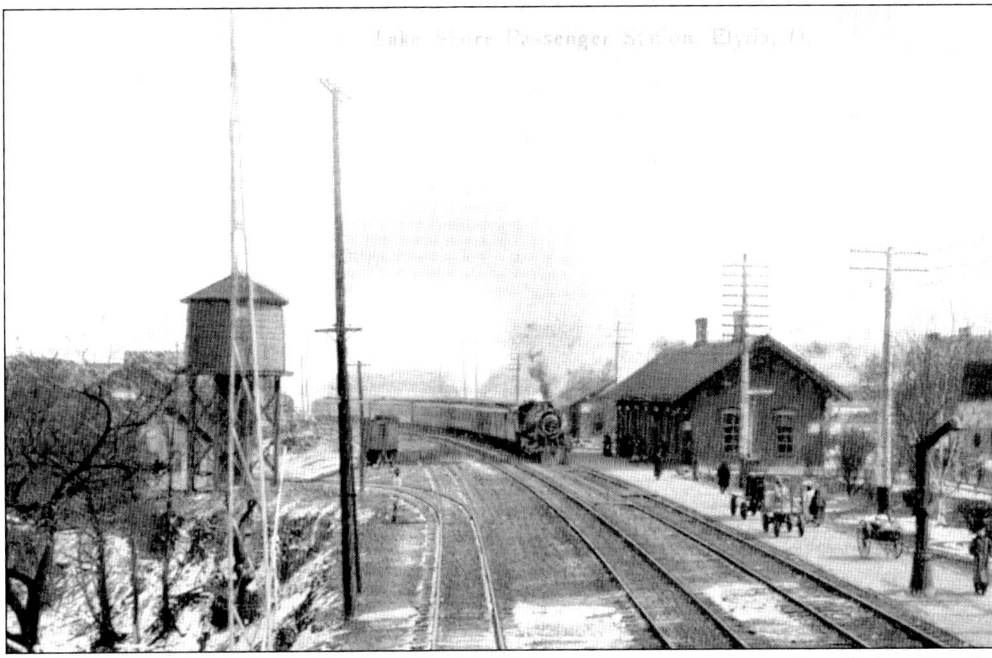

OLD PASSENGER STATION. In this view from the early 1900s, passengers bundled against the cold wait for the westbound train to arrive at the Lake Shore and Michigan Southern Railroad station in Elyria. The steam-powered engine can be seen in the distance.

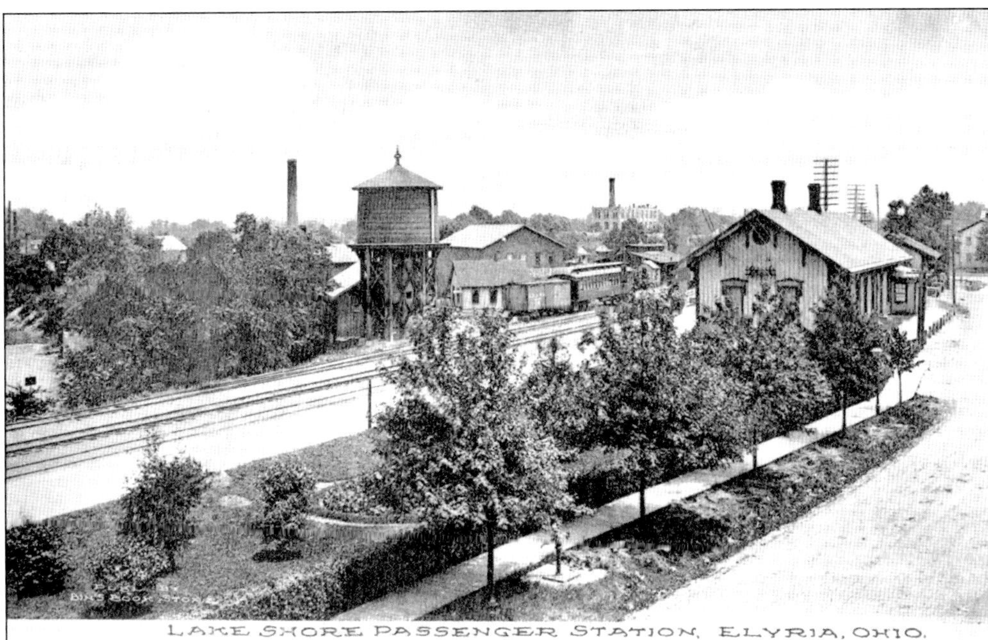

OLD PASSENGER STATION. Here is the same station as above, but in this postcard, the location of the building between the tracks and Depot Street on the right can be clearly seen. The railroad tracks had not yet been elevated. The Black River can be seen at the left edge of the card.

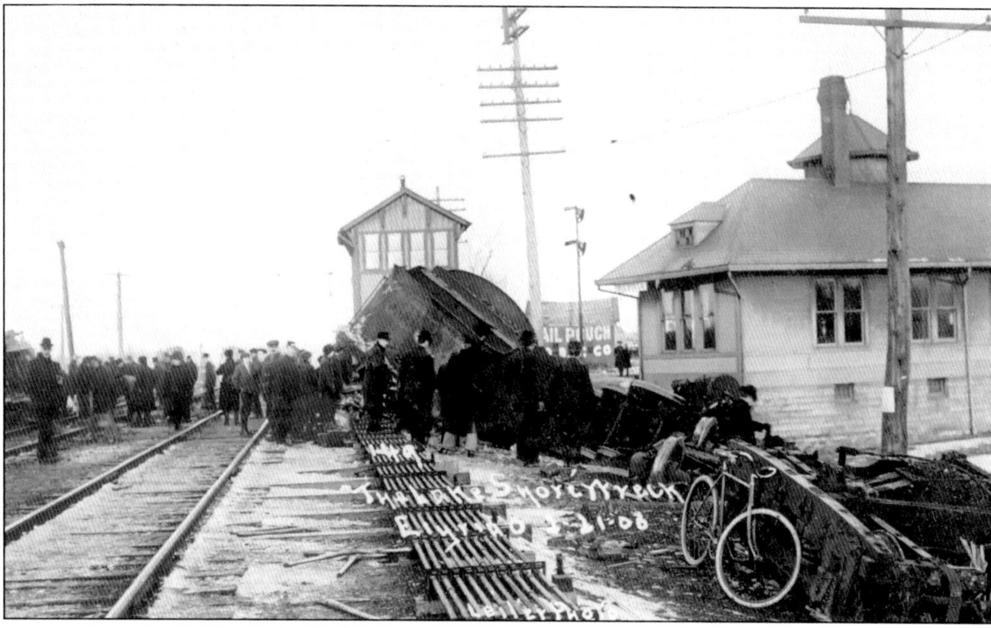

TRAIN WRECK. When many trains traveled through Elyria and Lorain County every day, there were inevitably more train wrecks. Photographs of these wrecked trains, along with other disasters, were frequently made into postcards. This card shows a train on the Lake Shore Line that derailed in Elyria in 1908.

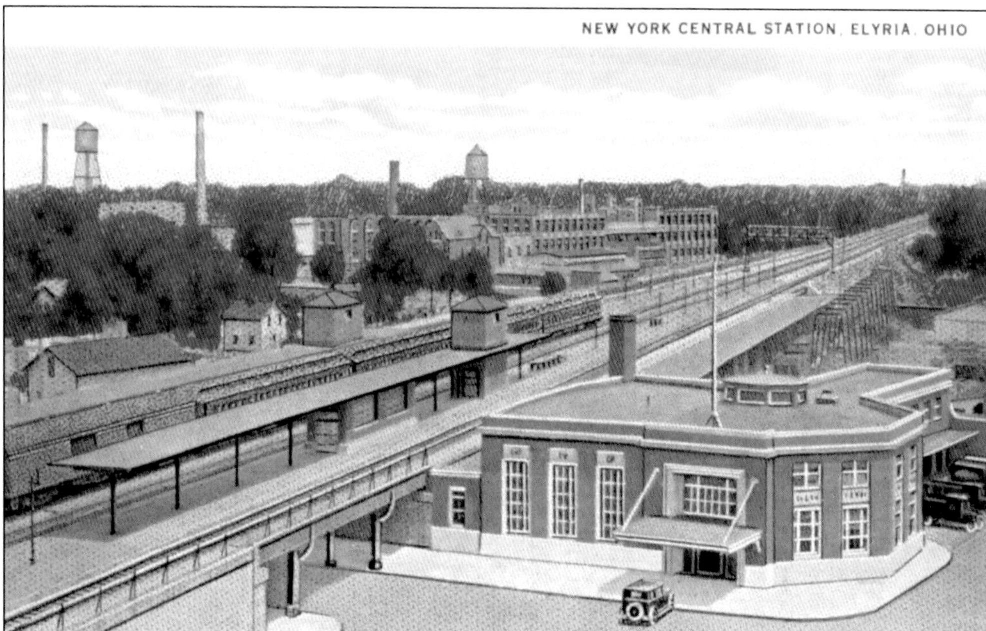

NEW YORK CENTRAL, ELYRIA STATION. In 1913, work began on elevating the east-west railroad tracks through Elyria, but was interrupted for several years by World War I. The Lake Shore and Michigan Southern became the New York Central Railroad in 1914, and their handsome brick depot opened in 1925 at the intersection of East Avenue and Depot Street.

Six

Cascade Park and the Falls

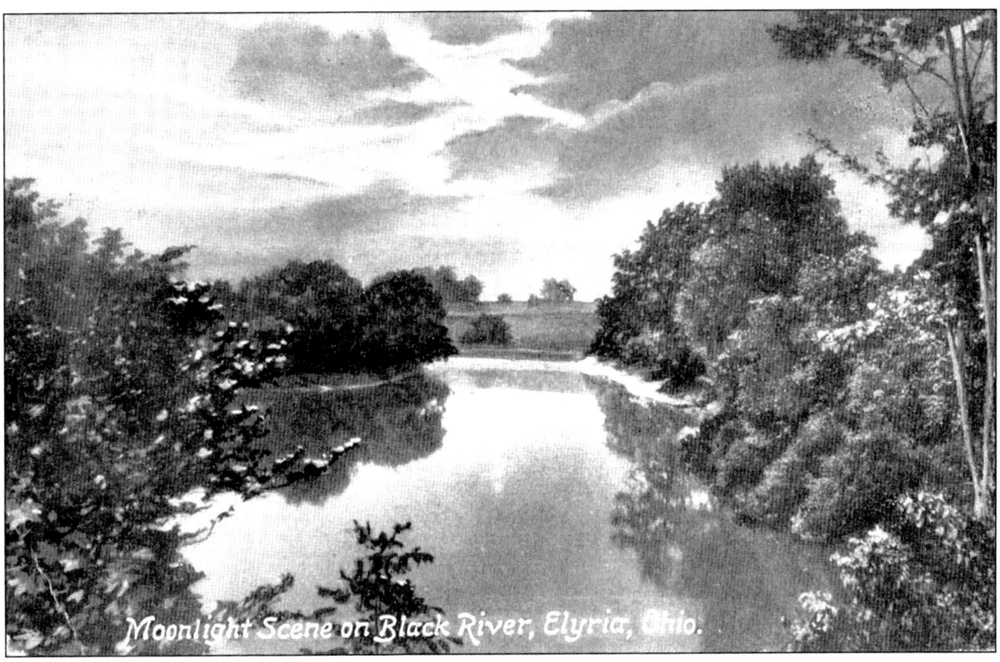

Black River by Night. Elyria was built at the intersection of the east and west branches of the Black River. The river has played an important role in the city's history. More than just an avenue of commerce, the river and surrounding parkland have been a refuge from everyday life to generations of Elyrians.

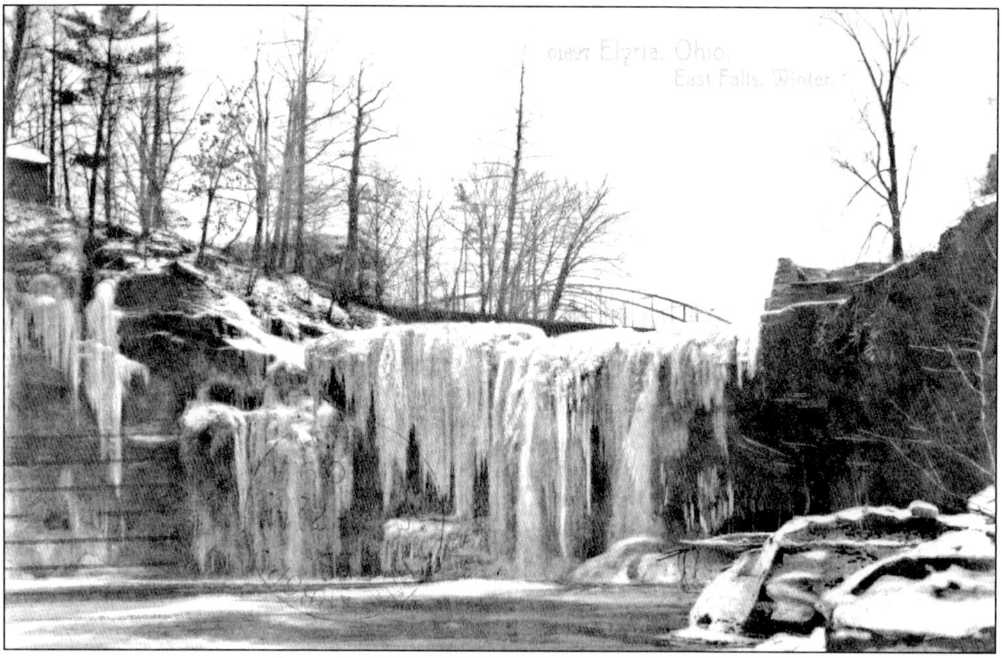

EAST FALLS, ***circa*** **1900.** This early view of the East Falls in winter includes a glimpse of the old iron bridge at Washington Avenue, which stood from about 1872 to 1904. The Washington Terrace Apartments would later be built behind the trees at top left.

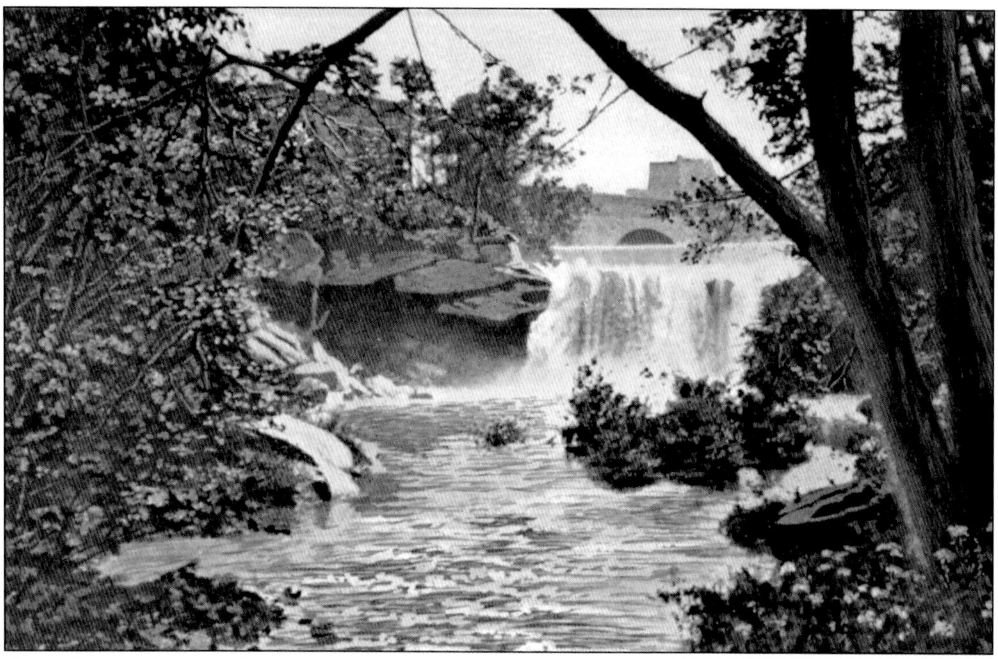

EAST FALLS, HIGH WATER. The power of the river during high water was no doubt the inspiration for installing mills both above and below the waterfall. The East Falls at one time turned up to five grindstones. Today, modern observation decks provide excellent views of the falls and the rainbows in the mist.

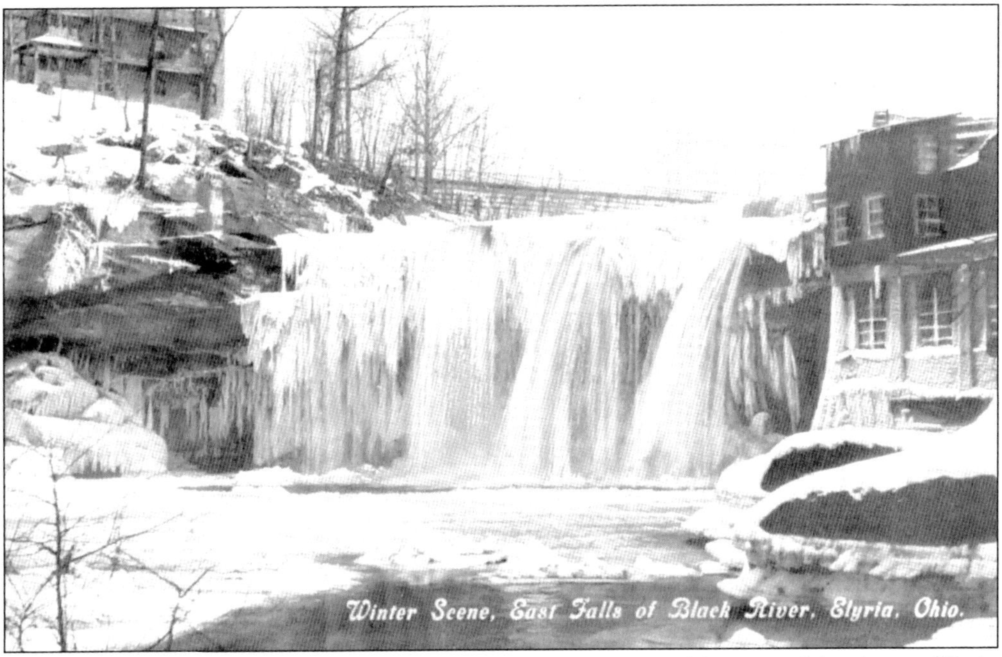

EAST FALLS IN WINTER. This card conveys some of the natural beauty of the frozen falls in winter. At left are the Washington Terrace Apartments. At right is the hydroelectric plant of the Elyria Milling and Power Company, which operated for a time in the early 1920s. The water powered two dynamos, which delivered power to parts of downtown.

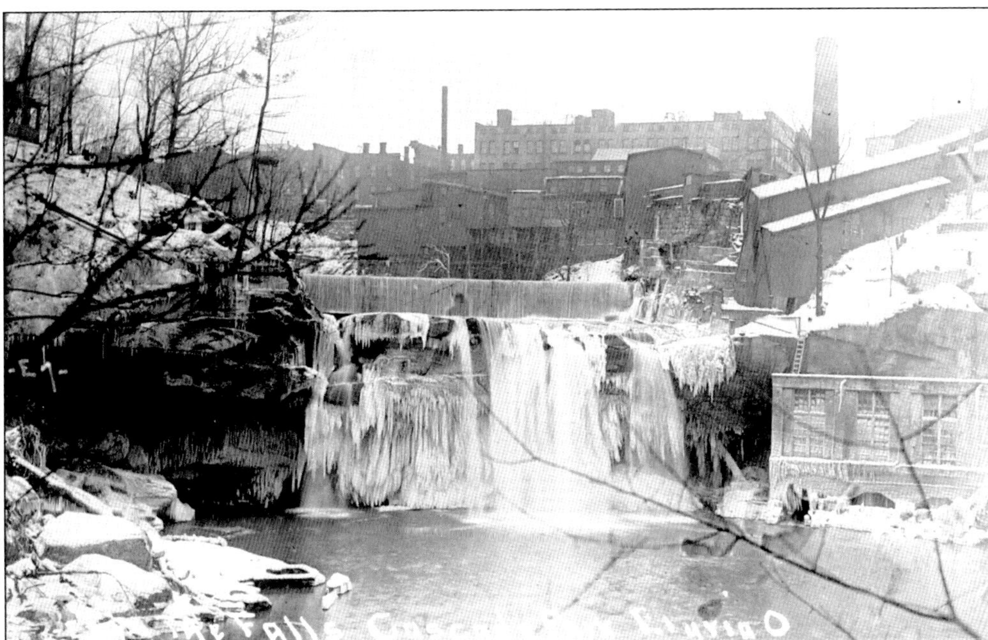

EAST FALLS AND BUSINESSES. This rare card provides a clear view of the dam above the falls, the Parsch Lumber Company, the Elyria Red Mill Company, and the hydroelectric plant at the foot of the falls. Only the dam and the broken shell of the power plant remain today.

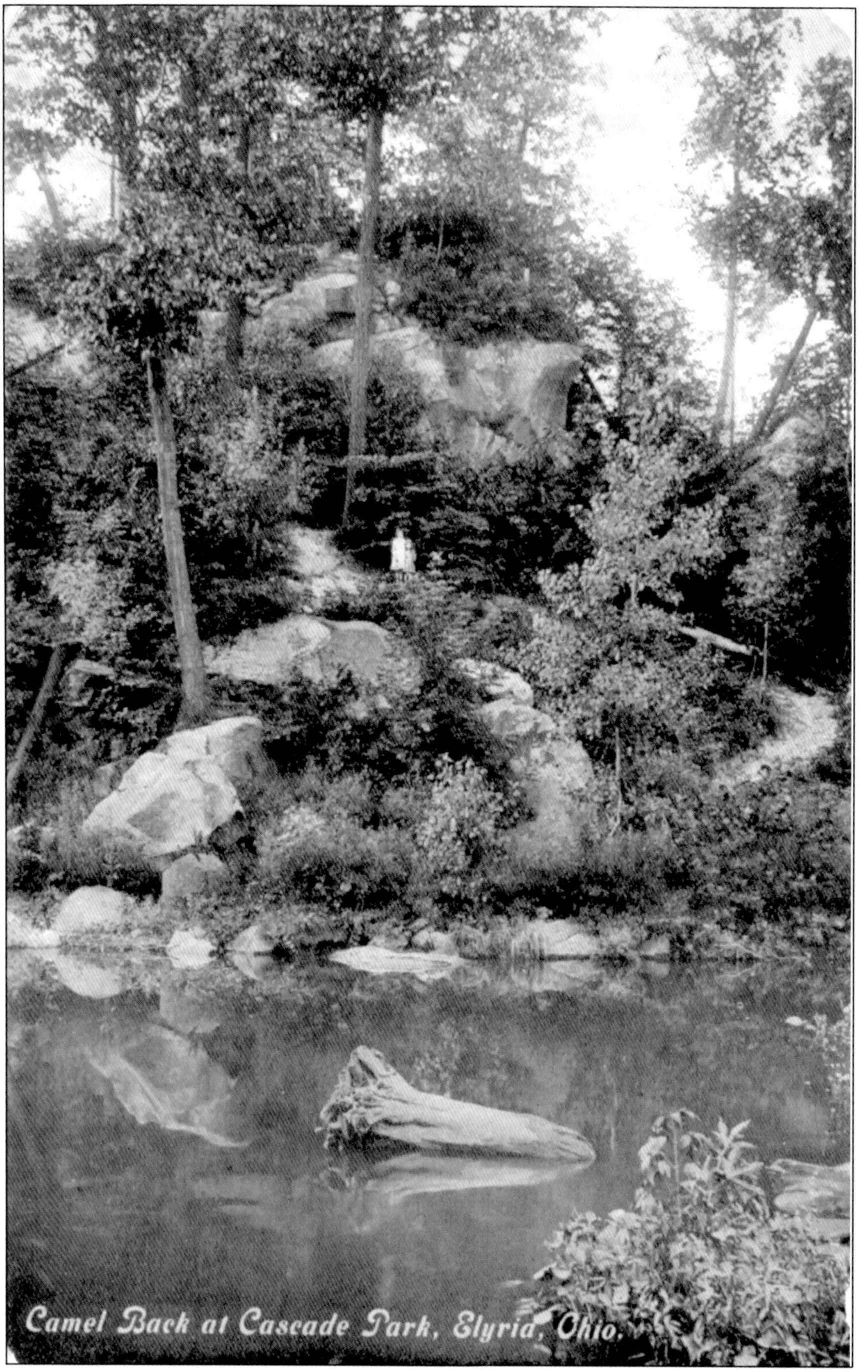

"CAMEL'S BACK," CASCADE PARK. Over the years, the more prominent features of the park have been given names, though some have fallen from use. This high rock out-crop near the junction of the east and west branches of the river is cut in two, forming a double hump. The taller of the two mounds is named Point Lookout, with a fine view to the south.

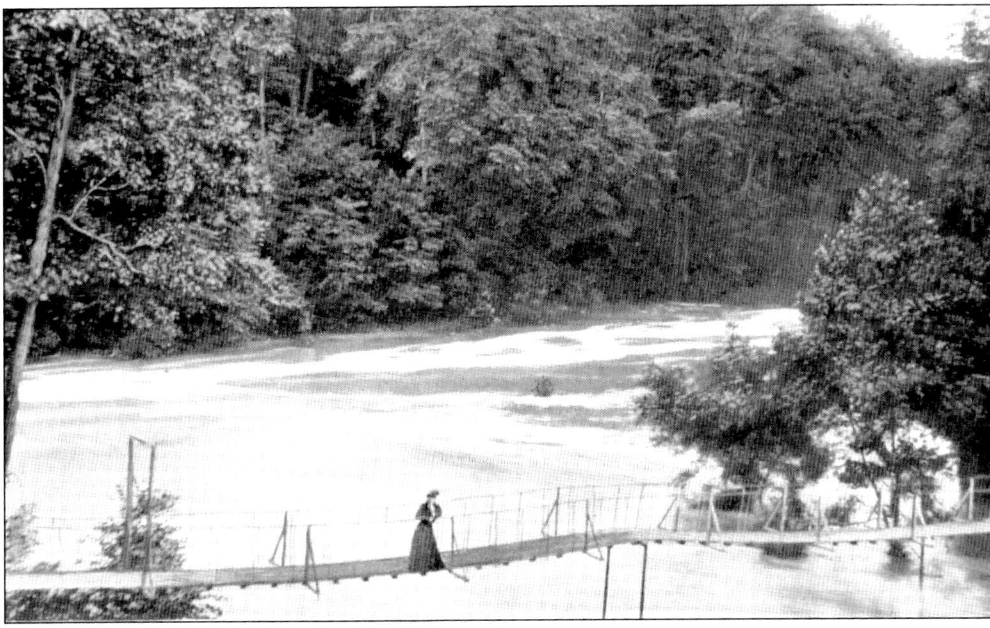

SUSPENSION FOOT-BRIDGE. This harrowing pedestrian bridge was suspended about 20 feet above the west branch of the Black River, just upstream of the junction with the east branch. The bridge, built in 1901, lasted only a few years, but the large iron anchors at either end remain to this day, sunk deep in the bedrock.

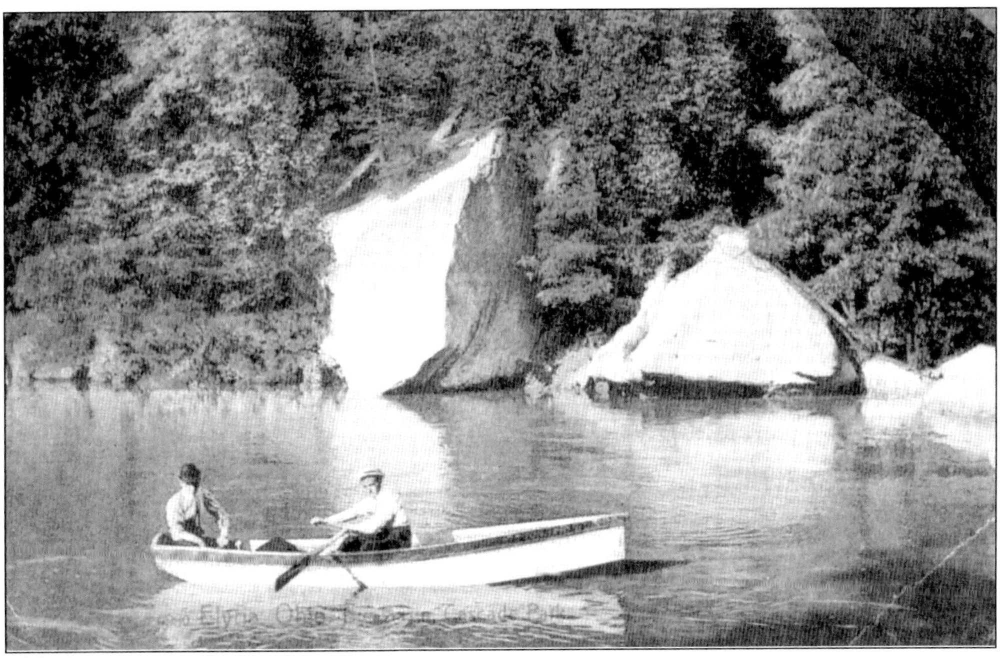

BOATING ON THE BLACK RIVER. During the early 1900s, pleasure boating on the river was very popular. After the Elywood parklands were added to Cascade Park, an auto ford was built across the river in 1929 to connect the two parks. The ford included a low dam built specifically to provide canoe-depth water upstream to the Basin, a popular picnic and launch area.

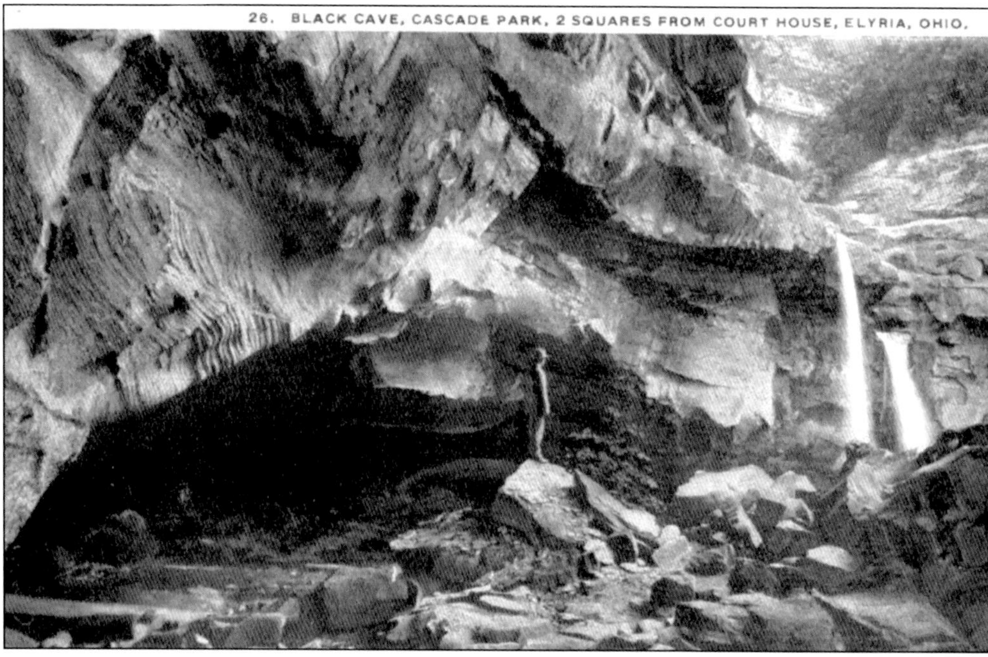

BIG CAVE, WEST FALLS. Along the south bank of the river at West Falls lies the gaping entrance to Big Cave. Some 120 feet wide and 90 feet deep, the cave is carved from the sandstone bedrock by the swirling waters of the Black River. Fine examples of flowstone rim the back of the cave, and enormous icicles adorn the west wall in winter.

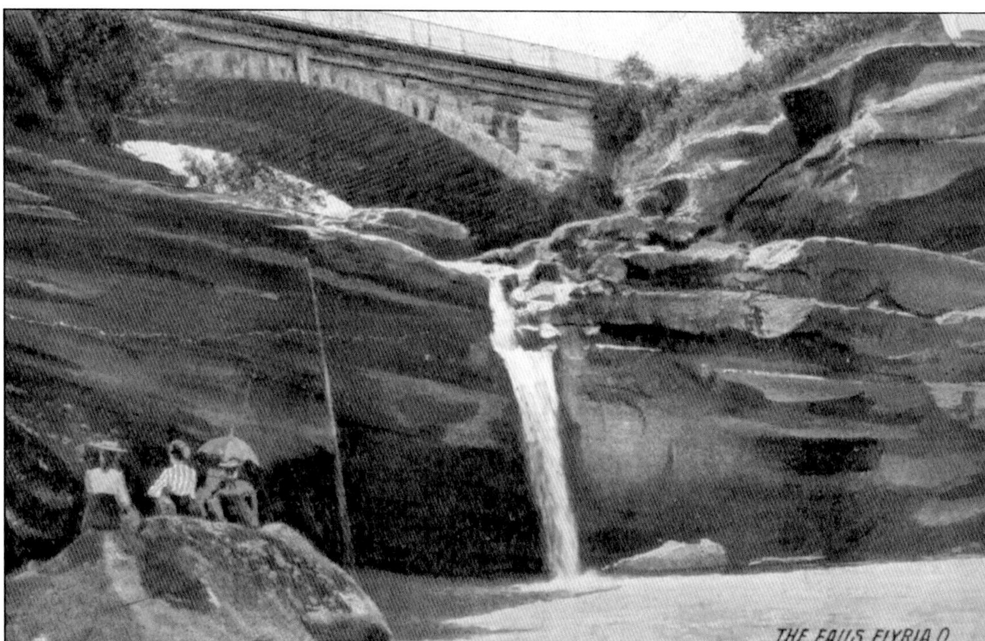

WEST FALLS, SUMMER. This huge boulder not far from Big Cave has provided an excellent view of the falls to Elyrians and out-of-town visitors for generations. The arching sandstone bridge of Lodi Street adds to the scenic beauty of this site.

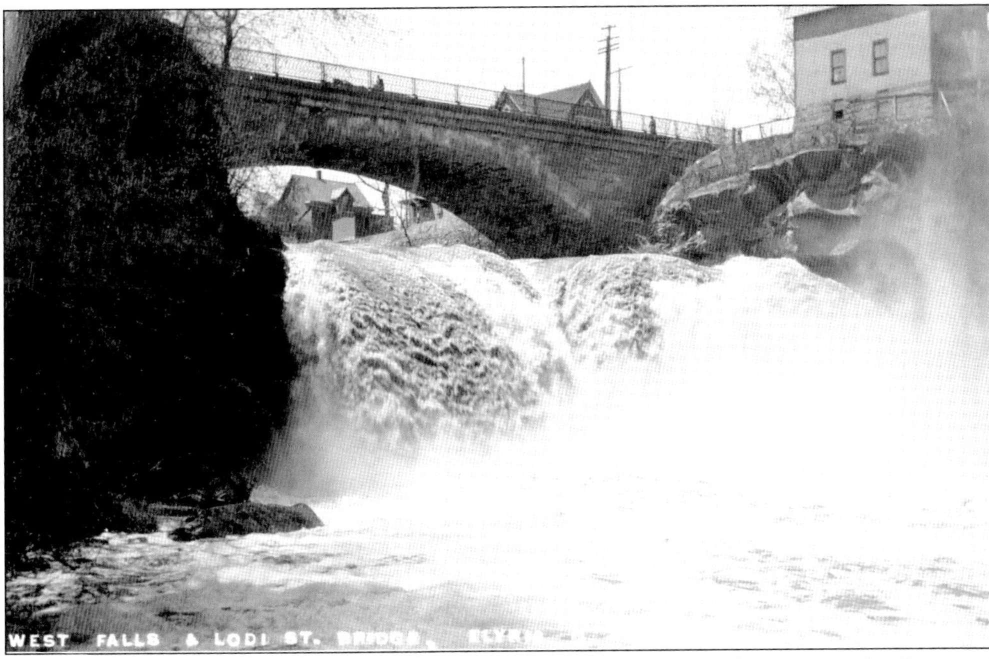

WEST FALLS, LATE WINTER. When spring rains combine with melting snow, the force and volume of water coming over the West Falls is truly awe-inspiring. The roaring waters produce a spray that rises high into the air, filling the river gorge.

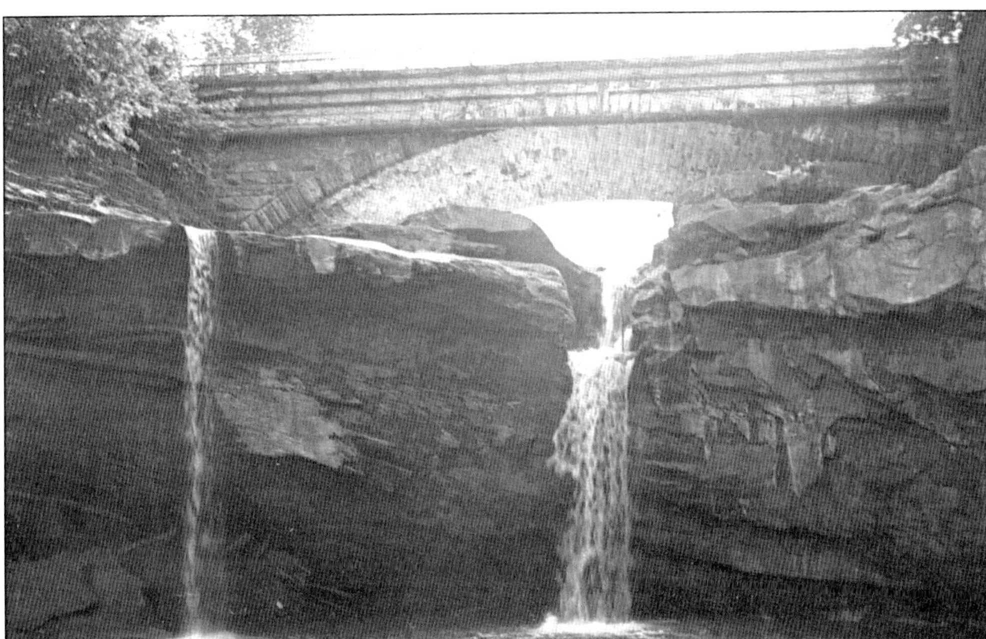

WEST FALLS, VIEW FROM THE RIVER. The low waters of late summer permit this straight-on view of the falls taken from mid-river. This is also a good time to explore the small and little-known Mink Cave or Mink Run, which is located behind and just to the right of the left flow, under the rock overhang.

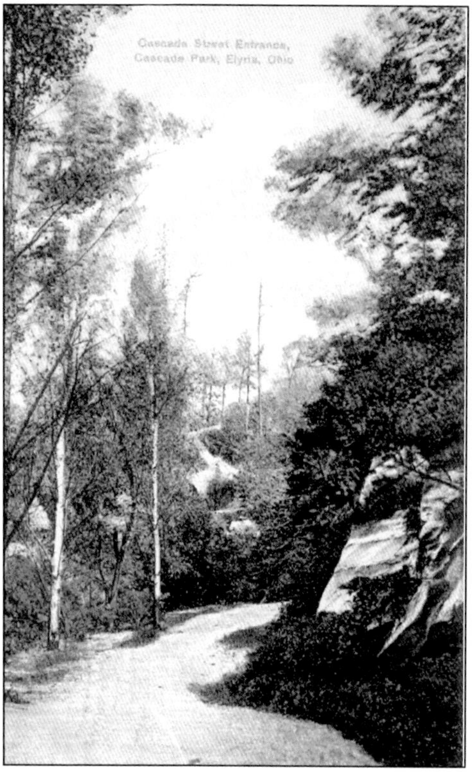

OLD ENTRANCE AT CASCADE STREET. For many years, visitors could enter Cascade Park by auto and follow this winding path as it descended into the scenic Black River gorge. The road crossed a ford near the junction of the two branches of the Black River and provided access to the present Cascade Park. Following the flood on July 4, 1969, this road was closed due to severe damage.

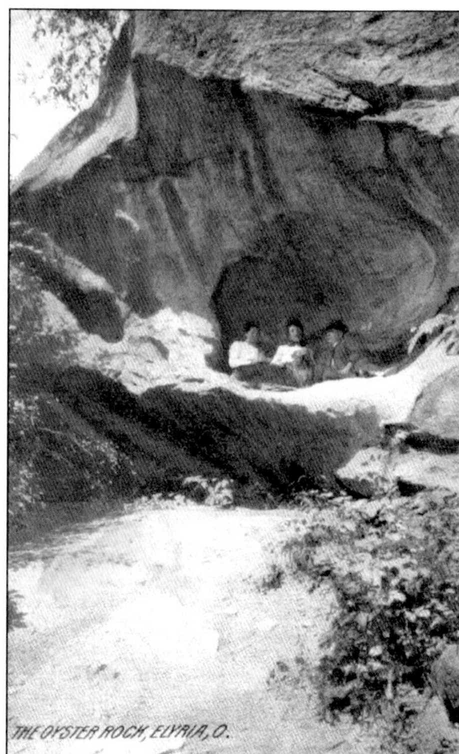

OYSTER ROCK, CASCADE PARK. This unusual hollow overlooking the Black River has fascinated park visitors for decades. The feature's name comes from it shape as well as the worn ridges along its back wall.

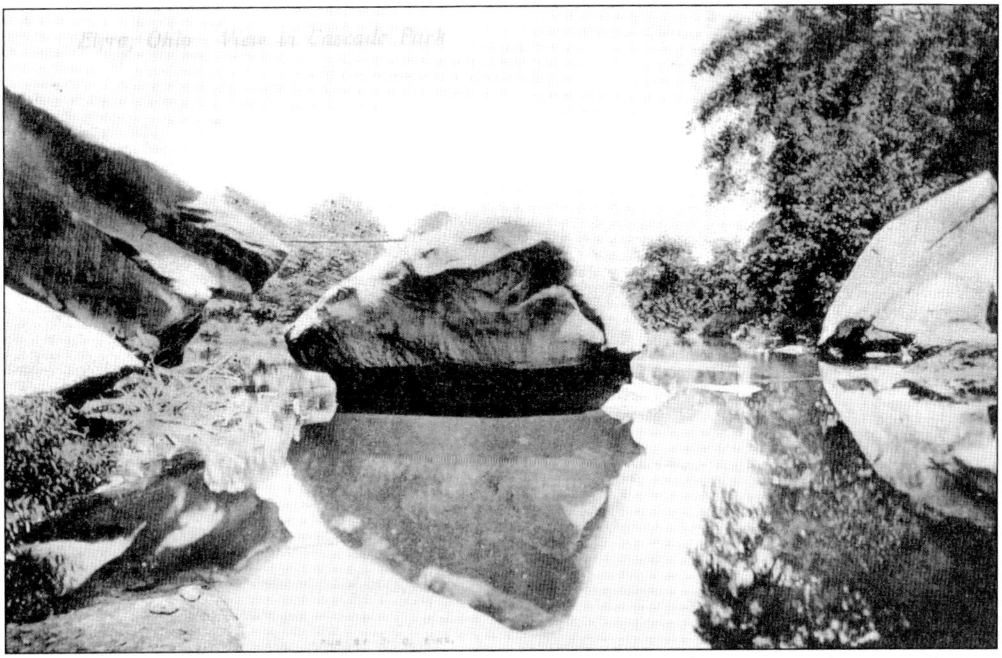

SPHINX ROCK, CASCADE PARK. Nearly every spring, young Elyrians must be rescued from Sphinx Rock in the middle of the Black River. In this early postcard, a wooden walkway connects Lookout Rock at left with Sphinx Rock. Sunset Rock is at right.

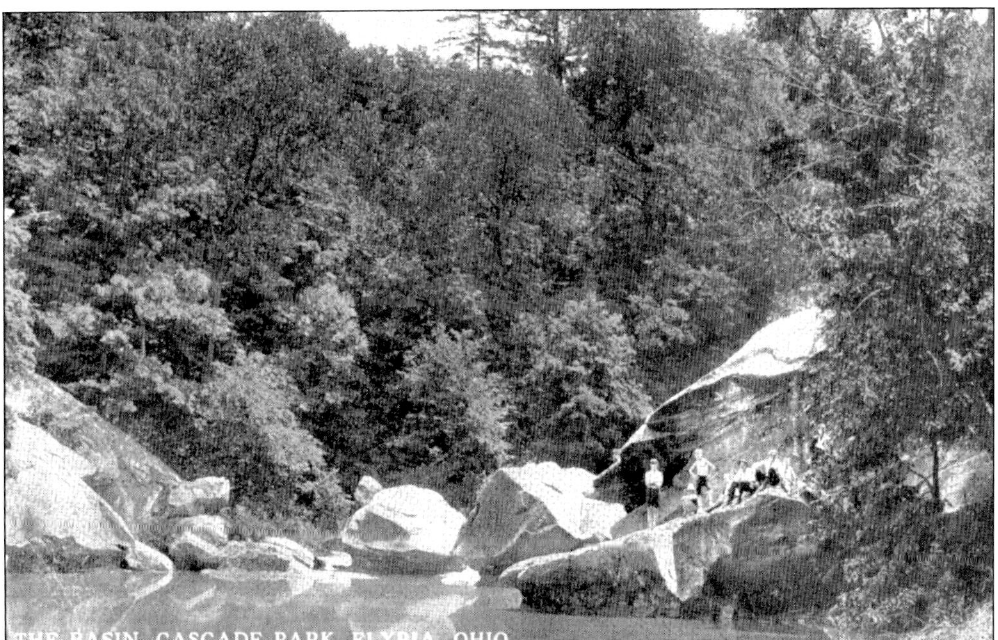

"THE BASIN," CASCADE PARK. The Basin refers to a wide section of slow-moving water just downstream from Sphinx Rock and ending at Violet Island. It was a popular destination for boaters and swimmers. In this image, the boys stand in front of Lookout Rock.

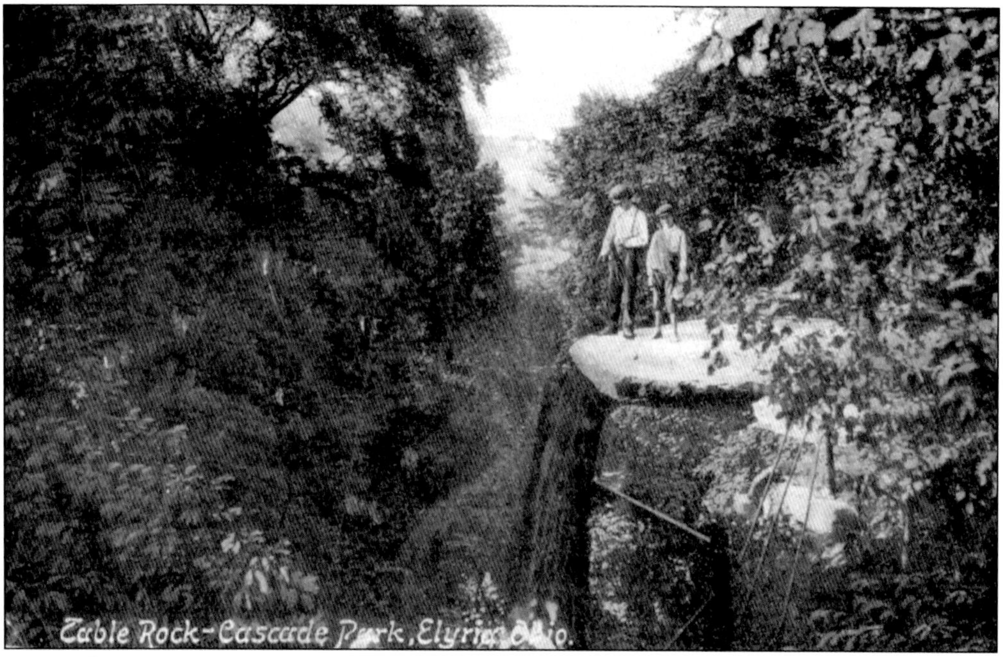

Table Rock, Cascade Park. This aptly named feature is located on Harmony Hill, between the Natural Bridge and the Camel's Back. It extends over a shallow cave where for many years a pen held a family of black bears kept by the city.

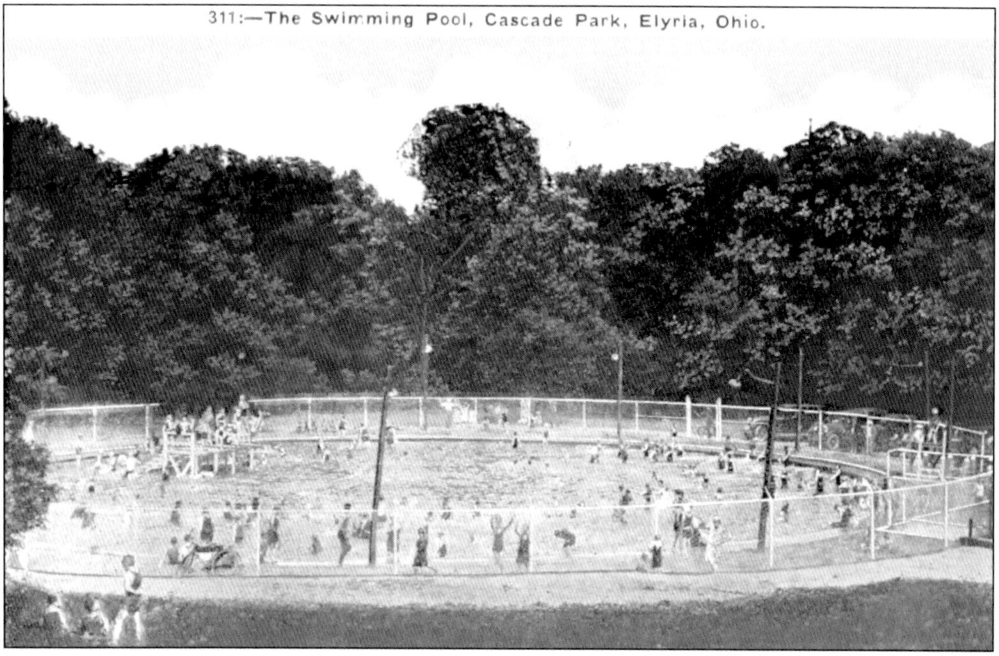

Cascade Swimming Pool. The round swimming pool in Cascade Park was the city's only public pool for many years. A submerged chain-link fence surrounded the deep end in the center of the pool. This wide view shows the pool in its beautiful, natural setting. There was a parking lot to the right and a brick bathhouse to the left.

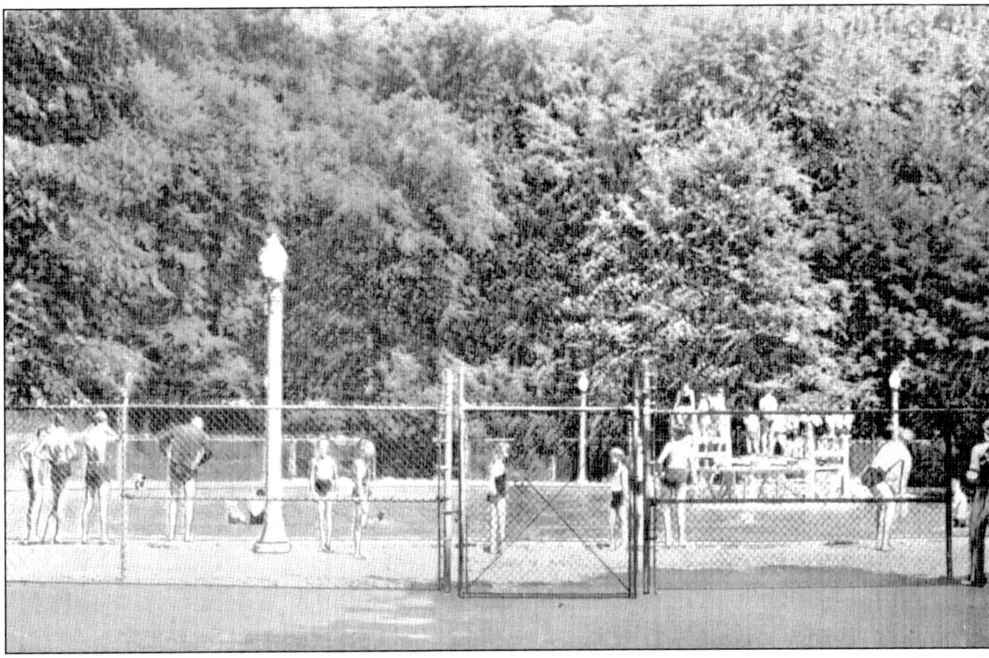

Cascade Swimming Pool. The Cascade Pool opened in 1926 thanks to donations from the Elyria Kiwanis Club. It was badly damaged in the July 4th flood of 1969, but was repaired and remained open until the close of the 1986 season.

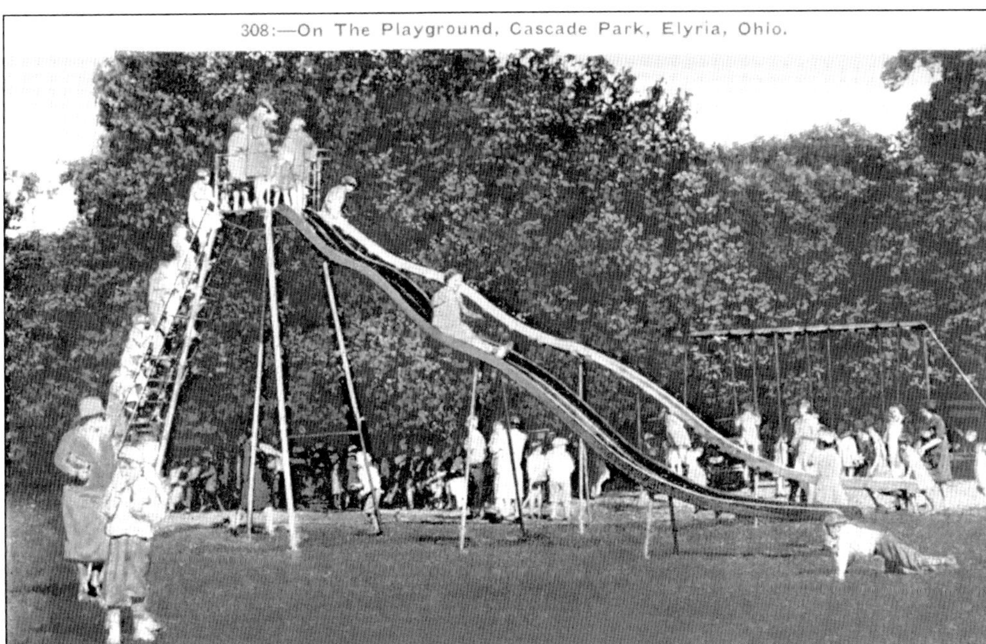

Playground, Cascade Park. To generations of Elyria children, a trip to Cascade Park was the highlight of a summer day. The playground contained swings for all ages, merry-go-rounds, and slides. The twin slides (seen here) were a big attraction, as was the snake slide with its corkscrew turns.

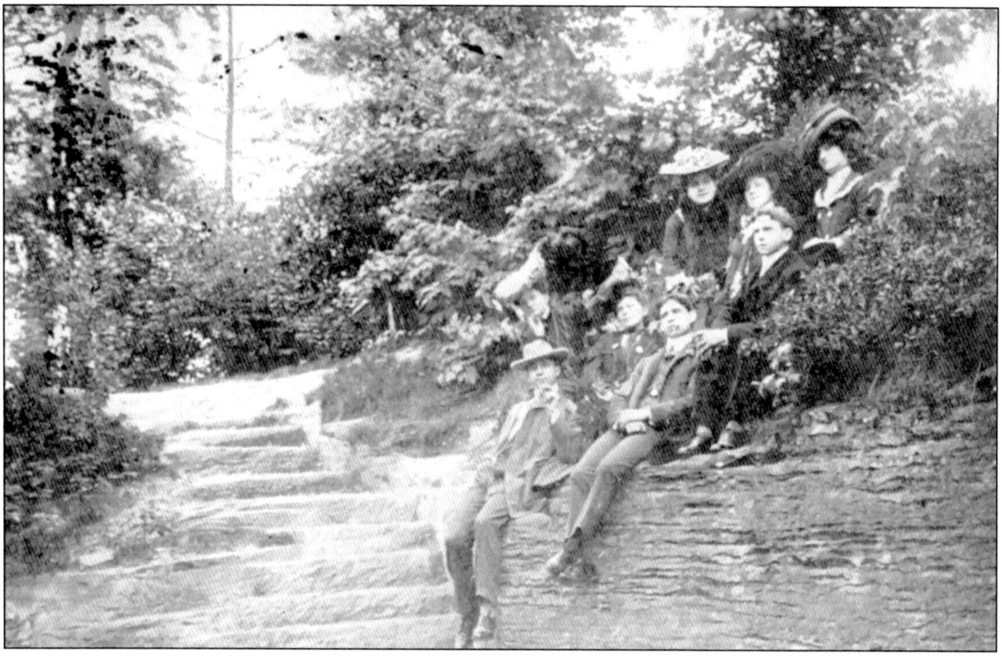

ANCIENT WATERFALL, CASCADE PARK. This jaunty party is posed atop a wide rock wall carved naturally by an ancient river. The steps at left lead to Harmony Hill and were carved by guarded jail inmates around the turn of the century.

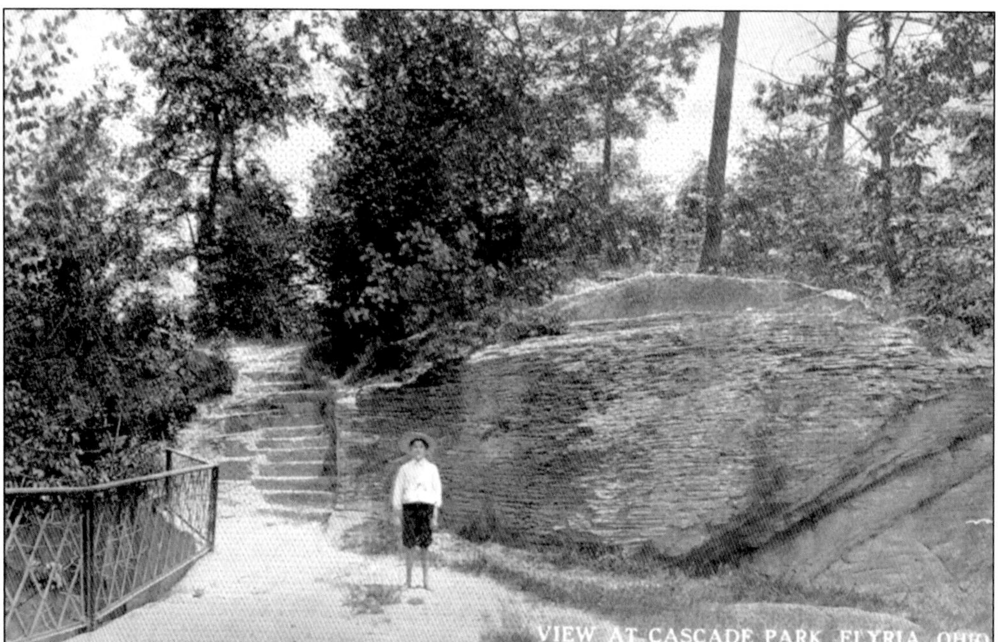

NATURAL BRIDGE, CASCADE PARK. A wider view of the above formations, this image includes the Natural Bridge area in the foreground at left. This precipice is actually the site of the ancient waterfall, and the cave hollowed out below lends the upper surface the shape of a natural rock bridge.

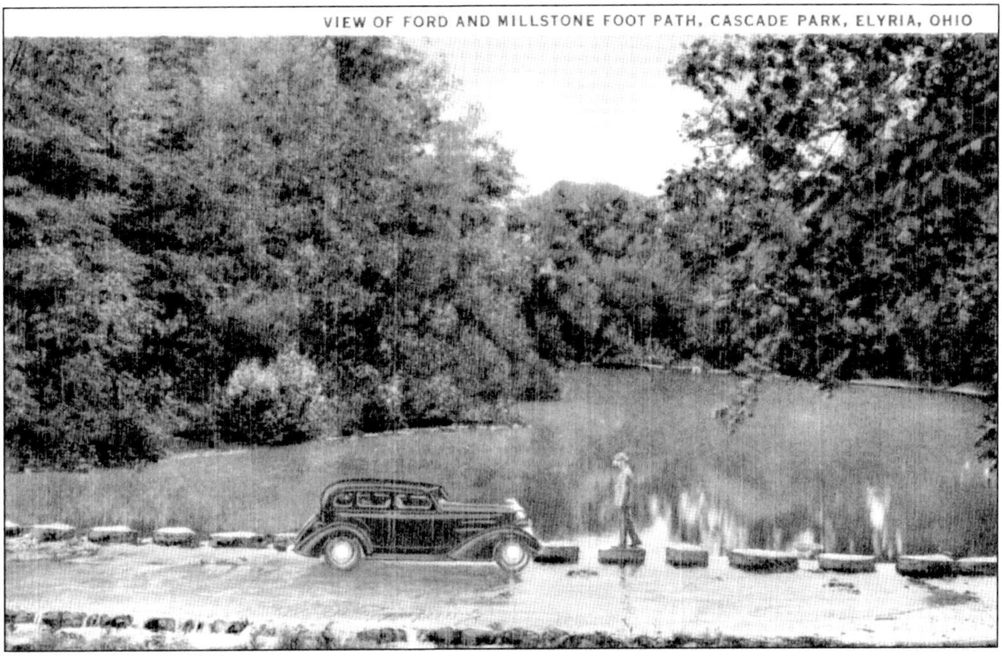

THE FORD, CASCADE PARK. This man-made feature has connected Cascade Park (at left) with Elywood Park (at right) since 1929. The stepping stones were convenient for pedestrians, but needed to be repositioned every spring. The Ford was remodeled in 1982, replacing the stepping stones with a raised sidewalk.

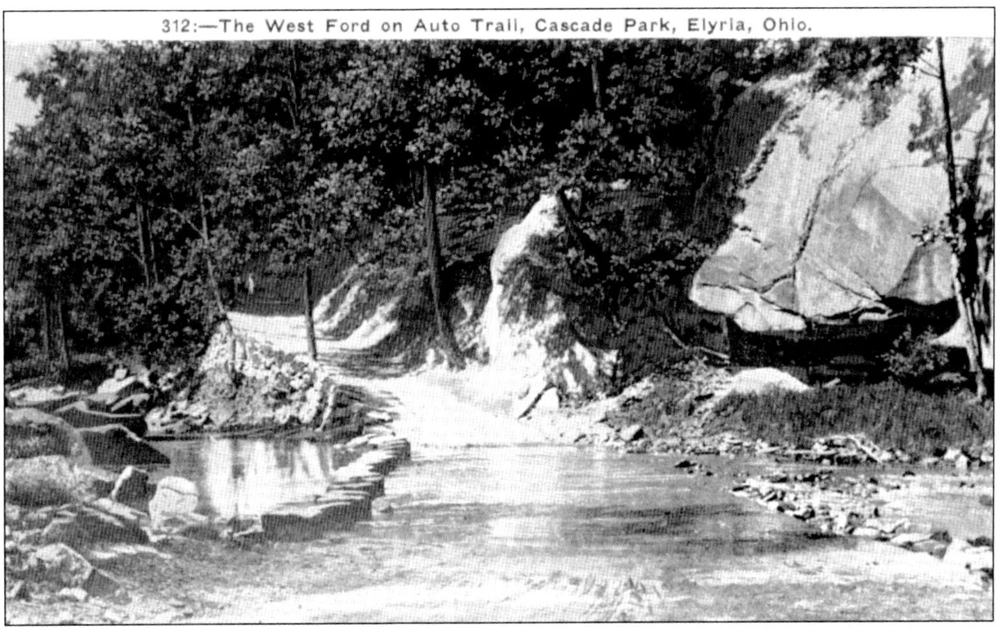

OLD AUTO FORD, CASCADE PARK. This ford and a nearby sidewalk once crossed the west branch of the Black River near the junction with the east branch. It led into Cascade Park up a winding road once used to supply an iron furnace near the West Falls. The ford and sidewalk both washed out in 1969 and were never replaced.

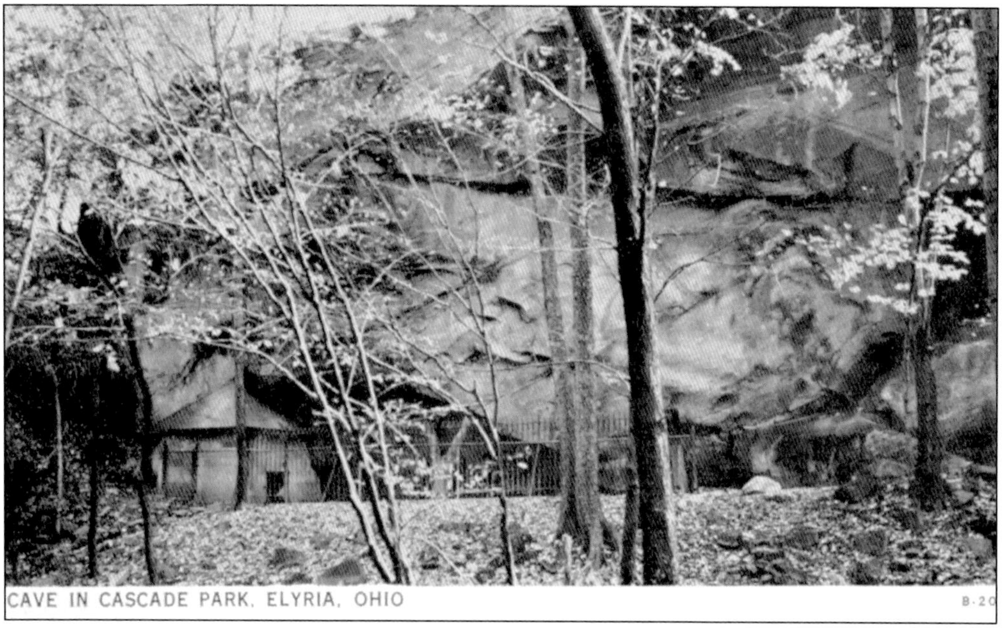

THE BEAR CAVE, CASCADE PARK. No trip to Cascade Park was complete without a visit to the Bear Cave. Nestled under a massive rock overhang, as many as three black bears at a time lived in the fenced-in cave area from 1920 to about 1980. Shelter houses were provided for the bears, and the smell was unforgettable.

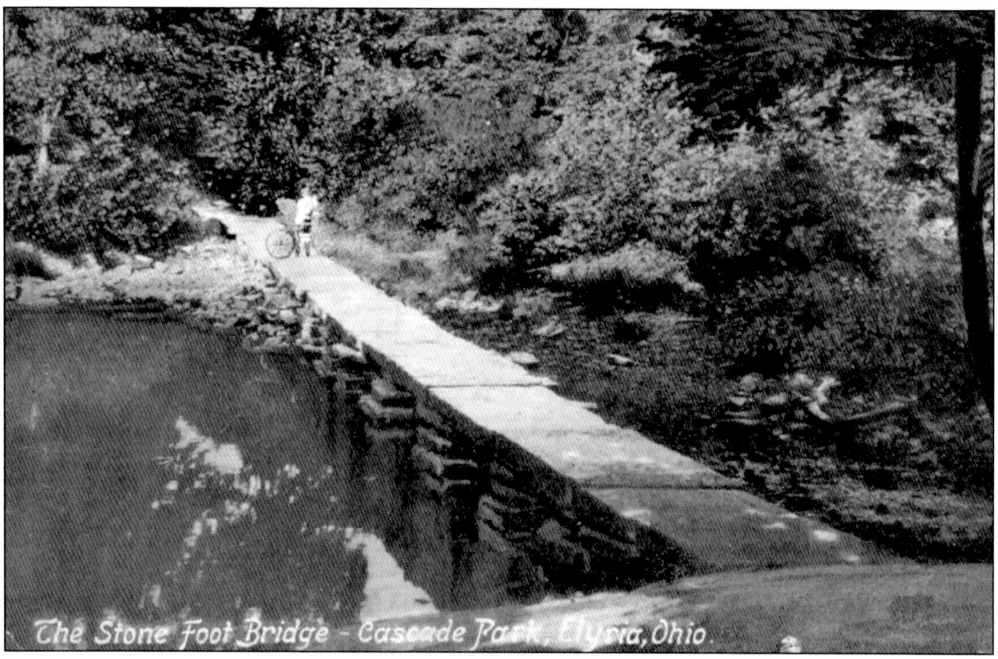

STONE FOOT BRIDGE, CASCADE. Though the exact location of this stone walkway is still debated, its charm is undeniable. Like many man-made structures over the years, the floodwaters of the Black River have erased this footbridge and most traces of where it may have been.

Seven

Gathering Spots

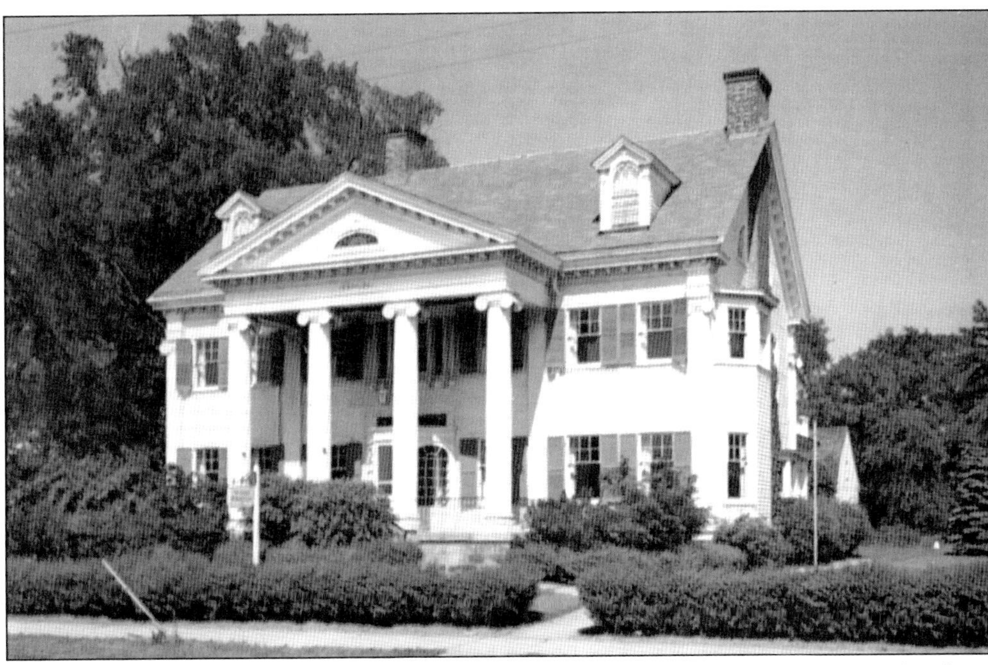

Montieth Hall, Elyria Women's Club. Montieth Hall is located on the east side of East Avenue across the street from the **Chronicle-Telegram** buildings. The house was built by the Reverend Montieth in 1835 and became a stop on the Underground Railroad. The Elyria Women's Club was founded in 1908 to promote women's suffrage. After having met at Montieth Hall for many decades, the Women's Club purchased the home in 1954.

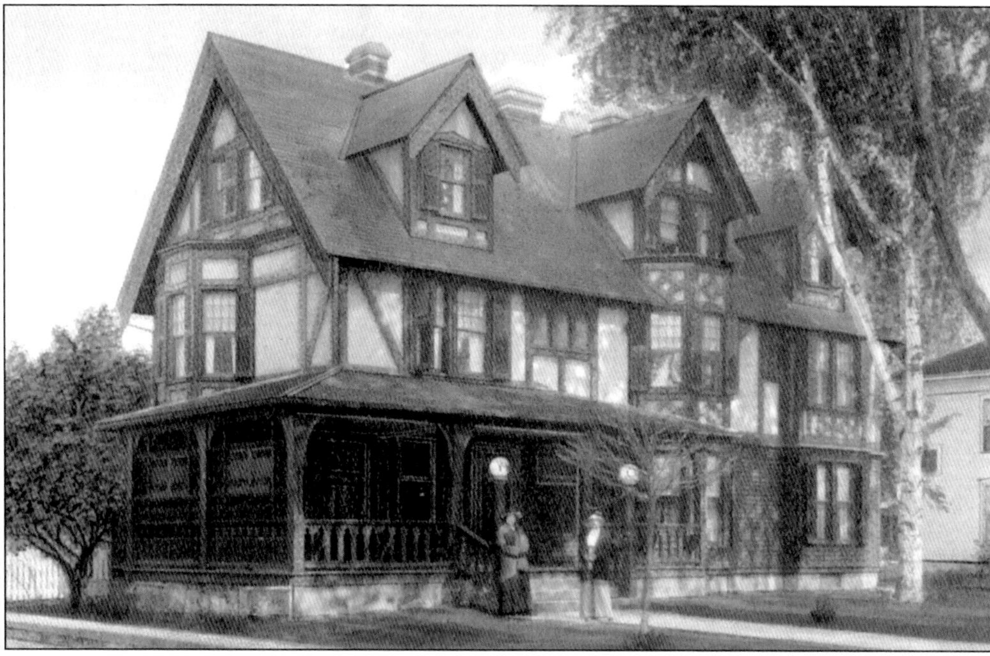

Elyria YWCA. The YWCA was formed in 1913 and purchased the W.E. Miller property on the east side of West Avenue between Third and Fourth Streets. The house was used as a meeting place and a women's residence, while the barn behind was used for social activities.

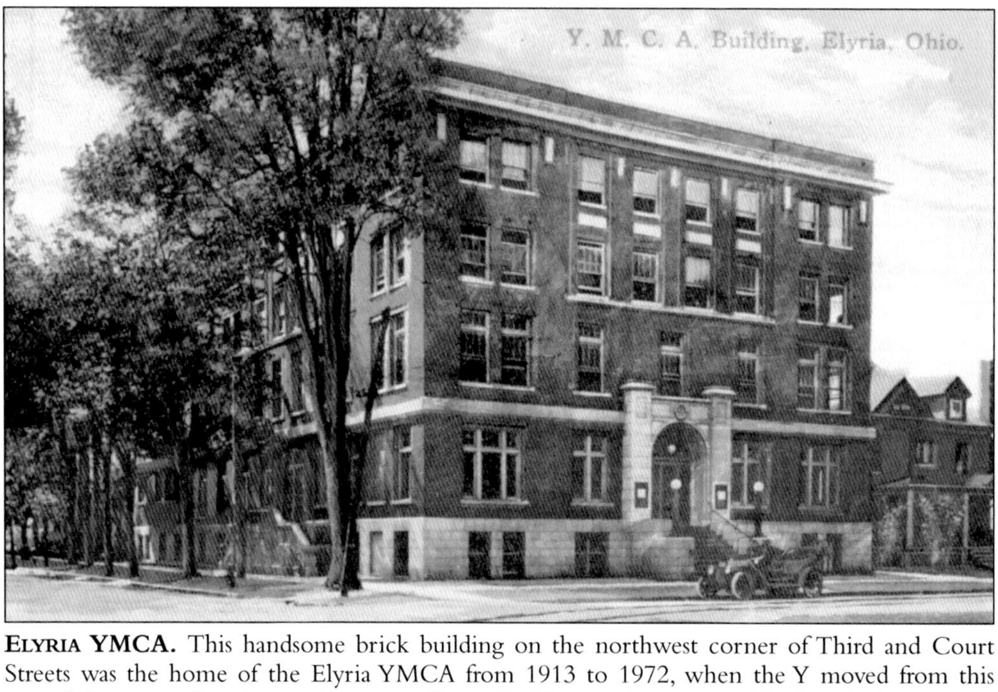

Elyria YMCA. This handsome brick building on the northwest corner of Third and Court Streets was the home of the Elyria YMCA from 1913 to 1972, when the Y moved from this central downtown location to the more affluent Washington Avenue neighborhood. The Y served as a residence hall for men, and generations of Elyria children learned to swim in the basement pool.

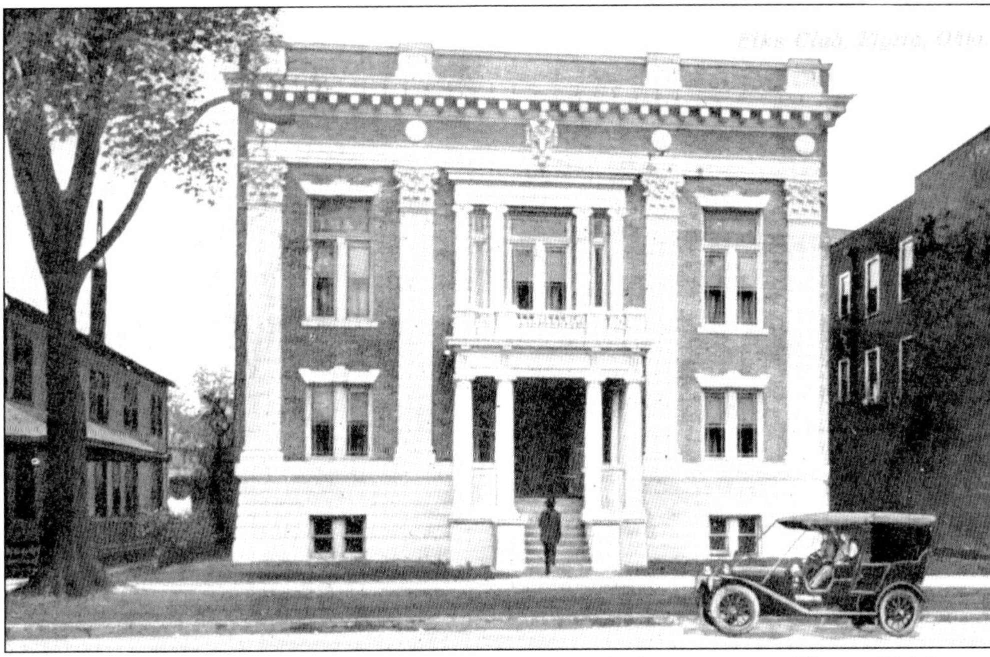

ELKS CLUB. The Elyria Elks built this brick structure with the imposing edifice at 246 Second Street in 1911 after the Elyria Block fire of 1909 destroyed their previous meeting rooms. A large ballroom originally occupied the second floor of the building, but has since been replaced by bowling alleys.

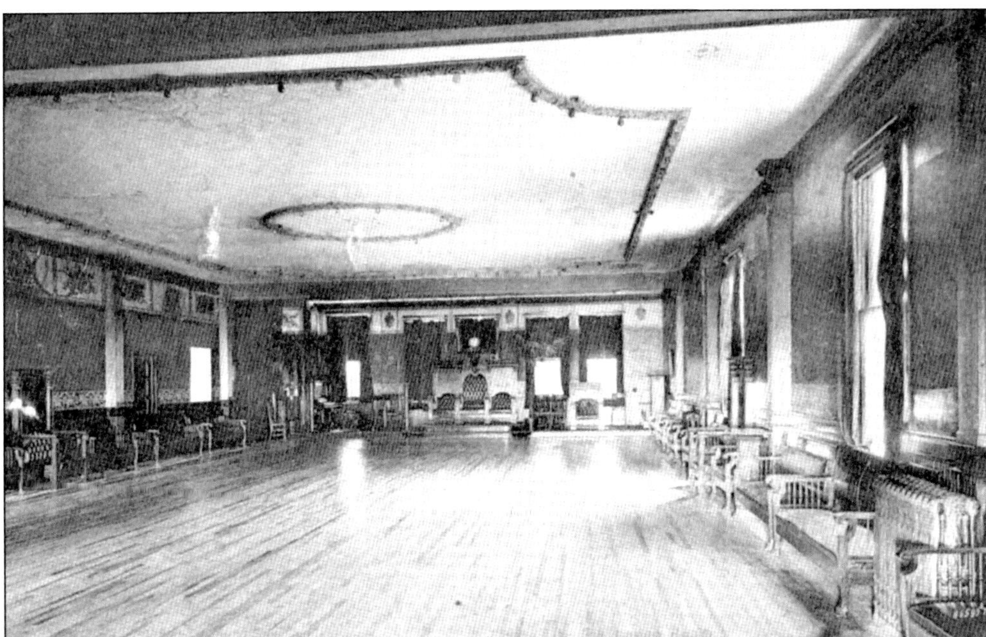

ELKS CLUB, LODGE ROOM. This unusual postcard shows the Lodge Room inside the Elks Club in the Elyria Block building prior to 1909, when the building burned to the ground.

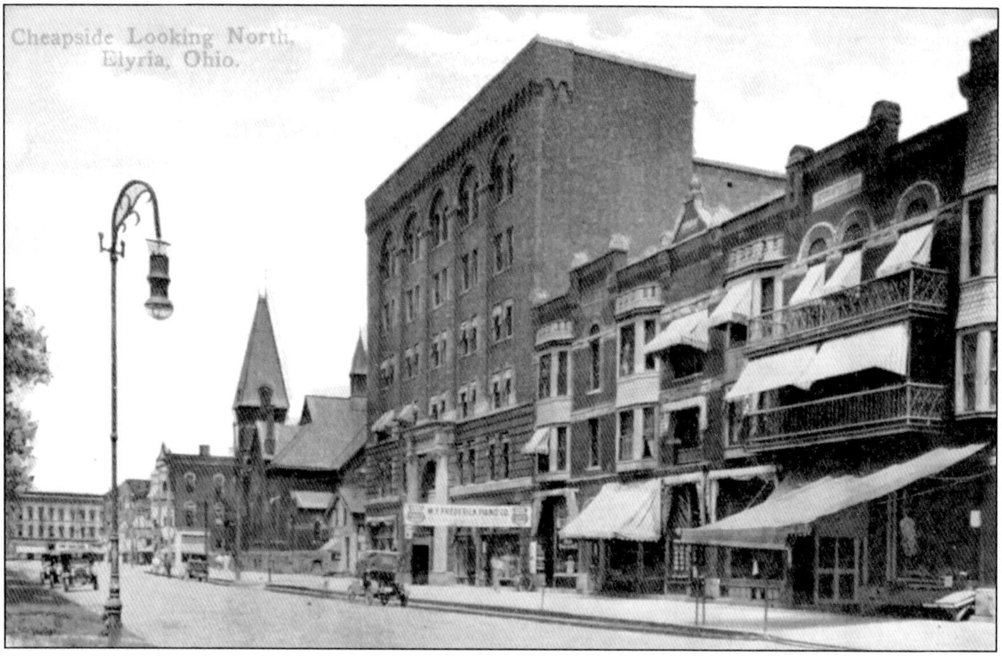

MASONIC TEMPLE LOOKING NORTH. Elyria's Masonic Temple was built in 1905 on the southeast corner of Middle Avenue and Temple Court. Many businesses were situated on the lower floor of the temple, including Wilmot Printing, Burns Drug Store, Seitz Bowling Alley, and for a time, the Elyria Post Office. The steeple of the First Baptist Church can be seen in the distance with the Endley Block at right.

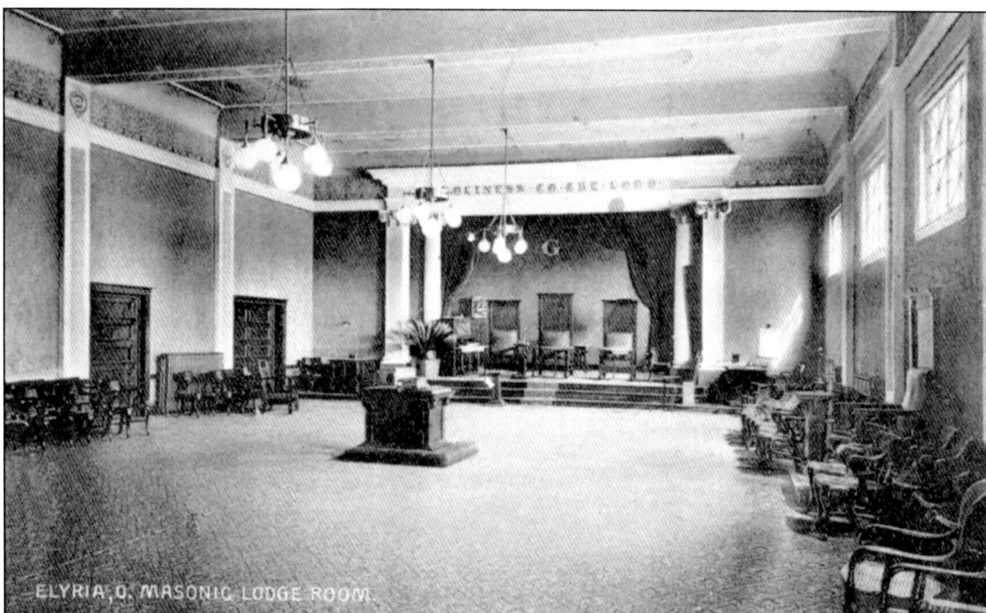

MASONIC TEMPLE, LODGE ROOM. Hanging electric lights illuminate the Masonic Temple's large, well-appointed lodge room in this pre-1915 interior view. The Masons were Elyria's oldest fraternal organization and counted the town's founder among its officers.

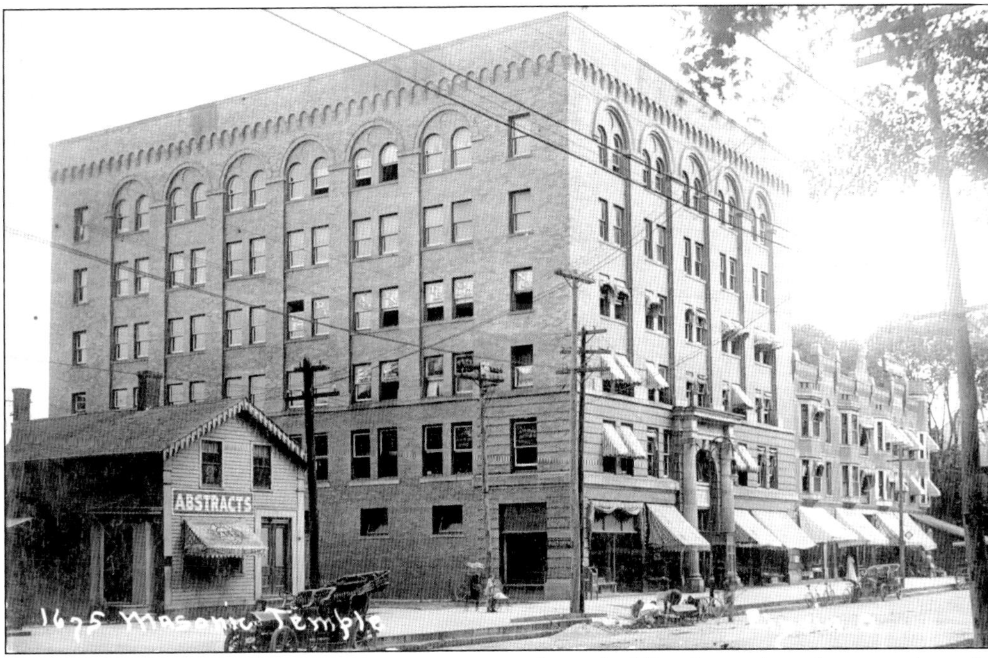

MASONIC TEMPLE LOOKING SOUTH. This magnificent building burned to the ground on the night of March 13, 1956. The firemen fought the fire from the roof of Bauer Dairy, which had replaced the small building at left. The Lorain County Administration Building now stands on this site.

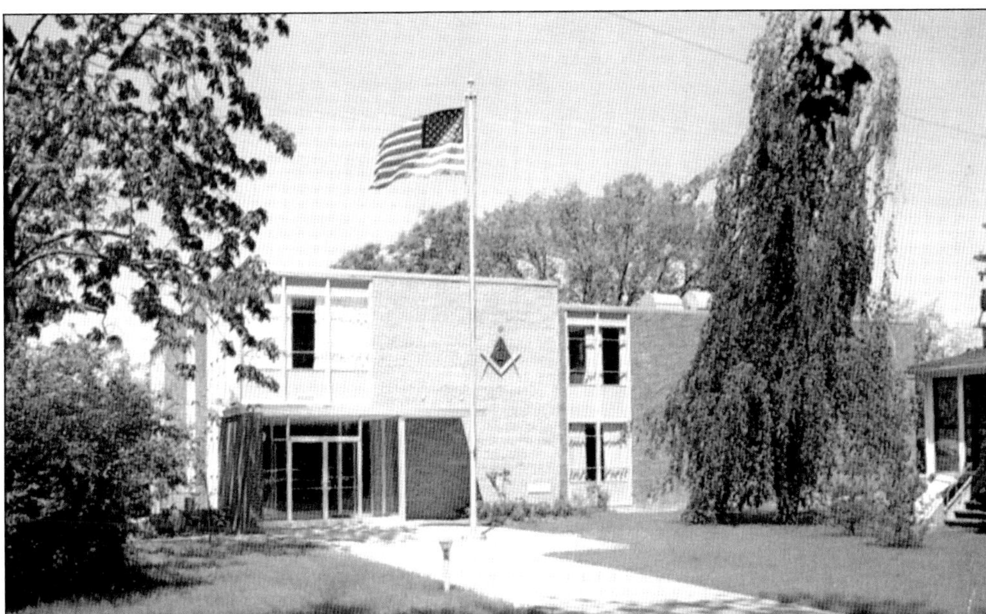

MASONIC TEMPLE, WASHINGTON AVENUE. Elyria's Masons built their new temple at 206 Washington Avenue in 1960, and the building reflects the architecture of that time. This property backs onto the Black River and affords an excellent view of the East Falls.

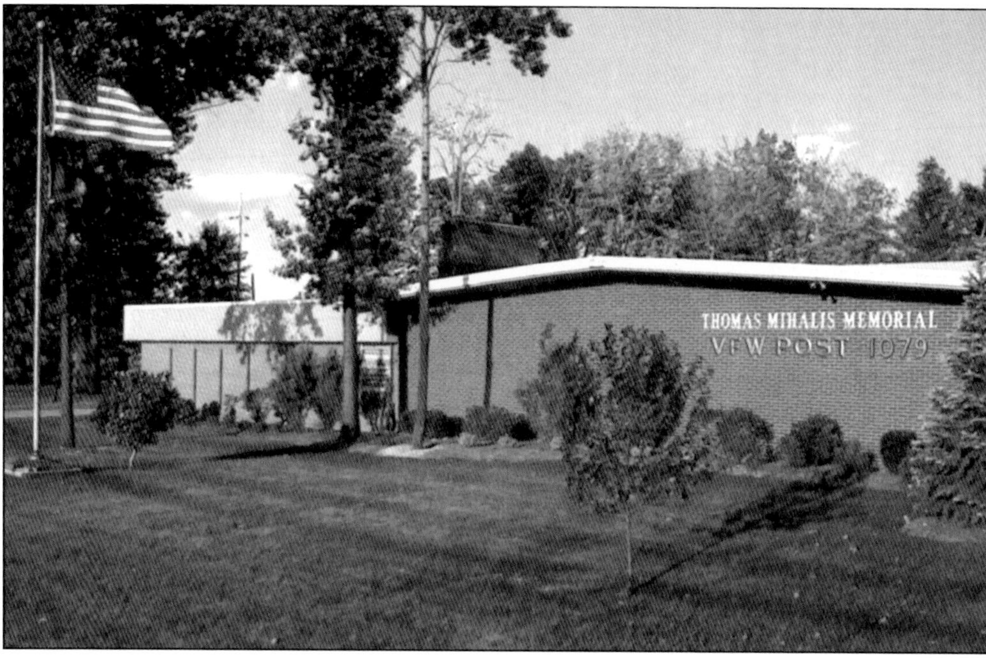

ELYRIA VFW BUILDING. The Thomas Mihalis Memorial VFW Post was built at 500 South Abbe Road in 1973, 50 years after the group first received its charter. The VFW had previously met in old City Hall, the Ely Block, the Wolf Block on Second Street, and on East Bridge Street.

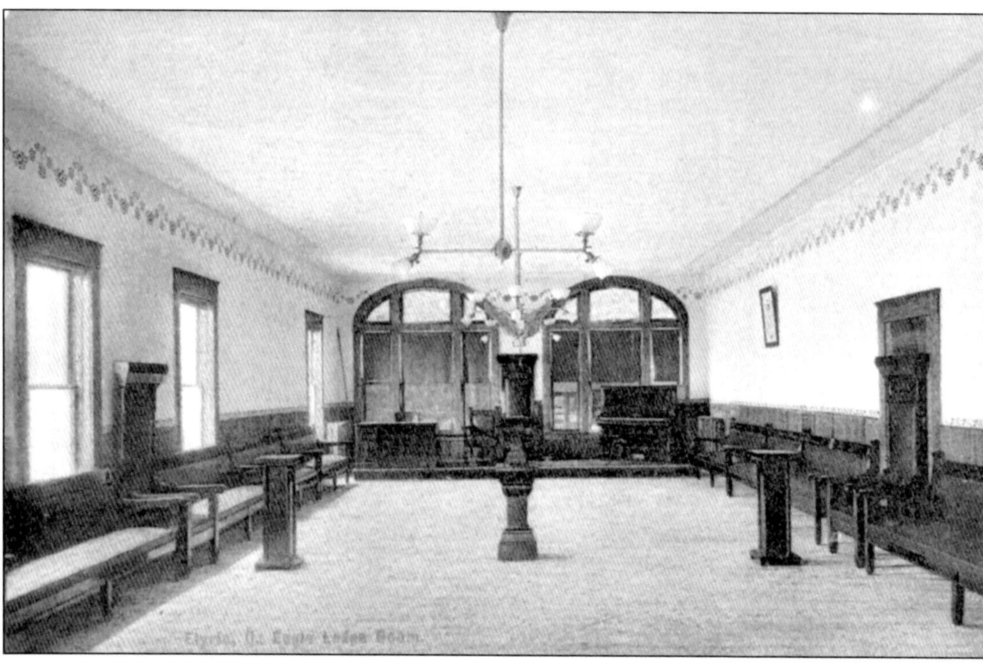

ELYRIA EAGLES LODGE ROOM. Elyria Eagles Aerie No. 431 was organized in 1903 and met in this lodge room until the club moved to its present location at 316 Broad Street in 1915.

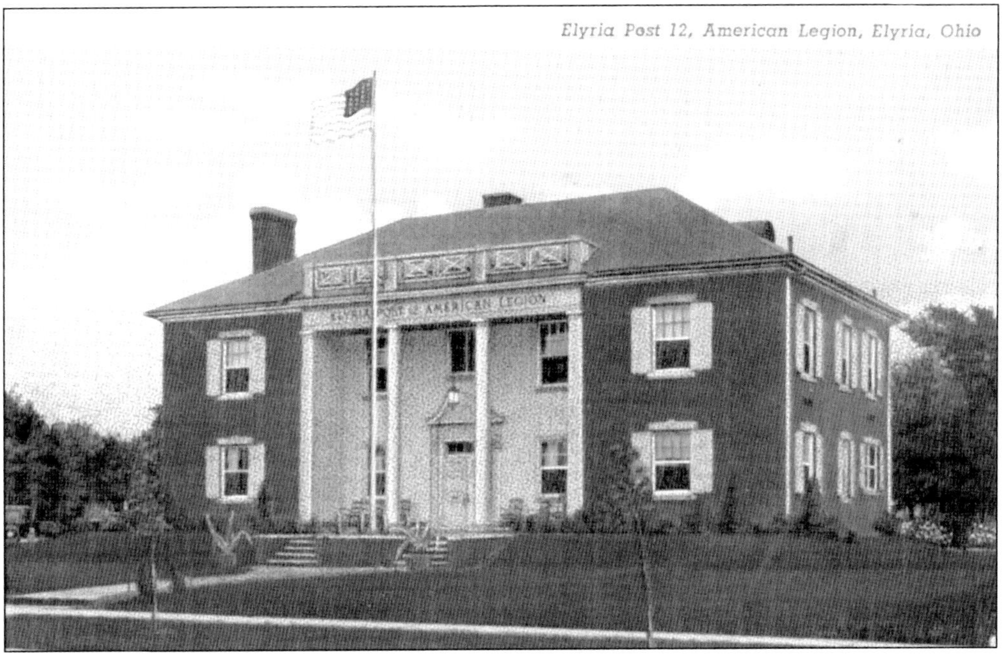

Elyria American Legion Hall. The Legionnaires of Elyria Post 12 moved into their present facility at the southwest corner of Gulf and Ohio Streets in 1930. Their charter dates back to 1919. Major additions have been made to the building since this postcard was printed.

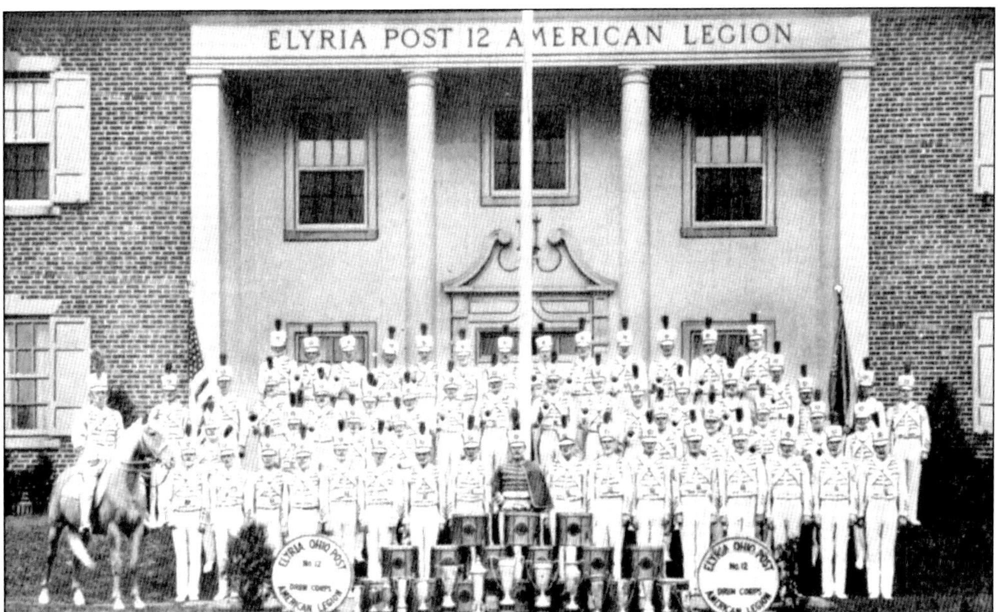

Elyria American Legion Drum and Bugle Corps. The Drum and Bugle Corps was formed in 1926. The corps started out with 35 members, which later grew to 60, including the Arabian mare, Cream Puff. They are pictured here with some of their many Ohio and national trophies.

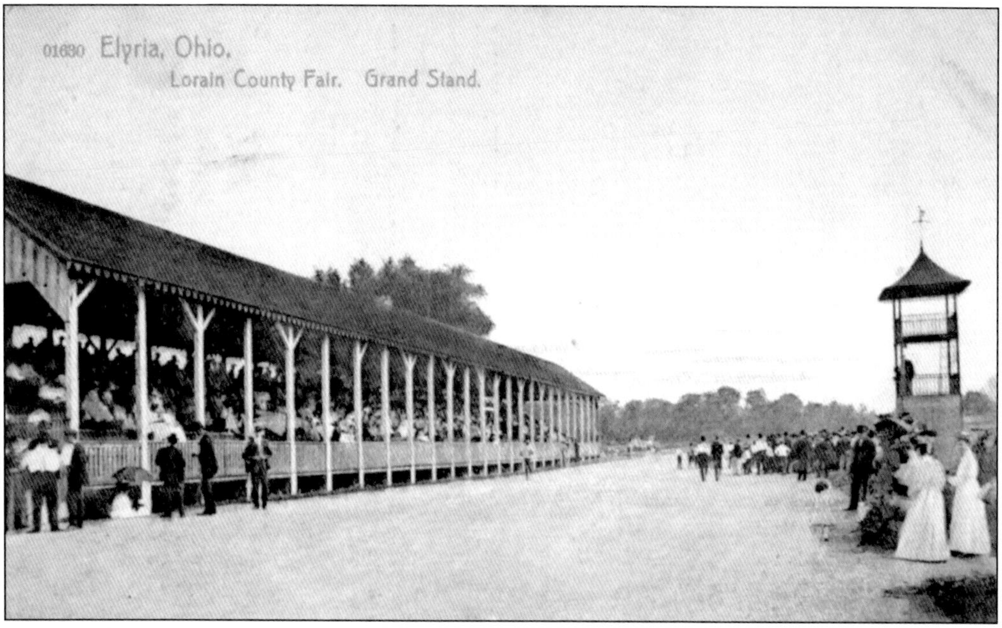

Lorain County Fair, Race Track. The Lorain County Fair moved to property on West 3rd Street in 1867, its second site in Elyria. Between fairs, the grounds were used for Elyria High School football games, and traveling circuses set up their tents at the fairgrounds after parading their animals from the downtown train depot.

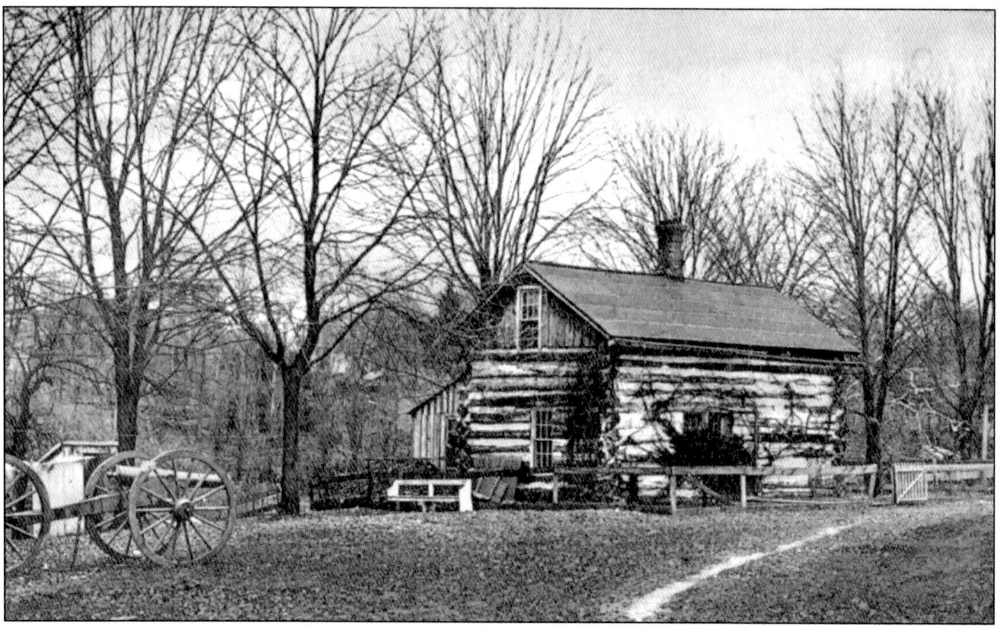

Lorain County Fairgrounds, Centennial Cabin. This cabin was constructed at the fairgrounds to celebrate the U.S. Centennial in 1876. It later served as the residence for the grounds keeper at the fair. In 1990, it was dismantled and moved to a site at one of the Lorain County Metroparks.

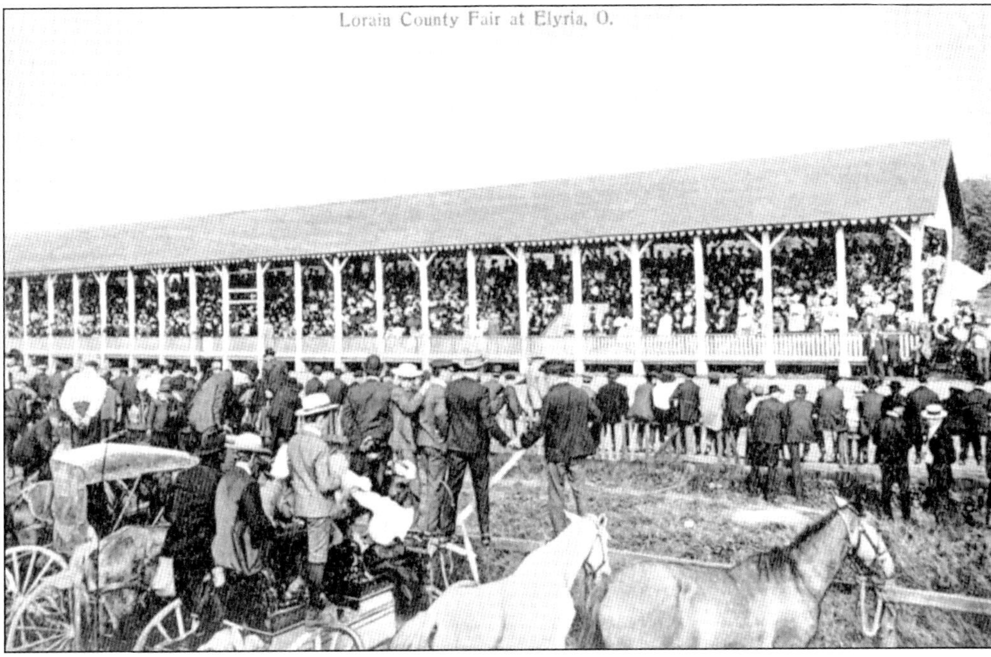

LORAIN COUNTY FAIR, RACE TRACK. The crowds that packed the large grandstand reflect the popularity of horse racing at the fair. It was the highlight of the fair for many Elyrians. The track was used for bicycle races and foot races as well.

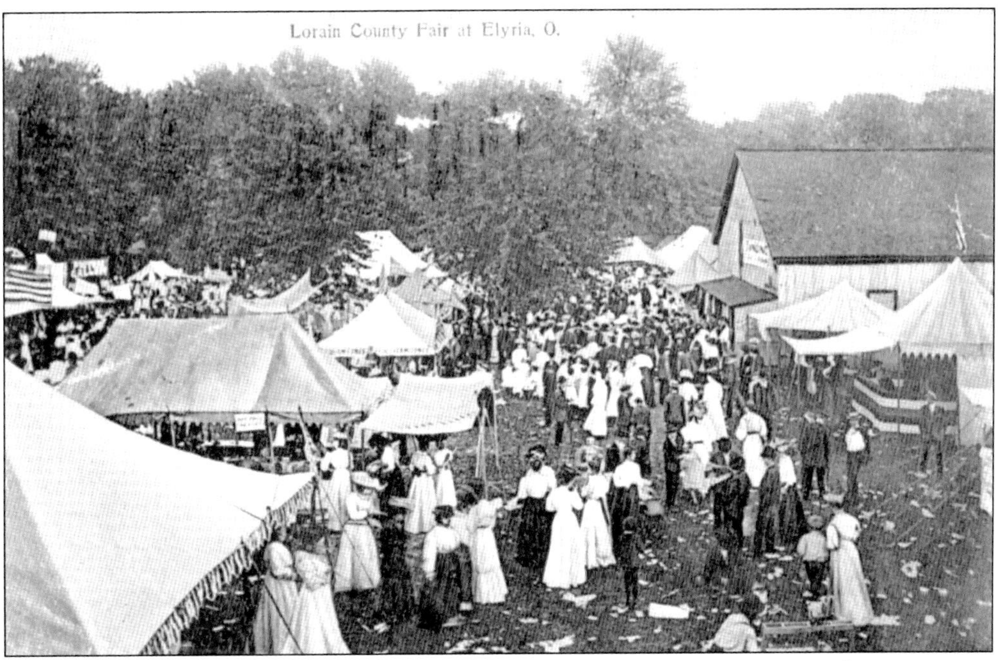

LORAIN COUNTY FAIR. Concession stands are an important part of the county fair experience, and it was no different a hundred years ago. The Lorain County Fair continued to be held at the West Third Street site until about 1940 when overcrowding forced it to merge with the Wellington Fair. The Sommers Mobile Home Park more recently occupied this site.

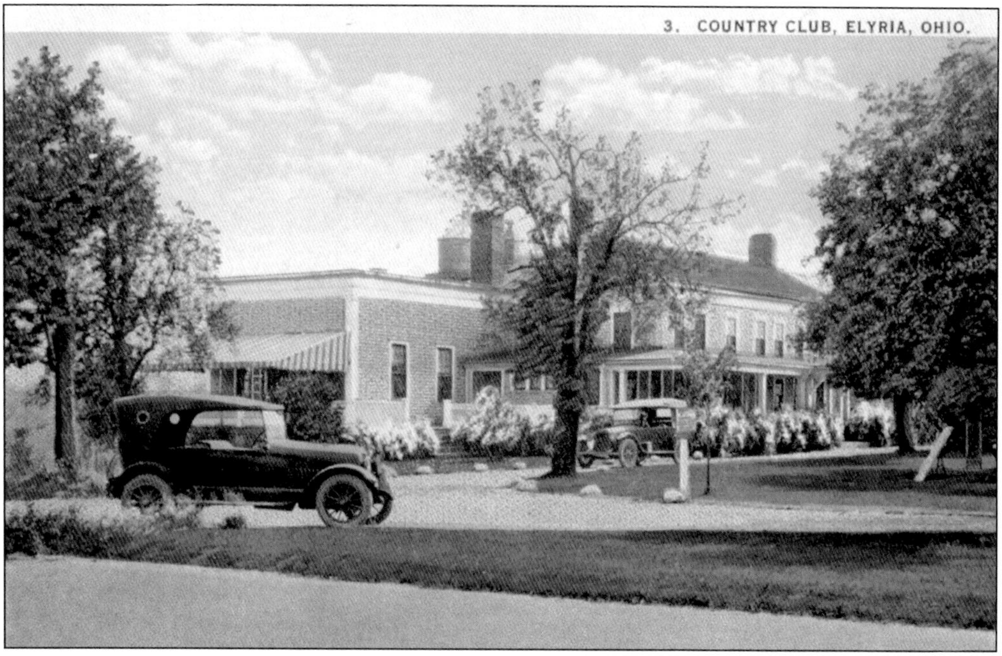

ORIGINAL ELYRIA COUNTRY CLUB. The Elyria Country Club was incorporated in 1905 and soon thereafter purchased the Clark house and farm on Oberlin Road, south of town at Stop 84 on the interurban line. The farmhouse became the clubhouse, and the pastures became the fairways and greens.

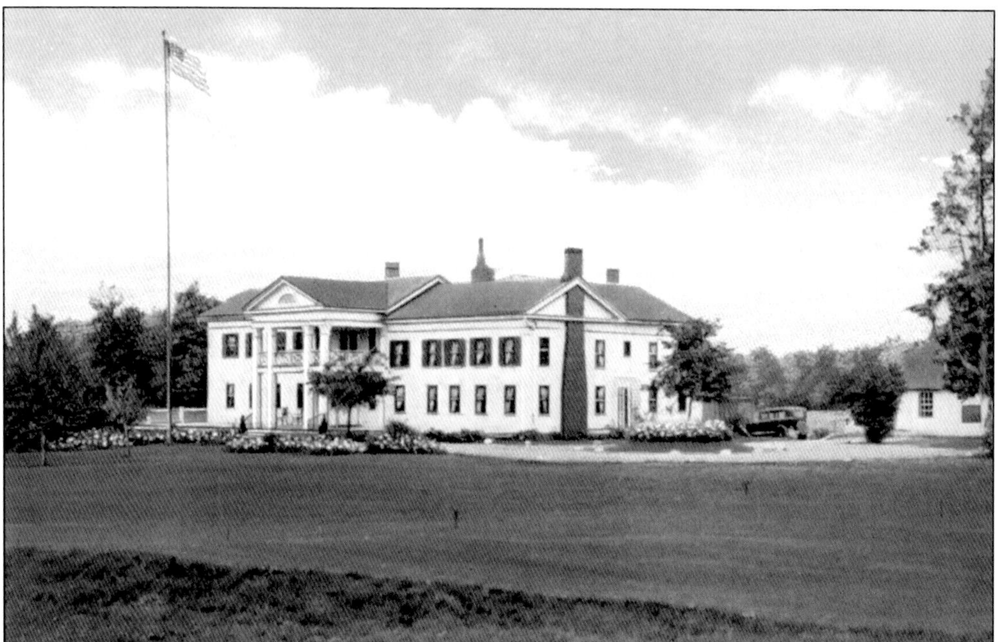

NEW ELYRIA COUNTRY CLUB. Additions and renovations were made to the original Clark farmhouse over the years. This is the clubhouse many Elyrians will remember with its "southern mansion" façade. A fire destroyed the clubhouse in1947.

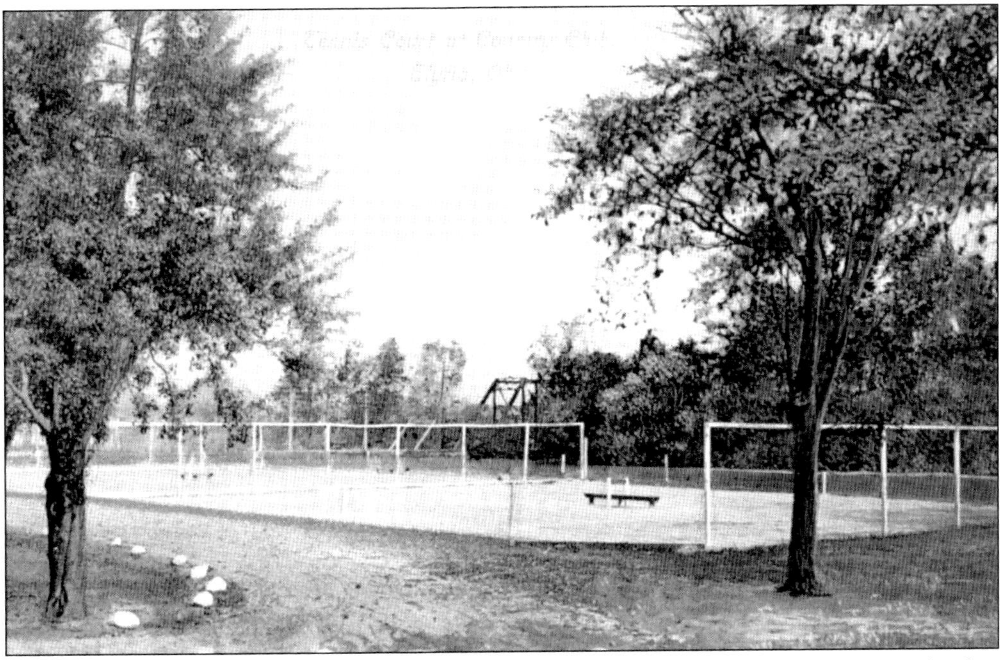

ELYRIA COUNTRY CLUB, TENNIS COURT. Among its other amenities, the club boasted this fine clay tennis court, and thanks to its proximity to the Black River, it had one of the few golf courses in the area with watered fairway and greens.

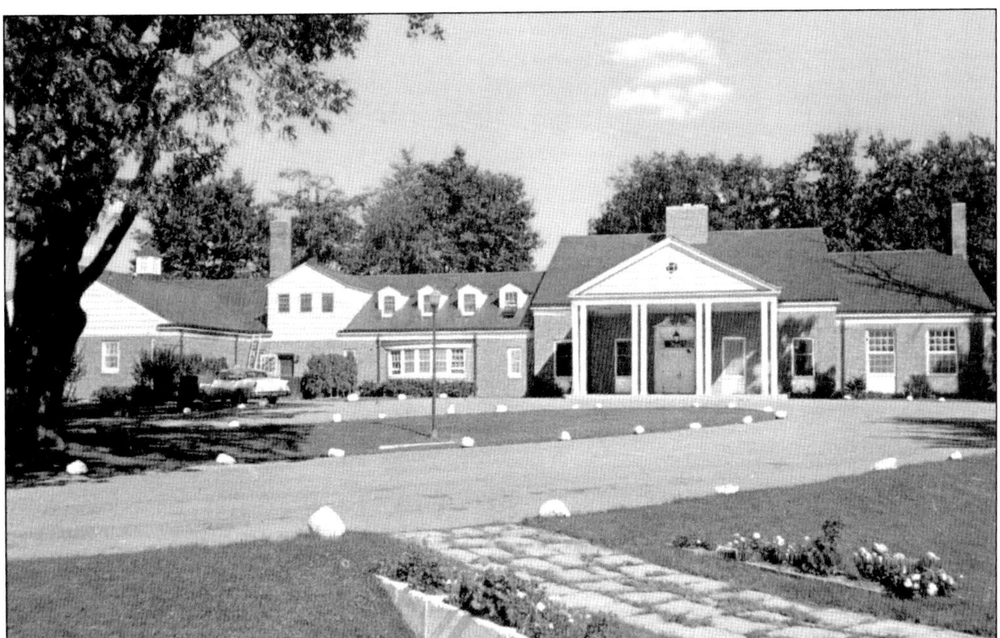

CURRENT ELYRIA COUNTRY CLUB. Two and half years after fire destroyed the old building, this new clubhouse opened in 1950 on the same property. In 1955, a swimming pool and bathhouse were added.

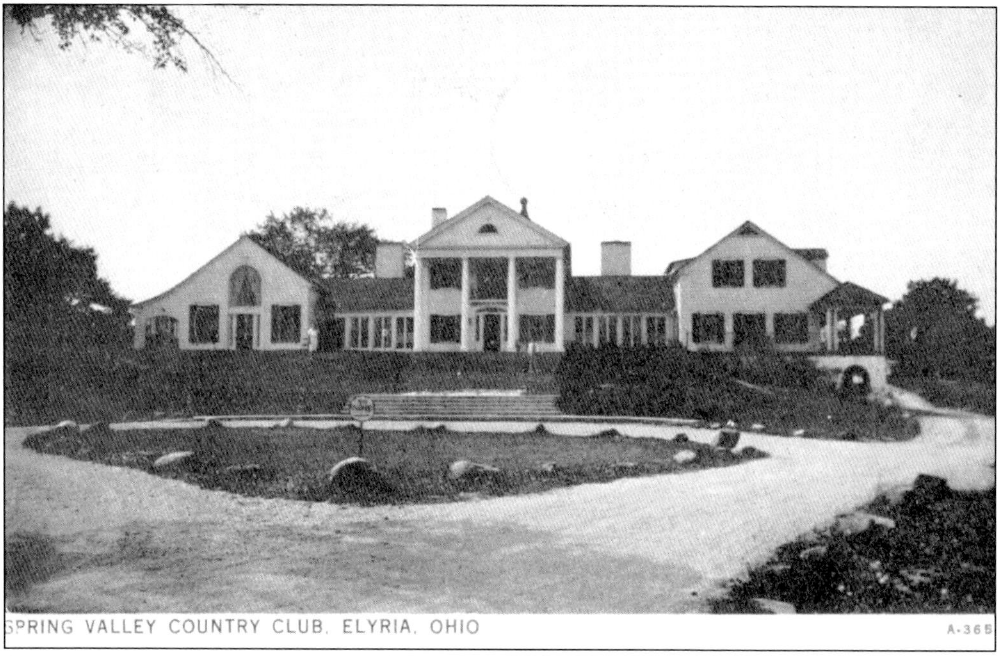

SPRING VALLEY COUNTRY CLUB. This former dairy farm was purchased in 1927 with the idea of using it as the centerpiece for an exclusive residential area. When these plans fell through, the property changed hands several times, at one time serving as a public golf course. It became a private, member-owned club in 1981.

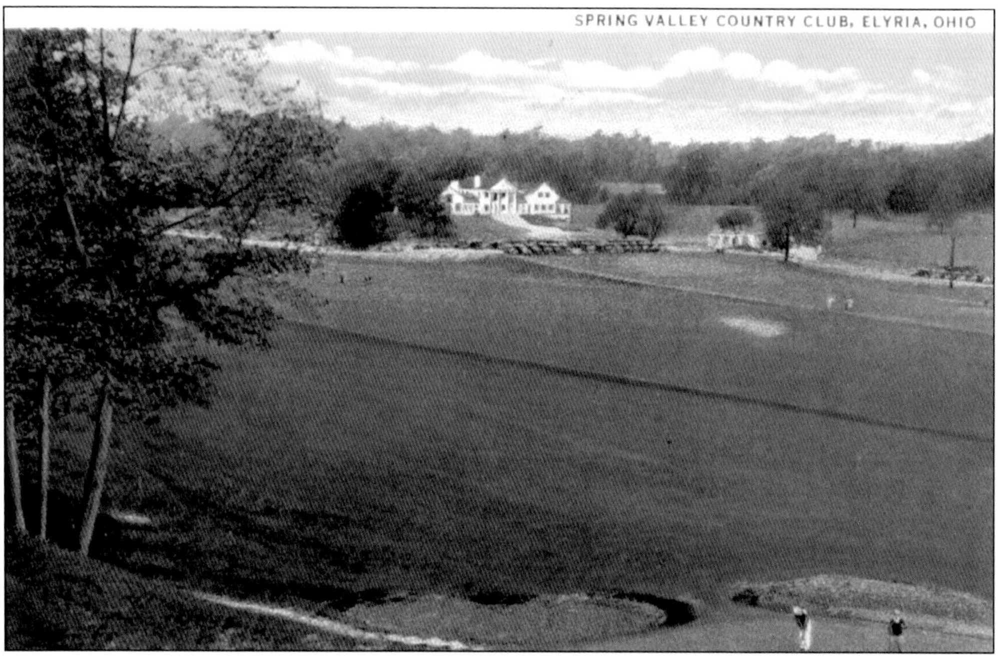

SPRING VALLEY COUNTRY CLUB GOLF COURSE. This view of the club's fine golf course shows the clubhouse in its beautiful setting as seen from Gulf Road. The original investors built the course in the late 1920s.

Eight

AROUND TOWN

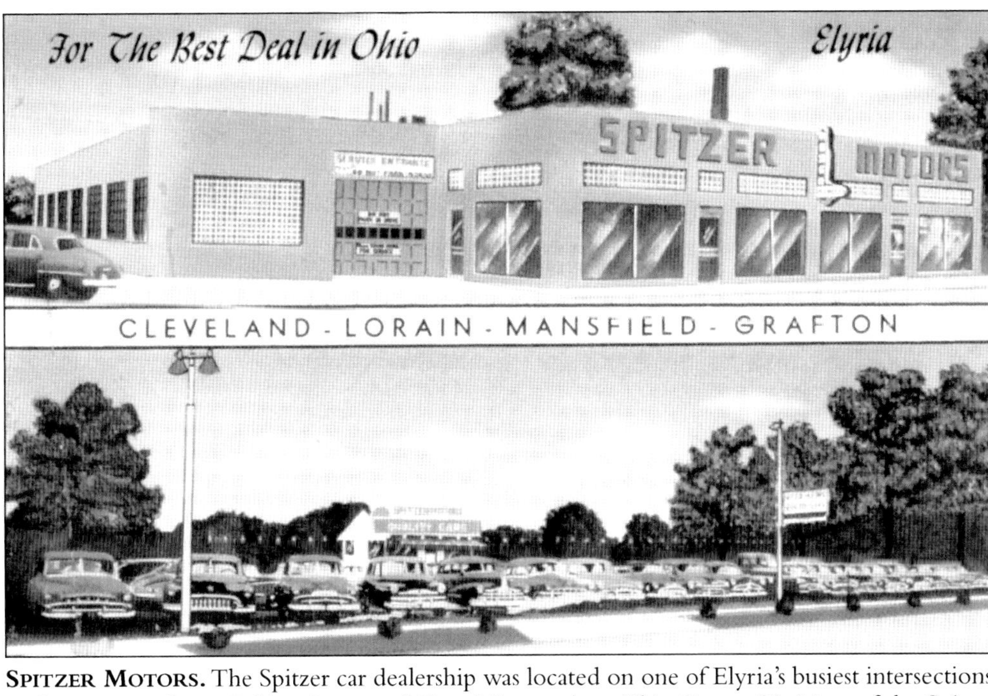

SPITZER MOTORS. The Spitzer car dealership was located on one of Elyria's busiest intersections, at the corner of East Bridge Street and Broad Street, then Ohio Route 20. Most of the Spitzer showroom buildings remain, although the dealership has left Elyria.

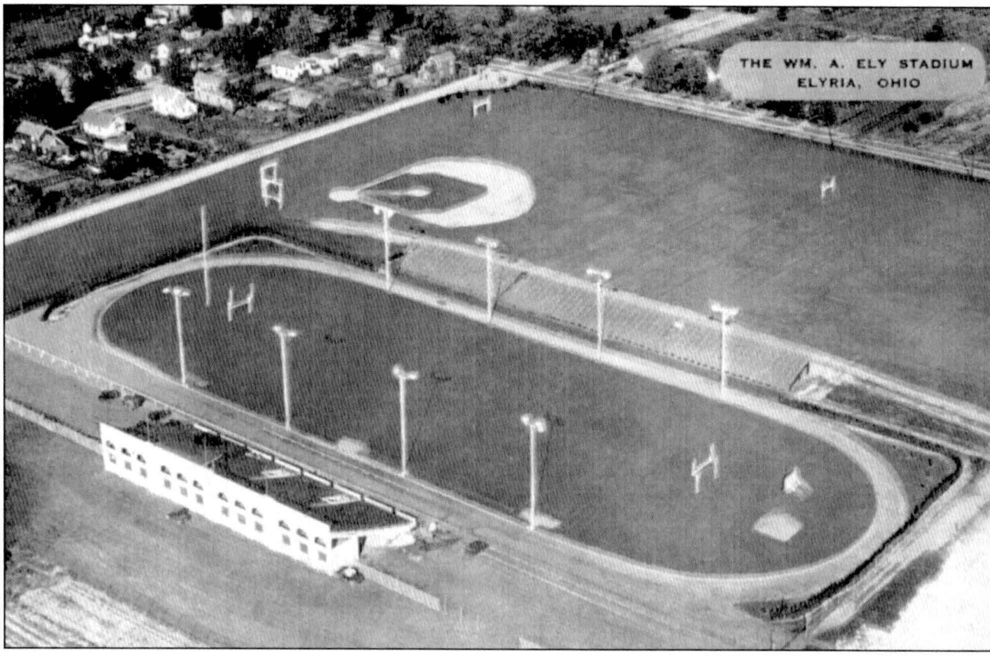

ELY STADIUM William Ely, grandson of Elyria's founder, donated the land at the south end of town for the stadium that bears his name. The stadium was completed in 1927, and although additions and renovations have been made over the years, it is still essentially the same—the home of the Elyria High School Pioneer football team and marching band.

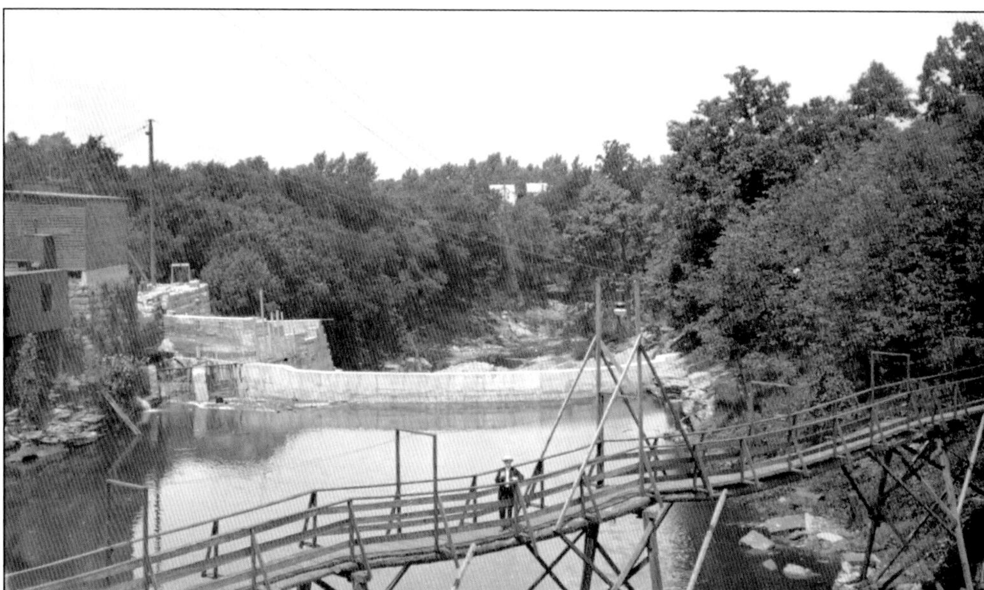

TEMPORARY WASHINGTON AVENUE FOOT BRIDGE. This interesting card shows the temporary bridge erected for pedestrian traffic after the destruction of the Washington Avenue Bridge by flood in 1913. From this bridge, it was possible to observe workers clearing the remains of the old bridge, repairing the mill dam, and constructing a new Washington Avenue Bridge.

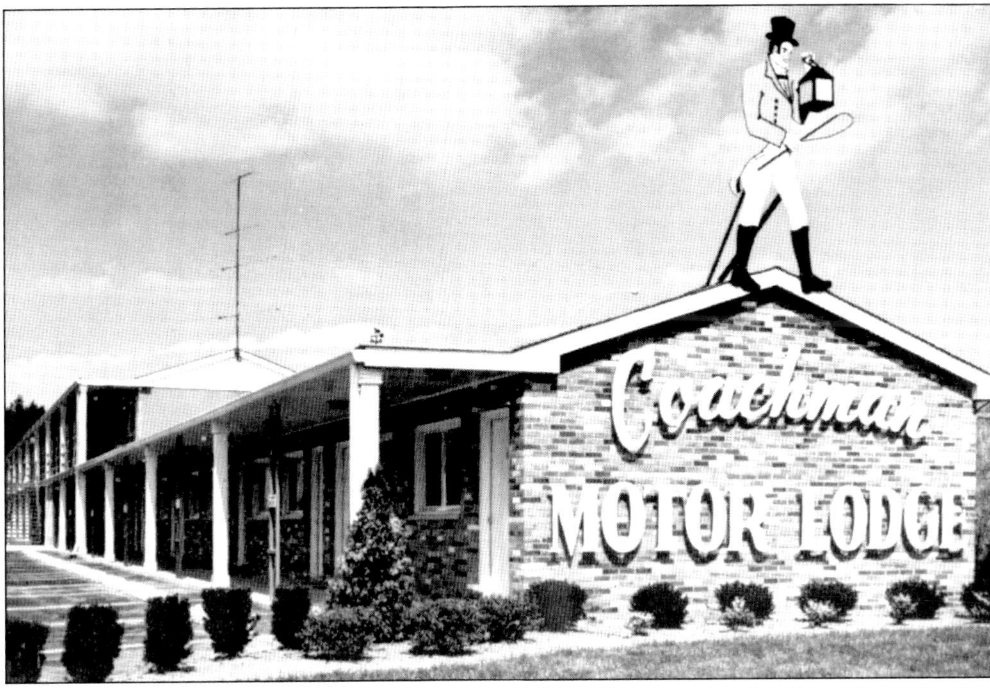

COACHMAN MOTOR LODGE. The coachman with his riding crop is a familiar sight to Elyrians traveling along Ohio Route 57. The motel is nestled against the embankment of the Ohio Turnpike on the west side of the road.

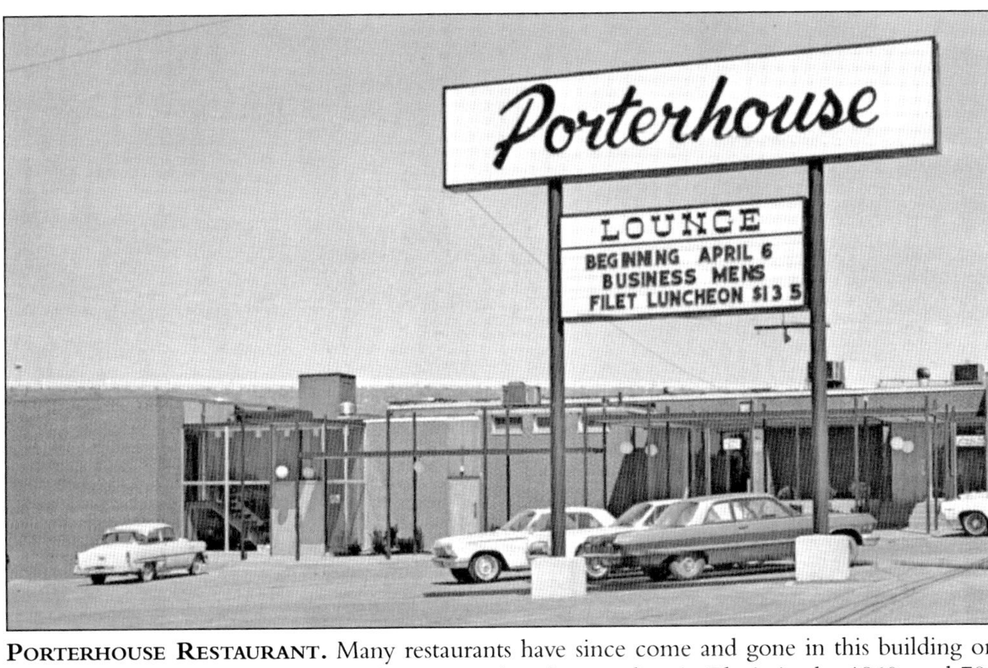

PORTERHOUSE RESTAURANT. Many restaurants have since come and gone in this building on Center Ridge Road, but the Porterhouse was the place to dine in Elyria in the 1960s and 70s. The location on Ohio Route 20 was ideal, down the street from the Bendix-Westinghouse plant. The Ohio Turnpike can be seen directly behind the restaurant.

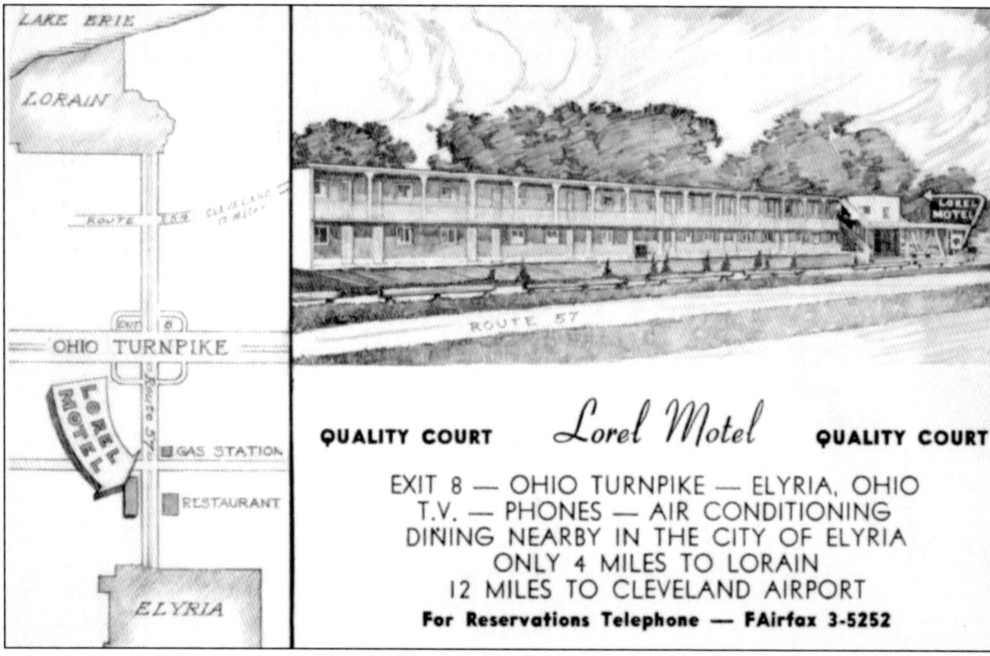

LOREL MOTEL. When the Ohio Turnpike was built in 1955, Exit 8 was located on Ohio Route 57, which ran north-south between Lorain and Elyria. Hotels and restaurants sprang up along Route 57, including the Lorel Motel.

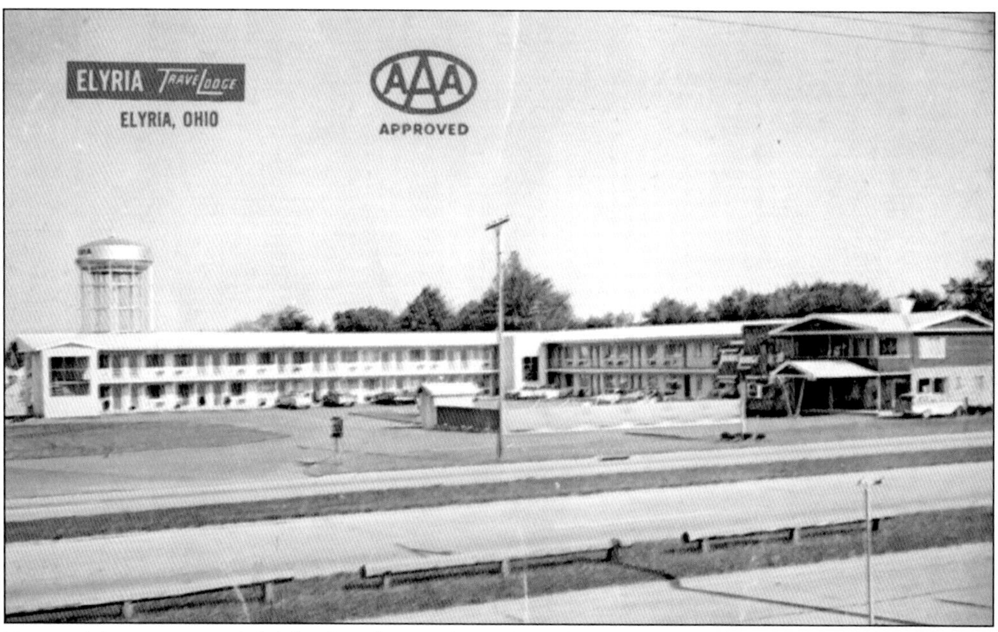

ELYRIA TRAVELODGE. This landmark motel stood on the corner of old Route 57 and the Route 57 bypass for many years. Ideally located just south of Exit 8 on the Ohio Turnpike, the Travelodge also boasted an outdoor swimming pool and was located next door to a turquoise-roofed Howard Johnson's restaurant. A large sleep-walking bear emblem was easily visible from the bypass.

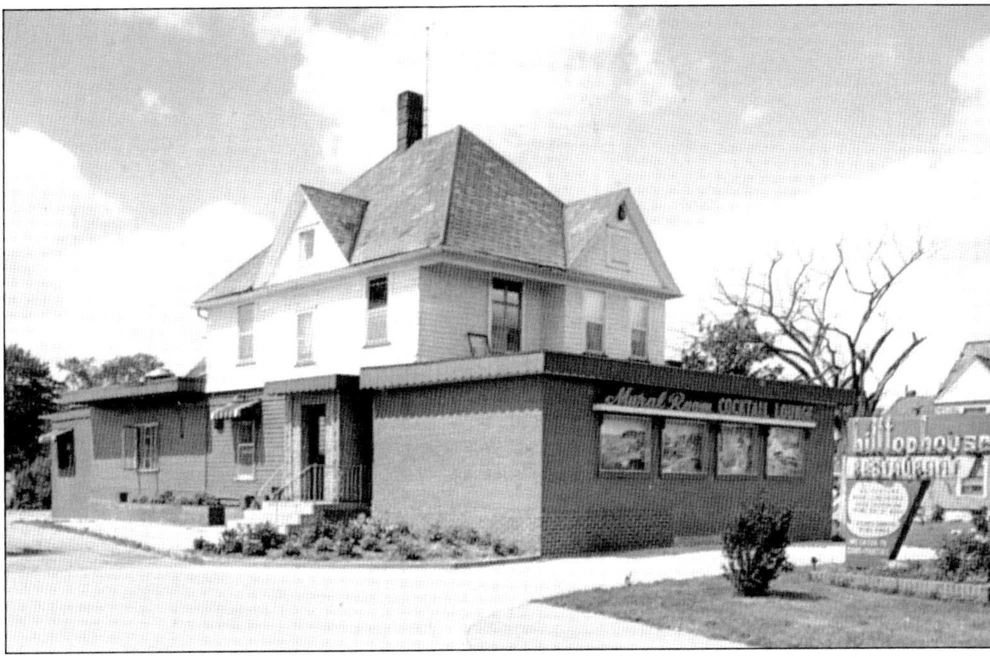

HILLTOP HOUSE RESTAURANT. This family restaurant was located on East Bridge Street, just northeast of the railroad underpass. It was a popular spot for business lunches, as well as special occasion dinners and parties.

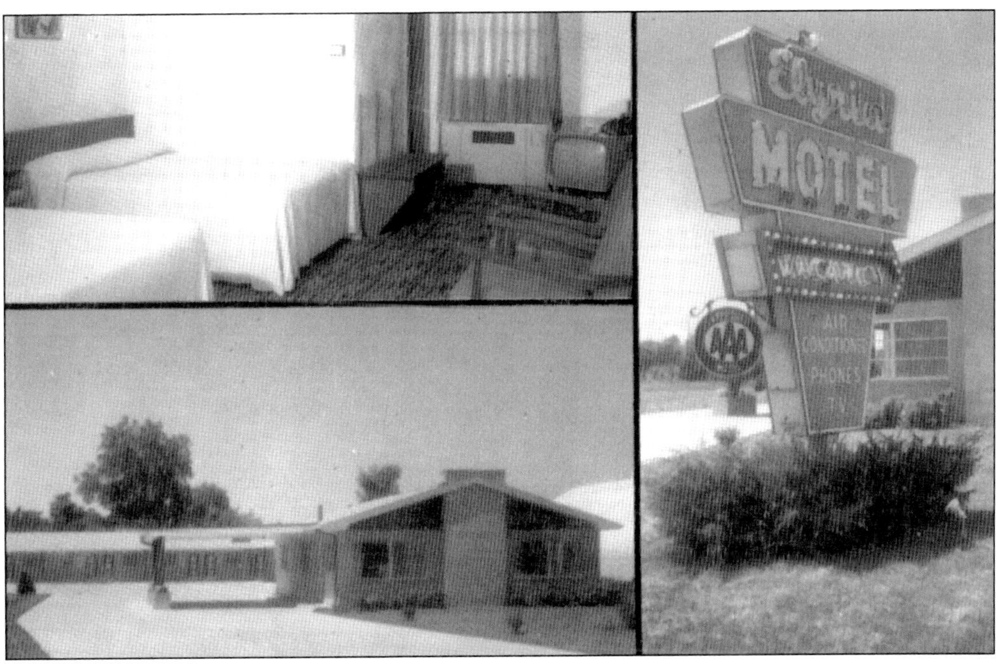

ELYRIA MOTEL. This motel is located just south of Elyria on Oberlin Road, then Ohio Route 20. It is typical of small motels across the country whose clientele declined as the interstates were built.

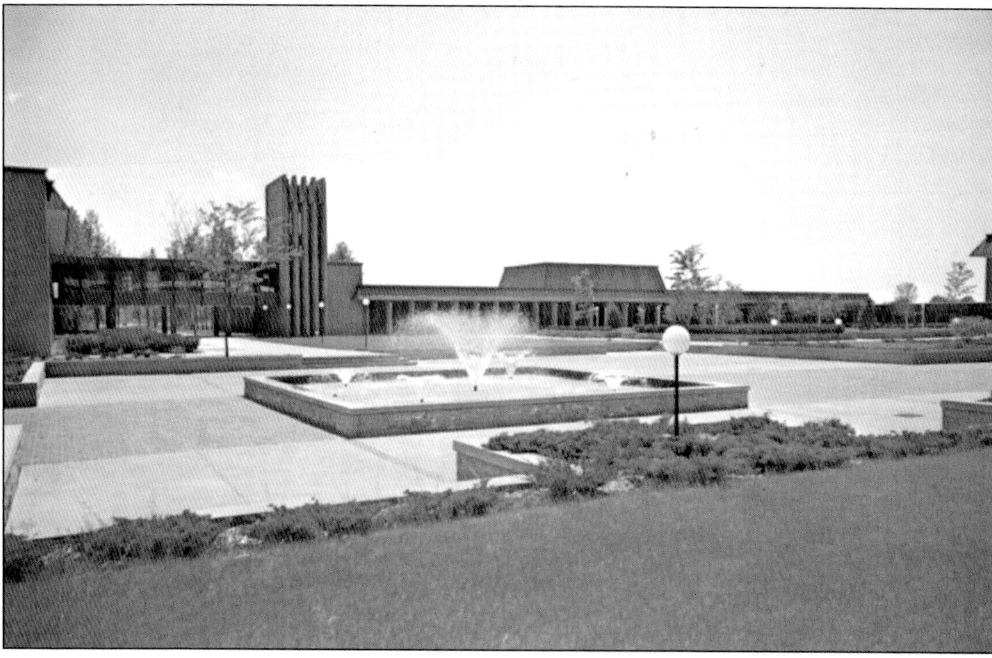

LORAIN COUNTY COMMUNITY COLLEGE. Ohio's second community college, LCCC opened in 1965 in the northeast corner of Elyria. Occupying 250 acres, the college continues to grow, and the six original buildings have been joined by high-tech and performing arts centers, among others.

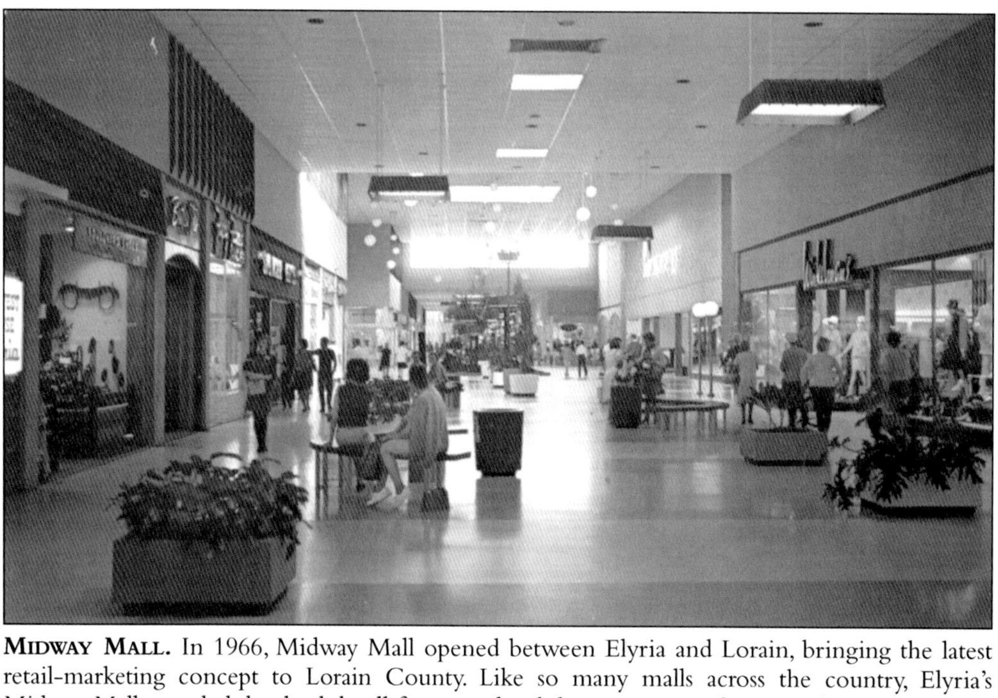

MIDWAY MALL. In 1966, Midway Mall opened between Elyria and Lorain, bringing the latest retail-marketing concept to Lorain County. Like so many malls across the country, Elyria's Midway Mall sounded the death knell for many local downtown merchants, with Sears, Penney's, and movie theaters abandoning downtown in favor of the mall.

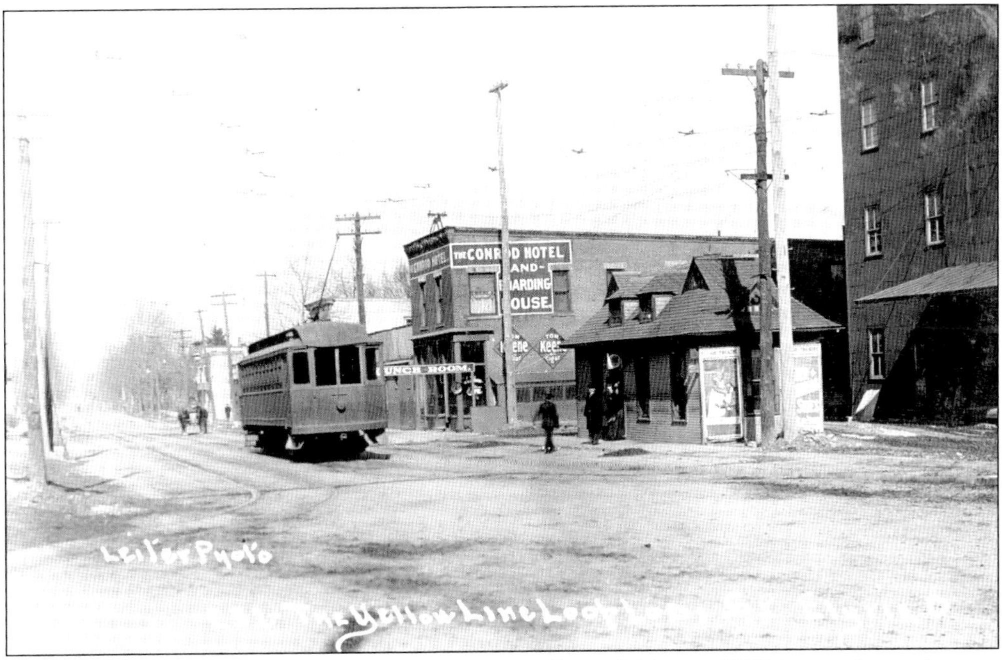

ELYRIA TERMINUS, LORAIN-ELYRIA INTERURBAN LINE. This pre-1910 image shows the area at the south end of the Yellow Line (Lorain-Elyria) trolley route. Here the tracks formed a loop for the return trip to Lorain. The image shows the Conrod Hotel, a small ticket office (3¢ each way), and the Red Mill at right.

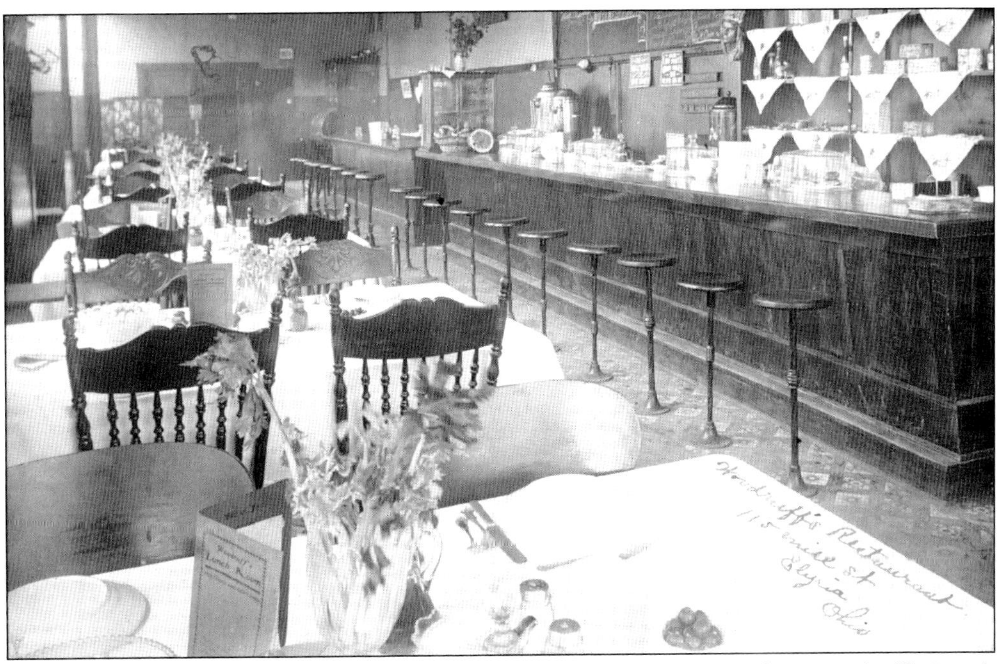

WOODRUFF'S RESTAURANT. At the time this rare interior photo was taken, Woodruff's Lunch Room was located at 115 Mill Street, near the Yellow Line turnaround shown above. The Elyria Police Department building and grounds now occupy this area.

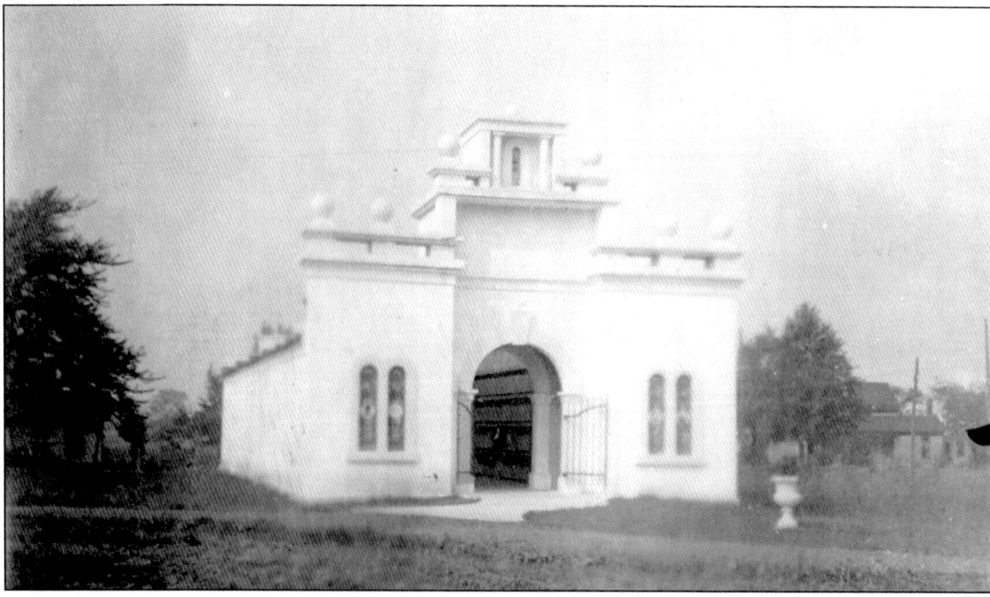

Ridgelawn Cemetery, Mausoleum Exterior. Elyria's oldest city cemetery, Ridgelawn, is bounded by Ridge Street, Columbus Street, Glenwood Street, and Gulf Road. Built around 1910, the mausoleum here seems to stand alone in the northeast corner of the cemetery. It is today surrounded by headstones and has been significantly remodeled, making it hard to recognize as the same structure.

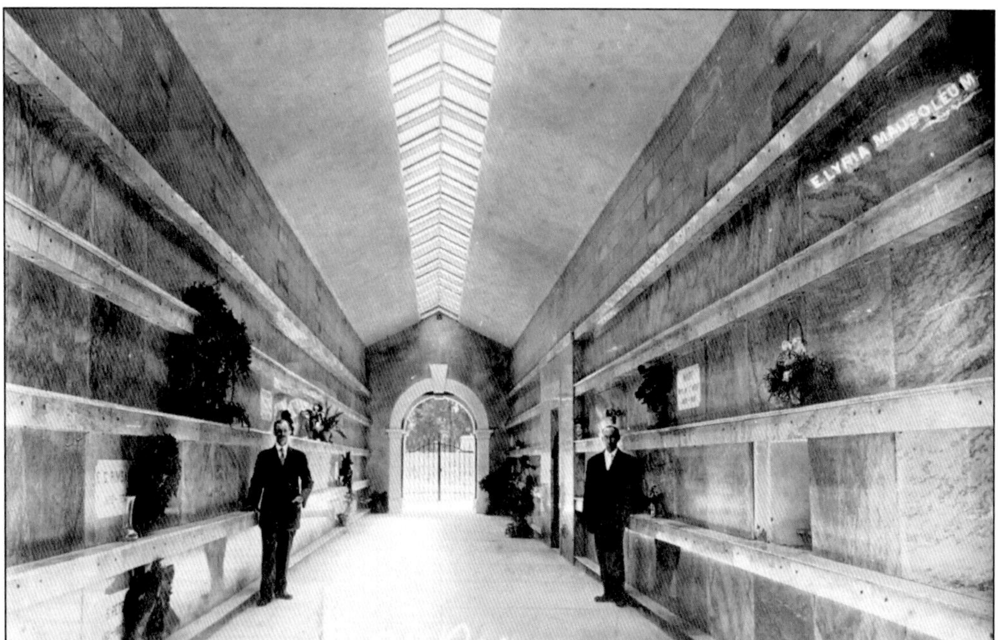

Ridgelawn Cemetery, Mausoleum Interior. This rare and somewhat macabre 1911 postcard shows the mausoleum's heavily marbled interior, the overhead skylights, and the nearly 200 available crypts. This postcard was actually mailed, and one wonders why this particular card might have been chosen.

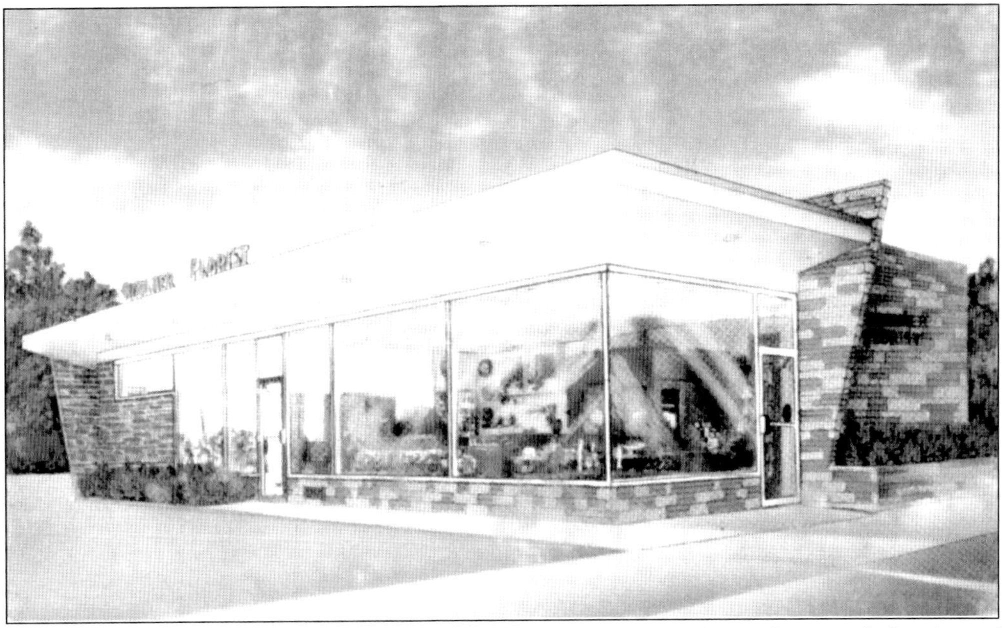

Botamer Florist. Even without its distinctive corner sign, this architectural drawing of Botamer's on the corner of Park Place and Clark Street is easily recognizable. The back of this advertising postcard touts this family-owned florist as "The Finest Drive-In Florist In Lorain County."

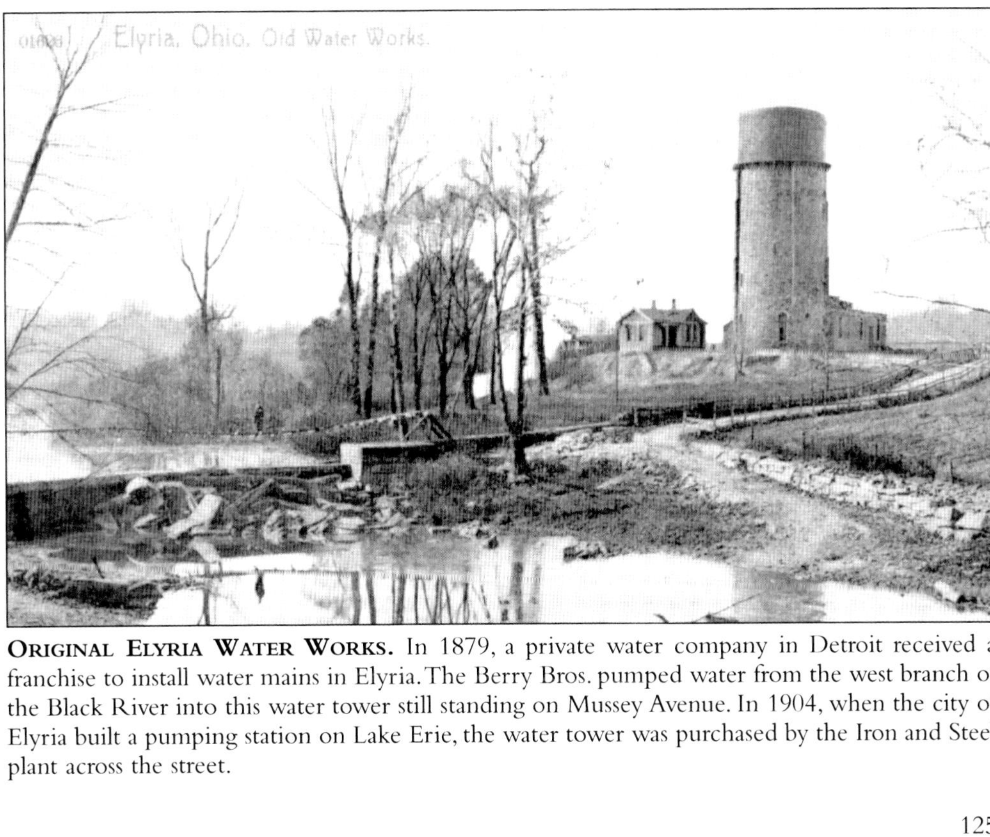

Original Elyria Water Works. In 1879, a private water company in Detroit received a franchise to install water mains in Elyria. The Berry Bros. pumped water from the west branch of the Black River into this water tower still standing on Mussey Avenue. In 1904, when the city of Elyria built a pumping station on Lake Erie, the water tower was purchased by the Iron and Steel plant across the street.

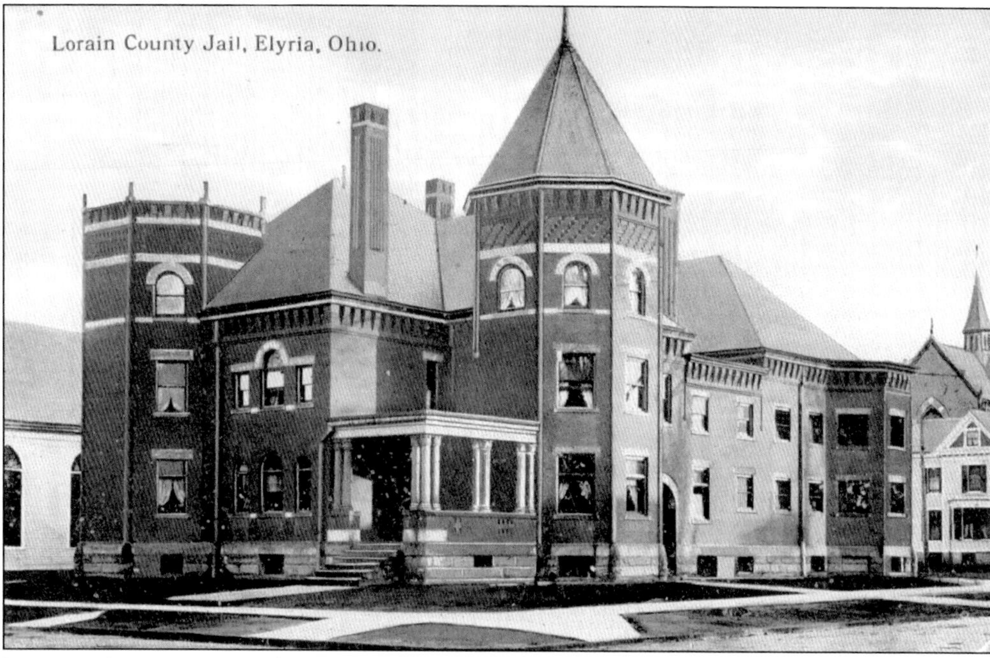

LORAIN COUNTY JAIL. This imposing brick building stood on the southeast corner of Middle Avenue and Third Street from 1893 to 1980. The buildings of the St. Mary's church complex can be seen all around the jail, with part of the school to the left, and the rectory and church building itself to the right.

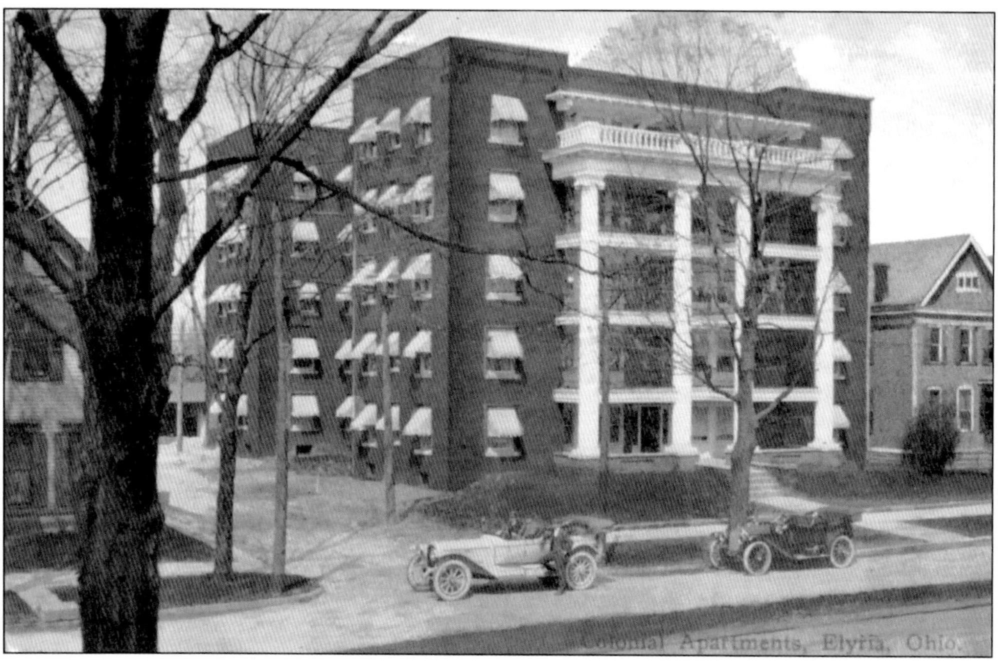

COLONIAL APARTMENTS. Built in the early 1900s, this handsome five-story brick apartment building stands on the west side of Middle Avenue between Fourth and Fifth Streets.

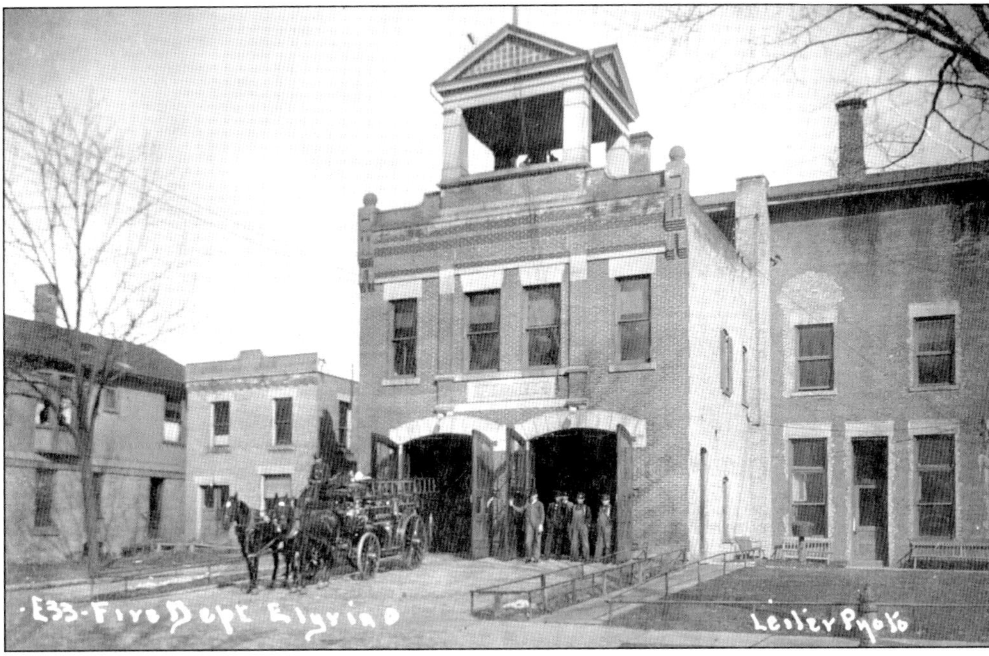

ELYRIA FIRE STATION NO. 1. City Hall underwent major renovations in 1904 when the second-floor opera house was replaced by much needed municipal office space. At the same time, this new fire station was added to the south rear of the building. The fire station included rooms for the firefighters, stalls for the horses, and a feed room.

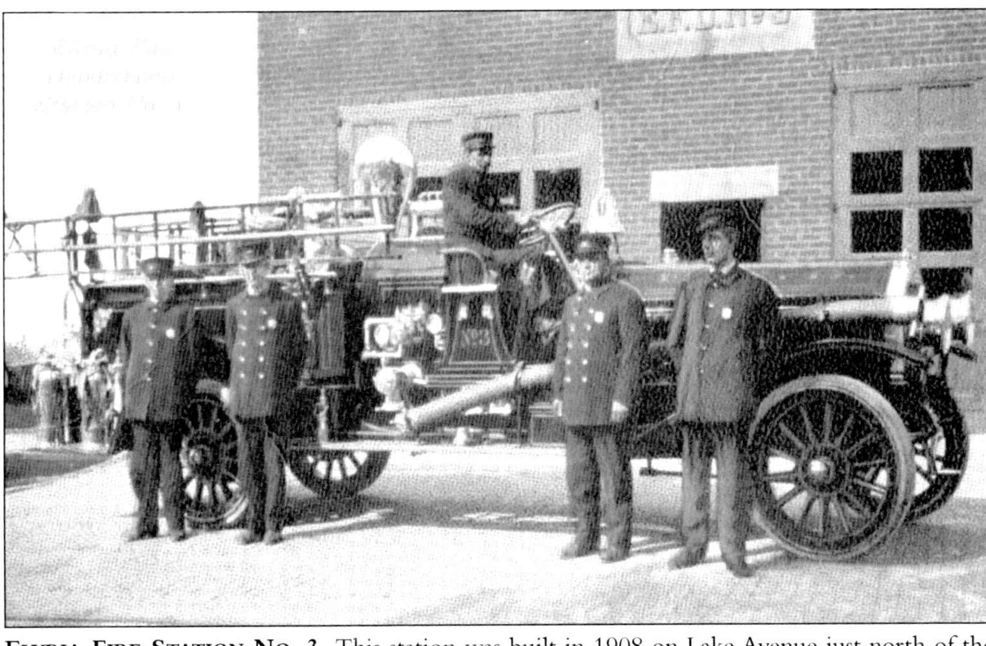

ELYRIA FIRE STATION NO. 3. This station was built in 1908 on Lake Avenue just north of the B & O Railroad tracks to serve the west side of town. Here, the firefighters pose with their new motorized pumper. Station No. 2 was built that same year at the corner of Clark and Winckles Streets to serve the east side.

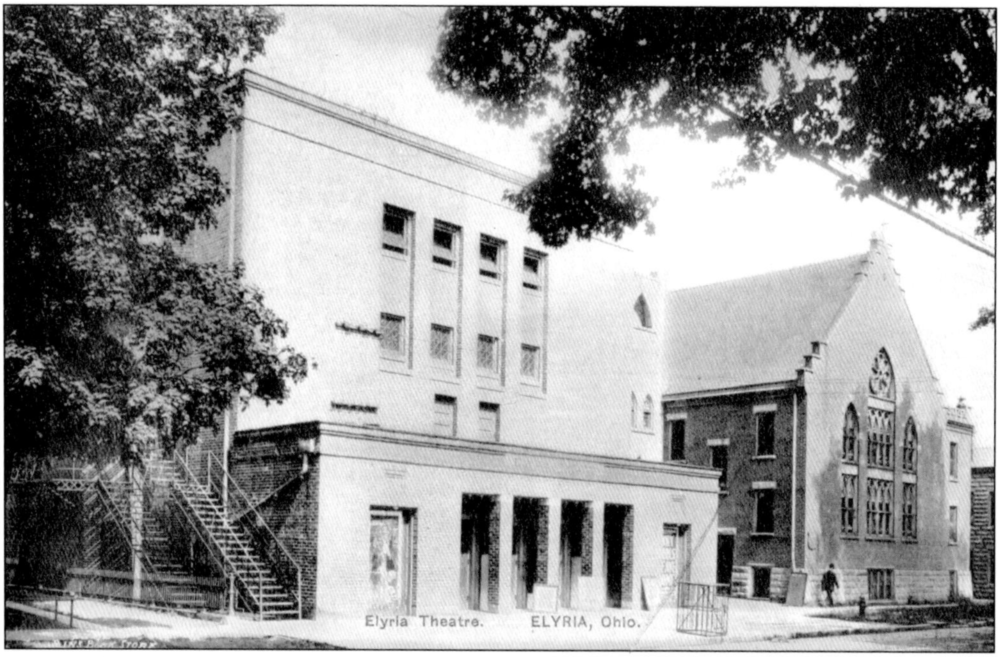

ELYRIA THEATRE. When the Opera House in City Hall closed in 1904, Elyrians needed a new venue for live entertainment. The Elyria Theatre, located on Second Street next to the Church of Christ, filled this void. The theater, later renamed the Rialto, included private boxes and a full orchestra pit. Both buildings above are gone now, as the space was needed for a bank parking lot.

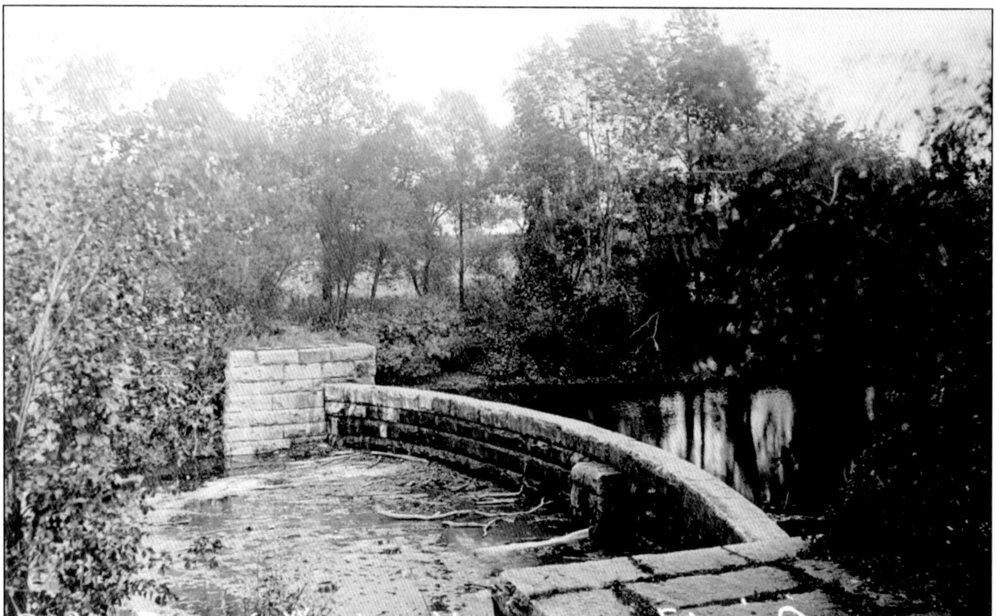

DAM AT COTTESBROOK. This dam is still located on the west branch of the Black River south of Elyria. It lies just south of the bridge on Oberlin Road and is one of the few remnants of businesses that once flourished here.